GUERRILLA
MARKETING

Other Books by Jay Conrad Levinson

The Most Important $1.00 Book Ever Written

Secrets of Successful Free-Lancing

San Francisco: An Unusual Guide to Unusual Shopping
(with Pat Levinson and John Bear)

Earning Money Without a Job

555 Ways to Earn Extra Money

150 Secrets of Successful Weight Loss
(with Michael Lavin and Michael Rokeach, M.D.)

GUERRILLA MARKETING

Secrets for Making Big Profits
from Your Small Business

Jay Conrad Levinson

Houghton Mifflin Company
Boston

Library of Congress Cataloging in Publication Data

Levinson, Jay Conrad.
 Guerrilla marketing.

 Bibliography: p.
 Includes index.
 1. Marketing. 2. Small business. 3. Advertising.
I. Title.
HF5415.L477 1984   658.8   83-18507
ISBN 0-395-35350-5
ISBN 0-395-38314-5 (pbk.)

Printed in the United States of America

S 10 9 8 7 6 5 4

I dedicate this book to Mike Lavin,
Thane Croston, Alexis Makar, Lynn
Atherton, Wally Bregman, Jan Schlesinger,
Leo Burnett, Steve Savage, Sidney Mobell,
and Norm Goldring — guerrillas all.

Acknowledgments

THE ACKNOWLEDGMENTS SECTION in a book may be the least enjoyable part of the book for the reader, yet writing the Acknowledgments is one of the most enjoyable parts for the author. It is only in the Acknowledgments that the people responsible for the spirit of the book receive the public recognition they deserve.

First on the list is Michael Larsen, my agent. Upon hearing me speak on marketing at a luncheon meeting, he dashed up to me and told me that I ought to write a book based upon my speech. From that moment on, *Guerrilla Marketing* started taking shape. Gerard Van Der Leun, my editor at Houghton Mifflin, has also earned my gratitude for believing in the book and for adding crucial touches of spark, style, and soul. Clay Morgan, my copy editor, is to be commended for his eagle eye, his sense of propriety, and his active blue pencil.

The people to whom this book is dedicated should also be singled out for the public appreciation they merit. Mike Lavin has always been a full-scale, high-energy practitioner of guerrilla marketing. Thane Croston has trusted guerrilla marketing with enough faith to build an empire. Alexis Makar has believed in guerrilla marketing to the point that she is now addicted to it. Lynn Atherton has appreciated guerrilla marketing and become so knowledgeable a student of it that she now teaches it to others. Wally Bregman showed me the value of fighting for one's beliefs with guerrilla-like tenacity. Jan Schlesinger possesses a deep understanding of guerrilla marketing and imparts it to all who have the privilege of working with her. Leo Burnett taught me more about marketing, guerrilla marketing, advertising, and life in general than any other mentor I've had, and I consider myself lucky to be able to make that statement. Steve Savage is the greatest guerrilla experimenter I know and is willing to take the risks that must be faced high on the ladder to the top, where he is now perched. Sidney Mobell was a true guerrilla long before I knew him, yet he allowed me to merge my own guerrilla tactics with his. And Norm Goldring has lived guerrilla marketing to the point that he is living proof of its success.

I also wish to thank the late Howard Gossage, who was the first to hire me as a professional guerrilla and teach me how much fun there is in the process of marketing.

During the writing of this book, I was constantly impressed by my daughter, Amy, who seemed to work harder while in college than I ever worked in real life. She served as an inspiration to me and continues to dazzle me with her mental acuity. And finally, I offer a deep bow and a warm kiss to my wife, Pat, who has always believed in me, encouraged me, understood me, put up with me, shared precious time with me, and loved me.

I am fortunate, indeed, to owe acknowledgment to so many superb people.

Contents

IV NON-MEDIA MARKETING

I
The Guerrilla Approach
to Marketing

IF YOU'RE EXCEPTIONALLY well funded and have stockpiles of money allocated to marketing whatever it is you are selling, you can take the standard approach and handle the marketing function with big bucks and textbook tactics. But if you're not well funded and have very little money for marketing, you might take a radically different approach and handle the marketing function with big ideas and guerrilla tactics.

Guerrilla tactics do not put textbook tactics to shame. But they do provide you with an alternative to standard expensive marketing. They enable you to increase your sales with a minimum of expense and a maximum of smarts.

You'll best understand the guerrilla approach to marketing once you study a standard marketing textbook. In the standard book, you'll learn of marketing goals and methods of attaining them. In this book, you'll learn of similar marketing goals and shortcuts to attaining them. You'll learn how to do what the big spenders do without having to spend big. Since very little comes to us for nothing, you'll have to do some extra work. But instead of relying on moneypower, you can rely on brainpower.

The guerrilla approach is a sensible approach for all marketers, regardless of size. But for entrepreneurs, for new businesspeople, for small businesspeople, it seems almost mandatory. As one guerrilla to another, I wish you well.

1
What Is Guerrilla Marketing?

MARKETING IS EVERYTHING you do to promote your business, from the moment you conceive of it to the point at which customers buy your product or service and begin to patronize your business on a regular basis. The key words to remember are *everything* and *regular basis*.

The meaning is clear: Marketing includes the name of your business, the determination of whether you will be selling a product or service, the method of manufacture or servicing, the colors, size, and shape of your product, the packaging, the location of your business, the advertising, the public relations, the sales training, the sales presentation, the telephone inquiries, the problem solving, the growth plan, and the follow-up. If you gather from this that marketing is a complex process, you're right.

This book can simplify the complexities, remove the mystique, show you exactly how any entrepreneur can use marketing to generate maximum profits from minimum investments. It can prevent you from making the many marketing mistakes made every day.

What this book can do for you

Put another way, this book can help make a small business big. It can aid an individual entrepreneur in making a lot of money as painlessly as possible. Very often, the only factor that determines success or failure is the way in which a product or service is marketed. The information in these pages will arm you for success and alert you to the shortcomings that lead to failure.

Every type of entrepreneurial enterprise requires marketing. There are no exceptions. It's not possible to succeed without marketing.

Assume that you have a fine business background and are well versed in the fundamentals of marketing as practiced by the giant corporations. Admirable. Now forget as much as you can. Marketing for you as an entrepreneur is vastly different than for an esteemed member of the *Fortune* 500. Oh, some of the principles may be the same, but the details are different. A good analogy is that of Adam and Eve. In principle, they were very much the same, but in important details, oh, boy, did they vary!

You're about to become a master of guerrilla marketing — the type of all-out marketing necessary for entrepreneurial success. Guerrilla marketing is virtually unknown to the large corporations. And thank heavens it is. After all, the large corporations have the benefit of big bucks. You don't. So you've got to rely on something just as effective but less costly. You've got to rely on guerrilla marketing.

Your size is your strength

I'm happy to report that your size is an ally when it comes to marketing. If you're a small company, a new venture, or a single individual, you can utilize the tactics of guerrilla marketing to their fullest. You've got the ability to be fast on your feet, to employ a vast array of marketing tools, to gain access to the biggest marketing brains and get them at bargain-basement prices. Now you may not need to use every weapon in your potential marketing arsenal, but you're sure going to need some of them. So you'd best know how to use them all.

It may be that you will require no advertising at all. But you will require marketing. It may be that word of mouth is so favorable, and spreads so rapidly, that your venture can reap a fortune just because of it. If so, you can be sure that the word of mouth was motivated by effective marketing in the first place.

In fact, a strong word-of-mouth campaign is part of marketing. And so are business cards. And so is stationery. And matchbooks. And the clothes you wear. And certainly your location is important in marketing. Every component that helps you sell what you are selling is part of the marketing process. No detail is too insignificant to be included. The more you realize that, the better your marketing will be. And the better your marketing is, the more money you will make. I'm not talking about sales. I'm talking about profits — the dear old bottom line.

That's the good news. Here's the bad: One of these days, you're going to be an entrepreneur no longer. If you successfully put into practice the principles of guerrilla marketing, you will become fat and rich and famous and will no longer have the lean, hungry mentality of the entrepreneur.

Once you've reached that stage, you will have to resort to the textbook forms of marketing, for you'll be too encumbered with employees, traditions, paperwork, management levels, and necessary bureaucracy to be flexible enough for guerrilla marketing. But somehow I have the feeling you won't mind that state of affairs too much. After all, Coca-Cola, Standard Oil, Procter & Gamble, and General Motors were all started by entrepreneurs. You can be damned certain that they practiced guerrilla marketing as much as possible in their day. You can also be sure that they do all their marketing by the numbers these days. And I doubt if they complain about it.

In time, some of those king-sized companies may be surpassed in size by companies that are now being founded and nurtured by entrepreneurs such as you. How will it happen? It will be the result of a combination of factors. And marketing genius will be one of them. Count on it.

At this point, I'm assuming you understand that you have to offer a quality product or service to be successful. Even the best marketing in the world won't motivate a customer to purchase a poor product or service more than once. In fact, brilliant marketing can speed the demise of an inferior offering, since people will learn of the shoddiness that much quicker. So do everything in your power to ensure the quality of whatever it is you'll be selling. And once you've got that quality, you'll be ready for guerrilla marketing. It is also mandatory for success that you have adequate capitalization — that is, money. Notice I didn't say that you need a lot of money. Sufficient capitalization to engage in guerrilla marketing will by itself be enough. That means you'll need enough cash or cash reserves to promote your business aggressively for at least three months, and ideally for a full year. It might take $300; it might take $30,000. That depends on your goals.

You must have quality

There are loads of small businesses throughout the United States. Many of them offer superb products and highly desirable services. But fewer than one-tenth of one percent of those businesses will make it to the point of phenomenal financial success. The elusive variable that makes the difference between merely being listed in the yellow pages and being listed on the New York Stock Exchange is the *marketing* of the product or service.

You now hold in your hand the key to becoming part of that tiny percentage of entrepreneurs who go all the way. By realizing that many facets of your business can fall into the category of marketing, you have a head start over those competitors who do not see that there is a difference between *advertising* and *marketing*.

The more aware of marketing you are, the more attention you will pay to it. And the increased attention will result in better marketing of your offerings. A great deal of marketing isn't merely poorly executed these days — it's not executed at all! I'd venture a bold guess

Be aware

that fewer than 10 percent of the new- and small-business people in America have never explored all of the marketing methods available to them. These methods include canvassing, personal letters, telephone marketing, circulars and brochures, signs on bulletin boards, classified ads, outdoor signs, advertisements in the yellow pages, newspapers, and magazines, and on radio, television, and billboards, direct mail, advertising specialties such as imprinted ballpoint pens, samples, seminars, and demonstrations, sponsoring of events, exhibiting at trade shows, and using searchlights, T-shirt ads, and public relations. Guerrilla marketing *demands* that you scrutinize every single one of these marketing methods and more, then use the combination that seems best for your business.

There are absolutely no advertising agencies that specialize in guerrilla marketing. When I worked as a senior executive at some of the world's largest (and smallest) advertising agencies, I found that they didn't have a clue as to what it takes to help an entrepreneur succeed. They could help the big guys, all right. But they were helpless without the brute force of big bucks. So where can you turn for help? The first place to turn is to this book. The next place is to your own ingenuity and energy. And finally, you will probably have to go to a marketing or advertising professional to get help with details in the areas where guerrilla marketing overlaps standard marketing. But don't expect the pros to be as tough in the trenches as you are. Most likely, they operate better from high in a posh skyscraper.

Excellence   Guerrilla marketing dictates that you comprehend every facet of marketing, then *employ with excellence* the marketing tactics that are necessary. To understand the nature of this idea, it may be useful to examine the real reason Japan was able to knock the United States off its perch as world leader in the TV, stereo, automobile, and electronics industries.

Industry in the United States has been able to turn out excellent products with a low percentage of rejects — 5 percent. That means that of one million manufactured items, only 50,000 were rejects. Industry leaders recognized that the cost to lower that number would be greater than the profit industry would realize by achieving perfection. So it became an economic truism that you could run a successful manufacturing operation if you limited your rejects to 50,000 per million units. And the public became used to the concept: They complained about lemons, but weren't really all that surprised at them.

Japan, after a monumental defeat in World War II, suffered from an image of poor quality. For years the phrase "Made in Japan" was enough to elicit a grin from a sophisticated purchaser. How did the Japanese overcome this problem? Japan decided to fly in the face of the economic truism that allowed for a 5 percent reject rate. Japan figured that if the public accepts products even though 50,000 per million are inferior, it might happily embrace products of which fewer than 50,000 were unacceptable. But according to the economists this would cost a ton of money.

The Japanese, having nowhere to go but up, figured it was worth it. They improved the quality of what they made to the point that right now, they have only 200 rejects per million units. Two hundred rejects versus our 50,000 rejects! And Japan is still working on methods for lowering that 200 figure.

How did Japan do it? By reducing mistakes. Every error that could possibly be construed as a mistake was noticed by people actually hired by industry to count mistakes. In the category of mistakes were included shoddy workmanship, tardiness, breaks that lasted too long, minor flaws in detail work, low morale, and anything at all that impeded production. Weekly, departments within Japanese industrial firms would meet with their hired mistake counters. They were told the number of mistakes made that week, and they worked to reduce that number. By working at it assiduously, they cut the number of mistakes dramatically.

Through almost totally eliminating mistakes, Japan took over leadership in the TV, stereo, automobile, and electronics industries. And as the number of mistakes went down, productivity went up. The country benefited in these two ways by this one action. In all businesses, there are numerous opportunities and numerous problems. The Japanese exploited their opportunities and solved their problems. So it is with guerrilla marketing.

Guerrilla marketing involves recognizing the myriad opportunities **Going all out** and *exploiting every one of them*. Like the Japanese, don't overlook a thing. In the marketing of any product, problems are certain to arise. Solve these problems and continue to look for new problems to solve. You won't have the luxury of neglecting the smaller opportunities or overlooking certain problems. You've got to go all out.

Going all out is the foundation of successful guerrilla marketing. By going all out, the Japanese completely reversed the reaction to "Made in Japan," to the point where the phrase now means excellent craftsmanship, attention to detail, and nearly zero defects.

Energy alone is not enough, however. Energy has to be directed by intelligence. Intelligent marketing is marketing that is first and foremost focused on a core idea. All your marketing must be an extension of this idea: the advertising, the stationery, the direct mailings, the telephone marketing, the yellow pages advertising, the package, the whole thing. But it is not enough to have a better idea; you must also have a better argument and a focused strategy. Today many large and supposedly sophisticated companies go to one expert for a trademark, another expert for an advertising program, yet another expert for direct-mail planning, and possibly one more professional for location selection. This is not only costly, it is nonsense. Nine times out of ten each of these experts is pulling in a different direction.

What must be done is to have all the marketing pros pull in a common direction — a preagreed, long-term, carefully selected direction. When this is done, a synergistic effect is automatically created and five types of marketing tactics do the work of ten. The preagreed direction will always be clear if you encapsulate your thoughts in a core concept that can be expressed in a *maximum* of seven words. That's right, a *maximum* of seven.

Here's an example. An entrepreneur wanted to offer courses in computer education, but knew that most people suffer from "technophobia" — fear of things technical. Advertisements for his proposed courses in word processing, accounting by computer, the electronic spreadsheet, and more produced little response. So he decided to restate the basic premise of his offering. At first, he stated it thus: "I wish to alleviate the fears that people have regarding computers, so that they will recognize the enormous value and competitive advantages of working with computers." Then, in an attempt to reduce this thought to a seven-word core concept, he reiterated his idea: "I will teach people to operate computers." This seven-word statement clarified his task. Clarified it for him, for his sales staff, for his prospective students.

Later, he developed a name for his company, a name that reduced his core concept to three words: Computers for Beginners. This bypassed the problem of technophobia, stated his premise, and attracted hordes of beginners. Before he started this business, his concept ran six pages. By reducing and reducing his basic thoughts, he was finally able to achieve the succinctness necessary to assure clarity. And clarity led to success. It usually does.

It's a pretty simple idea, this idea of centering all your marketing on a core concept. But you can be sure that when you begin to market your offering that way, you will be a member of an enlightened minority and well on your way to marketing success — a prerequisite for financial success.

2
Entrepreneurial Marketing: The Critical Difference

IN AN ARTICLE IN THE *Harvard Business Review*, John A. Welsh and Jerry F. White remind us that "a small business is not a little big business." An entrepreneur is not a multinational conglomerate but a profit-seeking individual. To survive, he must have a different outlook and must apply different principles to his endeavors than does the president of a large or even medium-sized corporation. Not only does the scale of small and big businesses differ but small businesses also suffer from what the *Harvard Business Review* article calls "resource poverty." This is a problem and opportunity that requires an entirely different approach to marketing. Where large ad budgets are not necessary or feasible, where expensive ad production squanders limited capital, where every marketing dollar must do the work of two dollars, if not five dollars or even ten, where a person's company, capital, and material well-being are all on the line — that is where guerrilla marketing can save the day and secure the bottom line.

A large company can invest in a full-scale advertising campaign run by an ad agency, and that company has the resources to switch to a different campaign if the first is not successful. And if the company is smart, it will hire a different agency the second time around. This luxury is not available to entrepreneurs, who must get it right the first time.

This is not to say that I hold the techniques employed by the big corporations in contempt; quite the contrary. While creating advertising for companies such as Alberto-Culver, Quaker Oats, United Airlines, Citicorp, VISA, Sears, and Pillsbury, I frequently employed big-company marketing techniques. I was acting properly. But to suggest that the individual entrepreneurs I advise employ the same techniques would be irresponsible, not to mention financially wasteful. Instead, I resort to the techniques of guerrilla marketing, techniques that might get me laughed out of a Procter & Gamble or Chrysler Corporation conference room.

The critical difference

Many of the approaches and some of the techniques overlap. Entrepreneurs must govern tactical operations by marketing strategy. And all their marketing efforts have to be weighed against that strategy. They also need to examine all of the marketing avenues available to them. The critical difference is the bottom line. They must keep a far keener eye on the bottom line than do the giant firms. They must spend far less money testing their marketing tactics. And their marketing must produce results at a fraction of the price paid by the biggies. They may not necessarily handle their marketing efforts better than large companies, but they will be more personalized and realistic in their use of marketing.

Large companies think nothing of producing five television commercials for purposes of testing. Small companies dare not even think the same thought. Large companies employ many levels of management to analyze the effectiveness of their advertising. Small companies entrust the judging to one individual. Large companies look first to television — the most far-reaching of all the advertising media. Small companies generally look first to small newspaper ads in local papers. Both are interested in sales that generate profits. But each must achieve its goals in a dramatically different way.

Often, large companies aim for leadership of an industry, or to dominate a market or large market segment, and they use marketing ploys designed to attain those lofty ambitions. But small companies, or individual entrepreneurs, can flourish merely by gaining a tiny slice of an industry, a fraction of a market. Different wars require different tactics.

Whereas large companies realize that they must advertise from the outset and continue to advertise with virtually no interruption, smaller enterprises may be able to advertise only in the beginning, and then rely solely upon word-of-mouth advertising. Can you imagine what would happen if Budweiser beer depended on word-of-mouth advertising? Miller Lite would sell a lot more six-packs.

An individual entrepreneur may be able to get enough business just by dealing with one gigantic company. An acquaintance of mine was able to survive financially (and in gracious style, I might add) merely by conducting small seminars for one large banking firm. No large company could exist off the income he was generating, but my friend was able to zero in on that one firm until he got his first assignment. After that there were others, and still others. This year, he is conducting his seminars for a large oil company. Working with companies of that size, he needs very few customers. Needless to say, his marketing was tailored to this reality.

A descriptive brochure sent to a single large corporation may result in enough business to keep an energetic telephone marketing trainer in the chips for a long time. Try finding a New York Stock Exchange–listed company that could do the same. Impossible.

Many entrepreneurs get all the business they need by posting signs on bulletin boards. A large company would never consider such a possibility. If it did, it would be known as Shrinking, Inc., in short order. The point is obvious: Sauce for the small goose is not necessarily sauce for the large goose. And vice-versa.

For example, business cards can be plain and straightforward for big-company executives. The executive's name, company name, address, and phone number are enough. Perhaps a title is also necessary. But for a smart practitioner of individual enterprise, that business card ought to contain a lot more information. For example, I know a typist whose card has all of the above, along with the message "Legal, theses, statistical, manuscript, résumé, and business typing." Her card does double duty. It has to. That is what guerrilla marketing is all about. **Business cards**

A business card can double as a brochure, a circular, a wallet-sized advertisement. The cost to produce such a card is not much more than one pays for a standard card. But the need is different. Lacking a large stockpile of dollars, the small businessperson must make use of all the advertising media available. A business card can be more than a mere listing of one's name, address, and phone number; it can be an advertising medium.

A huge corporation can run radio or television commercials and tell the audience, at the end of each message, to obtain the address of the nearest dealer by consulting the yellow pages. Now that's just dandy when you dominate that section of the yellow pages with the largest ad and the most recognizable trademark and line. But the individual entrepreneur dare not direct listeners or viewers to the yellow pages. That would only alert his prospective customers to the competition, or to the dominance of certain competitors. Instead, the astute entrepreneur directs his prospects to the white pages, where there will be no competitive ads, where his organization's small size will not appear as a detriment, and where recognizable promotion themes and symbols will not woo a customer away.

Perhaps the biggest difference between an individual businessperson and a large corporation is in the degree of flexibility each possesses. Here the balance tips in favor of the small business. Because it hasn't indoctrinated numerous levels of management and a gigantic sales organization in the tactics and strategies of its marketing plan, it **Flexibility** can make changes on the spot. It can be fast on its feet and can react to market changes, competitive ploys, economic realities, new media, newsworthy events, and last-minute offers.

I recall how a major advertiser once was offered an unbelievably good media buy for a fraction of its normal price. Because the offer did not fit into the company's engraved-in-bronze plan, and because the person to whom the offer was made had to check with so many bosses, the company had to turn down the offer. A tiny business then accepted it: a thirty-second commercial just prior to the Super Bowl, for the incredible price of $500. The cost of this commercial slot (in the San Francisco Bay Area) normally sold for ten times that amount. But because of lack of flexibility, the giant corporation was unable to get in on the bargain. Speed and flexibility are part of the very essence of guerrilla marketing.

A success-bound entrepreneur must learn to think about marketing and advertising on a different wavelength than does a corporate advertising executive. While you must think about the primary marketing tools much as the executive does, you must also develop a sixth sense for the other opportunities available to entrepreneurs. It may be that a personal letter or visit is in order. A corporate manager might never consider such mundane tactics. Perhaps a telephone marketing campaign is in order. Can you picture Coca-Cola getting involved in telephone marketing to consumers?

The *Fortune* 500 may have big bucks in the same way the Brontosaurus had a weight problem. But like the furry quick mammal, you've got the flexibility, the speed, the disregard of image, that enables you to use radio commercials and also hire high school students to hand out printed circulars on street corners. You don't have a body of rules to follow, a committee to answer to, a set structure to follow. You're a guerrilla. You *are* the organization. You answer to yourself. You make the rules and you break the rules. And that means you get to be amazing, outrageous, surprising, unpredictable, brilliant, and quick.

Word of mouth   You also just may be able to enjoy the rare luxury of sitting back and relying upon consistent word-of-mouth advertising. If you're really good at your work, that word of mouth might be enough to keep your coffers brimming. I know of no *Fortune* 500 companies that can enjoy that amenity.

Incidentally, please understand that what appears to be word-of-mouth advertising is often a combination of newspaper, magazine, radio, direct-mail, *and* word-of-mouth advertising. But it's the mouth that gets the credit and not the media. Don't delude yourself into believing that you can succeed with *no* media advertising. Winning with that strategy would be like winning the trifecta the first time at the track. It happens, but don't bet your boots or your business.

Still, it is possible to generate word-of-mouth advertising. There are several ways to accomplish this. The first, of course, is to be so good at what you do, or to offer products that are so obviously wonderful, that your customers will want to pass on the good word about you. Another way to get the ball rolling is to give brochures or circulars to your customers. This reminds them why they patronized you in the first place and spurs word-of-mouth endorsements. A third way to obtain positive recommendations is literally to ask for them. Tell your customers: "If you're really satisfied with my service [or products], I'd sure appreciate it if you'd tell your friends." Finally, you can *bribe* your customers. Tell them, "If I get any customers who mention your name, I'll send you a free gift [or give you a ten percent discount next time you're in]." Which of these methods should you employ? As a guerrilla, you should use *all* of them.

The point to remember is that *no* large corporation can succeed by means of word-of-mouth advertising alone, and some entrepreneurs can. But do yourself a favor and don't leave everything up to the recommendations of your happy customers. They probably have more important things to talk about. Even for a guerrilla, consistent marketing is crucial to success.

An overall marketing plan for a person engaged in individual enterprise might consist of a listing in the yellow pages, a mailing of circulars and business cards, a posting of signs, and a follow-up telephoning to those prospects to whom the promotional material was sent. That four-pronged effort (yellow pages, mailing, sign-posting, and telephoning) might be all it takes to get a business off and running. You can be certain that no big company has a marketing plan so short and simple — and inexpensive.

Imagine a staple gun and a handful of circulars as the only marketing tools necessary to conduct a business. IBM would boot me out of their corporate offices for suggesting such a thing. But many a successful home-typing service uses these devices and none other. A typist I know started out by typing her circulars, thereby lending credibility to her typing ability. Then, she posted them with her staple gun on bulletin boards throughout local college campuses. These days, she posts no more circulars, and her staple gun gathers dust. Word of mouth has taken over, and she gets all the business she needs through referrals.

Entrepreneurs can enjoy month after month of profitable business merely by advertising in the classified pages. I'm sure you've seen rafts of ads by independent contractors while perusing the classified ads. You do look through them, don't you? The classified ads are recommended reading for entrepreneurs. They give you ideas. They alert you to the competition. They clue you in as to current prices. You'll read a lot more about them in chapter 13. The point I'm making here is that classified ads are an important tool for independent businesspeople. They are not a tool for large companies. I doubt if the most professional advertising agencies in the world are well-versed in proper use of the classified pages. But the classified pages may be invaluable to free-lance earners.

In "How to Start and Run a Successful Home Typing Business" (Pigi Publishing, Huntington Beach, California, 1980), Peggy Glenn, the author, lists an eleven-point advertising program:

1. Hang fliers on campuses and near student gathering places.
2. Ask each school department to allow you to post your fliers.
3. Post a flier in the faculty lounge.
4. Post your flier at placement offices and counseling centers.
5. Leave fliers at the graduate study office.
6. Advertise in the campus newspaper.
7. Post a small sign on the community library bulletin board.
8. Post fliers for special groups such as engineers.
9. Visit a few college departments to see if they need your help.
10. Visit the principals of schools in your community with fliers.
11. Visit private and special schools in your area, leaving fliers.

She admits that this is *a lot* of advertising. To a typist, it is. To a large company, it isn't. And that seems to illustrate clearly how marketing is different for entrepreneurs.

Still, there are three highly significant marketing secrets that must be known by all advertisers, large and small, if they are to succeed. Even the tiniest of entrepreneurs must be aware of them. And that awareness will begin the moment you start reading the next chapter.

3
The Three Most Important Marketing Secrets of All

IT AMAZES ME that these secrets are secrets at all. Instead, they ought to be truisms, engraved on brass plaques in the offices of all who market or plan marketing. Yet these proven gems of marketing wisdom have somehow escaped the ken of large and small marketers alike. I sincerely believe that it is next to impossible to market a product or service successfully unless these secrets are known and put into practice. I also believe that merely by learning these secrets, then living by them, you're 50 percent of the way toward a successful marketing campaign.

If you have a small business and want it to become a large business, forget it — until you put these secrets into practice. And if you allow these concepts to become part of your mental marketing framework, you've got a giant head start on those who do not.

So as not to keep you in suspense any longer, I'll reveal the secrets right here and now. They can be summarized in three words: *commitment, investment, consistent.*

The big three

1. You must be *committed* to your marketing program.
2. You must think of that program as an *investment.*
3. You must see to it that your program is *consistent.*

Let's start with the first. If you're not committed to a marketing or advertising program, it's probably not going to work for you. I tell my clients that the single most important word for them to remember during the time they are engaged in marketing is *commitment.* It means that they are taking the marketing job seriously. They're not playing around, not "testing the waters." They have no room to "test" the marketing function — they must act. Without commitment, marketing becomes practically impotent.

You evolve a marketing plan, revise and rerevise it until it is *a powerful plan for your purposes.* You put it to work, and then you stay with it, no matter what (in most cases). You watch it slowly take effect, rise and falter, take a bit more effect, slide back a bit, start taking hold even more, stumble, then finally grab on and soar, taking you with it. Your plan is working. Your cash register is ringing. Your bank balance is swelling. And it all happened because *you were committed to your marketing program.*

Patience is profit

Let's examine that last paragraph. What if you weren't patient enough during the time your plan "slowly" took effect? You might have changed the plan. Many entrepreneurs do. What if you dropped the plan the moment it faltered? You would have lost out. Many marketers do. What if you lost your cool when your sales slid backward? You might have scrubbed the plan. Suppose you dropped it when it stumbled, as virtually all marketing plans do, at least temporarily. Disaster would have ensued. But because you stayed with the plan, because you were committed to it, it finally took hold and did what you wanted it to do. Your success was very much due to your understanding of the concept of commitment. If you had not been in touch with the essence of the concept, you probably would have taken one of the many tempting opportunities to kill the plan — and would have killed your chances along with it. But you understood what commitment means, and it paid off for you.

A winner

A new business was starting out in Boulder, Colorado. The owner of the business had heard about me, so he flew out to California to talk with me. We hit it off. We discussed the idea of commitment to a marketing program. He admitted that he knew zilch about marketing and turned the whole thing over to me. I developed a marketing plan, secured his approval, then reiterated the necessity for him to commit himself to the program. Mind you, I'm talking about a guy with one little store in a relatively small town.

The marketing started and nothing happened. Six weeks later, my new client called me to tell me he was still committed to the program, but that he hadn't seen much proof of it working for him. He also let me know that he was completely relaxed about the whole thing because he felt he understood about commitment. After twelve weeks, he called to tell me he was beginning to see hints that the program was taking effect. After six months, he opened his second store. After nine months, he opened his third, and at the end of the year, he had five stores. He remained committed to the marketing program and within six years had forty-two stores in Colorado, Iowa, Kansas, Wyoming, and Missouri.

I sincerely doubt that he would have progressed to a point where he could even have justified a second store if he had not stayed with the plan, if he had not understood what I meant about commitment. He had many chances to waver, many chances to become a disbeliever. He had a ton of reasons to veer from the plan. Naturally, it was a well-conceived plan, a plan perfect for his purposes. Commitment to an unwise plan is just plain stupid. And you won't have any way of knowing if your plan is good or bad at the outset — except for your own intuition and the counsel of others in whom you believe. But once you believe in your plan, you've got to back that belief with patience. Patience is another way of saying commitment.

My advice to you is to create a sensible plan, then stick with it until it proves itself to you. How long might that take? Maybe three months, if you're lucky. Probably six months. And maybe even as long as a year. But you will never, never, never know whether the plan is working within the first sixty days. Commitment is directly related to time. The longer you live by a plan, the deeper your sense of commitment. If your boat sinks in the ocean and you start swimming to shore, you should not give up if you haven't hit the beach within one hour — even five hours. To survive, you've got to be committed to swimming to that beach. Think of that when you consider altering your marketing plans after a short time.

In working with small clients, I consider the greatest stumbling block to be their inability to understand commitment. And this brings us to the second of the three most important marketing secrets of all — investment. Marketing and advertising should be considered *conservative investments*. They are not miracle workers. They are not magic formulas. They are not instant gratifiers. If you don't recognize that marketing is a conservative investment, you'll have difficulty committing yourself to a marketing program.

Marketing is not instant gratification

Suppose you buy a blue-chip stock. If it drops after a few weeks, you don't sell it. You hold onto it, hoping it will go up. And in all likelihood it will. Such is the nature of a conservative investment. Think of marketing the same way. If it doesn't produce instant results, that's because most marketing doesn't. If it does produce instant results, good for you — but don't figure it will always be that way.

Also, don't expect marketing to suddenly double your sales. Although that has happened, it is unusual. Marketing will contribute to slow but steady increases for you. At the end of a year, you'll be able to say that you've invested X dollars in marketing and received X plus Y in sales. Just the way conservative investments are supposed to pay off. Recognizing this, you'll feel good about making a conservative investment in marketing the next year, and the year after that. If you expect more from marketing, chances are you'll be disappointed. If you expect only that, chances are you'll be gratified. And successful.

A loser   Stupid example time: I worked with a client who had never engaged in newspaper advertising. We developed a marketing plan, a creative strategy, and a media plan. We discussed commitment. Then we ran the ads. After four weeks, my client called to tell me he was dropping the entire advertising program. When I inquired why, he told me he had expected his sales to at least double by this time. Yes, he admitted, I had explained that advertising does not work this way. But no, he decided, he didn't want to spend money that didn't produce instant sales.

I wish I had informed him up front that his advertising expenditure was a conservative investment. Perhaps he would have better understood its powers. But instead, he dropped the plan and lost his money. Obviously he didn't have an iota of understanding of the investment concept. People don't invest money and then pull out when there is zero chance of recapturing the expense. But he did. And mind you, he was no dummy in real life. Only in marketing. He was expecting miracles, instant results, dramatic changes. Marketing just does not work that way. So don't expect it. Don't plan for it. Don't lose money because of it. In fact, whenever you spend one dime for any type of marketing, you should actually use the term *investing* to describe your expenditure. By *investing* your money in marketing, you'll earn a lot more money than by *spending* your money in marketing. See the difference?

In the middle of the stream there is no other horse   The third major marketing secret is to make your marketing *consistent*. Don't change media. Don't change messages. Don't drop out of the public eye for long periods. When you are ready to market your product or service, be prepared to put the word out consistently. Consistently means regularly — and for a goodly period of time. It means that instead of running a couple of large newspaper ads once every few months, you'll run smaller newspaper ads, and run them frequently. Instead of airing fifty-five radio commercials in one week every few months, you run twelve radio commercials per week every week. You can even drop out of sight one week out of four. As long as you are a consistent marketer, you can pull out of the media for brief periods.

Consistency equates with familiarity. Familiarity equates with confidence. And confidence equates with sales. Provided that your products or services are of sufficient quality, confidence in yourself and your offering will attract buyers more than any other attribute. More than quality. More than selection. More than price. More than service. Confidence will be your ally. And consistent marketing will breed confidence.

Customer confidence

I have a client now who has been with me for about ten years. When she first started marketing her product, she spent a fortune advertising on television. Could she afford it? Of course not. But she believed that television was her key to success. With the number of dollars she had to invest, television was her key to doom. We'll discuss TV in greater detail later, but for now, suffice it to say that unless you can utilize a medium effectively, you should not utilize it at all.

My client was able to salvage her business from her disastrous TV experience, and she came to me. We talked about commitment, investment, and consistency. Since that day, she has run a tiny ad every Sunday in the newspaper, and her sales have continued to rise. Without increasing her marketing expenses, she has dramatically increased her sales. It happened over a period of several years. Her store has quadrupled in size, and her profits have followed suit. The key was consistent advertising. She calls her tiny Sunday newspaper ad her "meal ticket." And she's right. She tells me that almost everyone who comes into her store says they've seen the ad. You'd find that hard to believe if you saw the size of the ad. But you'd find that easy to believe if you knew that she's been running that and similar ads in the same newspaper on the same day for years. People are familiar with her operation. They're confident in her offerings. And they buy from her.

Familiarity breeds profits

These three secrets — being committed to your marketing program, investing in it with the expectation of a conservative return, and promoting consistently — are the most valuable secrets you'll learn in this book. They are also extremely difficult rules to follow.

Your friends, employees, coworkers, partners, family, and suppliers may advise you to change your marketing plan when they don't see instant results. These same well-meaning people will question a marketing program that does not produce a dramatic increase in sales over a short period of time. And they'll be the first to tire of your marketing, become bored with your ads or commercials, be ready for a major change in your message or media. But your customers won't feel that way at all. They'll go through the process of developing confidence in your offering, and you should do every-thing in your power not to undermine that process. Now that you know these secrets, you won't.

So when you do develop your marketing plan, don't give it your stamp of approval until you are ready to commit yourself to it. Don't okay it until you are ready to invest in it with a realistic expectation of return. And don't commence implementing it until you are pre-pared to stay with it on a consistent basis. This is not to say that you can't make changes. Of course you can. And maybe you should. But you can make changes while remaining consistent.

There. Now you can never say you weren't made fully aware of the three most important marketing secrets of all. Merely by knowing them and making them a cornerstone of your business, you have a head start on your competition. Now, let's increase that head start. Let's examine what it takes to develop a successful plan in the first place.

4
The Blueprint: Secrets of Successful Market Planning

IN ORDER TO ENGAGE in successful marketing, you absolutely *must* start out with a marketing plan. But how do you develop one? You engage in research, attend to all details, and give the matter quite a bit of deep thought. Rest assured, the difference between many a success and failure is market planning and nothing else.

A word that you should now start to use and understand is the word *positioning*. Positioning means determining exactly what niche your offering is intended to fill. Recently, I read of an airline that commenced operations during a time when most airline business was drastically down. By establishing a solid marketing plan, the new airline took off with astounding speed. It positioned itself as a high-frequency, no-frills airline that specialized in flights of less than two hours and in connecting passengers with long-distance routes of other airlines. That was a unique position. No other airline in the region offered such benefits. Success came rather easily.

Positioning

To attract further attention, the airline held seat-clearance sales, gave away free fifths of Chivas Regal and Jack Daniel's, and introduced other innovations into a rather staid industry. None of this happened by accident. All of it came as a result of intelligent market planning and brilliant positioning.

One of the best-known names in American advertising circles is David Ogilvy. After placing several billion dollars' worth of advertising, Mr. O. listed thirty-two things his advertising agency had learned. Of the thirty-two, he said that the single most important decision had to do with *positioning* the product. He claimed that marketing results depended less on how advertising was written than on how the product or service was positioned.

The market plan or positioning strategy should serve as the springboard for marketing that sells. When doing your own market planning, review your offering with regard to your objectives, the strengths and weaknesses of your offering, your perceived competi-

Questions and criteria

tion, your target market, the needs of that market, and the trends apparent in the economy. This should be instrumental in your establishment of a proper position. Ask yourself basic questions: What business are you in? What is your goal? When you know the true nature of your business, your goal, your strengths and weaknesses, your competitors' strengths and weaknesses, and the needs of your target market, your positioning will be that much easier to plan.

Once you zero in on a position for your product or service, you should measure it against four criteria: (1) Does it offer a benefit my target audience really wants? (2) Is it a real honest-to-goodness benefit? (3) Does it truly separate me from my competition? (4) Is it unique and/or difficult to copy?

Unless you are completely satisfied with your answers, you should continue searching for a proper position. When you have finally answered the questions to your own satisfaction, you'll end up with a sensible position — and that should lead you to your goal. Accurate positioning doesn't just happen. It takes a lot of clear thinking, quite a bit of effort. But it's the key to marketing that works. And no guerrilla would think of doing one speck of marketing without a proper marketing plan that includes a positioning statement.

Just prior to starting on your marketing plan, you should practice thinking big. At this point, your imagination is not a limiting factor, so let it expand to open your mind to all of the possibilities for your venture.

The positioning paragraph

If you want, you can make your finished plan up to ten pages long. But at first, try stating it in one paragraph. Suppose you call your business Prosper Press and you intend to sell books about free-lancing. Let your paragraph start with the words:

"The purpose of Prosper Press marketing is to sell the maximum number of books at the lowest possible selling cost per book. The target market will be people who can or do engage in free-lance earning activities." Let the paragraph continue, "This will be accomplished by positioning the books as being so valuable to free-lancers that they are guaranteed to be worth more to the reader than their selling price. The major value of reading the book will be stated in the title of the book, so that it is communicated as clearly as possible." (This statement could also apply to a certain book on marketing, but we will let that pass.)

And the paragraph might end, "Marketing tools to be utilized will be a combination of classified advertising in magazines and newspapers, direct mail, sale at seminars, and publicity in newspapers and on radio and television. In addition, direct-sales calls to bookstores will be employed. However, the thrust of the business will be mail order. Thirty percent of sales will be allocated to marketing."

That's a long paragraph. And it's a simplistic paragraph. But it does the job. It's for a product rather than a service, for an earning venture that entails hardly any contact with the public. This mail-order venture requires very little in the way of marketing, considering all the options. It works beautifully in real life; has worked since 1974.

The plan starts with the purpose of the marketing — that is, it starts with the bottom line. From there, it connects with those who contribute to that line — the target audience. Next comes the positioning statement, which explains why the offering has value and should be purchased. The marketing tools are then listed. And the cost of the marketing wraps it up.

Now let's try it for a computer tutor.

"The purpose of Computer Tutor marketing is to book 100 percent of the time the company has for computer education, at the lowest possible cost per hour. The target market will be small local businesspeople who can benefit from learning how to operate a small computer. The company will be positioned as the prime source of one-on-one, guaranteed instruction in the operation of small computers. This positioning will be made possible by establishing the credentials of the educators, the location of the operation, and the equipment. Marketing tools to be utilized will be a combination of personal letters, circulars, brochures, signs on bulletin boards, classified ads in local newspapers, yellow page advertising, direct mail, advertising specialties, free seminars, sampling, and publicity in local newspapers, on radio, and on television. Marketing and positioning will be intensified by office decor, employee attire, telephone manners, and location selection. Ten percent of sales will be allocated to marketing."

Most marketing plans, especially when reduced to one paragraph, seem deceptively simple. But *unless* they are simple, they are difficult to execute. A complete marketing plan, which can run as little as three paragraphs — the marketing plan, the creative plan, and the media plan — or as long as ten or even one hundred and ten pages (not recommended), should serve as a *guide*. It need not spell out all the details.

The chairman and chief executive officer of the Coca-Cola Company recognized this need for simplicity when he said, "If I had to state our business plan in one sentence, it would be this: 'We are going to build on our marketing strength in order to achieve profitable growth in the decade ahead.'"

Naturally, the marketing plan does identify the market. It lays out the framework for creating the advertising — as will be seen in the next chapter. It specifies the media to be utilized, along with costs, as will be seen in chapter 6. And that's really all it has to do.

A business plan may require support documents such as results of research, the overall competitive situation, financial projections, and other details. But to include those details in the marketing plan itself is to muddy the waters. A good road map lists the name or number of the highway wherever appropriate, not wherever possible. Like maps, marketing plans with too many details are difficult to follow.

The briefer your marketing plan, the easier it will be to follow. Bolster it with as many support documents as you wish. But don't include support information in the plan itself. Leave the details for other times, other places, other documents. The marketing plan should be the essence of simplicity. If it is not, chances are you haven't thought it through enough.

Expanding your plan   Once you have given your plan the proper thought, brevity, and focus, you can expand it in those areas pertinent to your business. While expanding it, never forget that your prime purpose is to obtain maximum profits. These profits will be obtained if you clearly list your goals — all of them, including timing, budgets for everything, and projections. Without projections, you'll not have a measuring stick. Your expanded plan should look first to the long range, then to the near future. By looking far enough into the future, you will realize what it takes to get you where you want to go in the style you desire.

You might want to consider what market share you are targeting, what key personnel may be necessary to command that share, what inside services you'll need, and what outside services can be utilized to negate the need for inside services. And whether you list all the potential pitfalls in writing or not, you should think about how to deal with them. If you know what to expect in the way of obstacles, you'll better be able to surmount them as they pop up. And pop up they will.

Many expanded marketing plans include a situation analysis. This entails learning about your key customers, your expected competition, the possibilities, the probabilities, and the reality of the marketplace at the moment. While you are analyzing your situation, always remember to keep your eye on your bottom line. Don't let business get in the way of the purpose of business. The means should not interfere with the end.

Computers now enable us to project results based upon hypothetical instances. An expanded marketing plan or business plan may examine those "what if" situations. It should have the framework for incorporating alternative courses of action based upon contingencies. If you wish, it can embrace lists of objectives, priorities, monitoring methods, problems, opportunities, and responsibilities. But an expanded marketing plan is more of a luxury than a necessity. And too many entrepreneurs get waterlogged with details to the point that the flame of their initial thrust grows dim and turns to smoke. Huge corporations do the same when they get carried away with technology and distracted from their original dreams.

Yearly, you should reexamine your marketing plan — whether brief or expanded. Your goal should be to maintain it. The conservative philosophy should apply: If it is not necessary to change, it is necessary not to change.

But whatever bells and whistles you have attached to your basic plan, whatever M.B.A. documentation you have affixed to it, you must still know who you are, where you are going, and how you will get there. You must start with a bare-bones marketing plan, short and simple. And you should not confuse a marketing plan with a business plan. A longer plan can go into details of growth, exact expenditures, and details. But the plans I have included a few pages back are enough to enable you to start and succeed. The first example is for a real company. The second is for a fictional company. These plans can be implemented by entrepreneurs who have a bent toward either mail-order book marketing (you can write or buy the books) or computer education (you can do or delegate the teaching). Both follow a simple formula that can serve as the basis for virtually any venture.

Such plans allow for some flexibility, but not a great deal. For example, Computer Tutor may run only one magazine ad one time in one regional edition, and run radio commercials every single day of the year. The marketing plan would still be fulfilled. **A little flexibility, but not too much**

A good marketing plan should not allow for too much flexibility. After all, the plan is created to be followed. If you want changes, make them *before* you write the plan. *And don't forget to commit yourself to it.*

Once you have positioned your business with a marketing plan and can start, where do you go? You go on to develop a creative plan **What is to be done** that tells what your advertising is going to say. And finally, you create a media plan that tells the exact media details: costs, names of newspapers or radio stations, dates and sizes of ads, frequency of advertising, advertising specialties to be employed, tacks for obtaining free publicity, and the identity of your business. Notice that I use the word *identity* and not the word *image*. *Image* implies something artificial, something that is not genuine. *Identity* is more evocative of what your business is all about and comes across as honest because it really is.

Okay, you've got a marketing plan that tells how you'll promote your earning endeavor. You've got a creative plan that dictates your message and your identity. You've got a media plan that tells exactly where you'll spend your money. Now, if you've got the rest of your earning act together — the financial side, the legal issues, the accounting, the ability to offer a lot of quality in either your products or your services, and the right mental attitude — you can start earning money.

Many people start at this point, get frigid feet when they see the early results, and stop marketing while they think things over. Think but do not stop. Stopping is not a good idea. If after starting a business and embarking upon a marketing program — which is to say, investing serious cash in promoting the business (serious being anywhere from $100 per month to $1,000,000 per month) — you decide to stop marketing for a while, turn immediately to this page and read the following list of reasons why you *should* continue to market:

Ten truths you must never forget

1. *The market is constantly changing.* New families, new prospects, new lifestyles change the marketplace. Nearly one-third of the people in America will move this year. Nearly five million Americans will get married. When you stop advertising, you miss evolving opportunities and stop being part of the process. You are not on the bus. You are not in the game.
2. *People forget fast.* Remember, they're bombarded with tons of messages (an estimated 2700) *daily.* An experiment proved the need for constancy in marketing by running advertising once a week for thirteen weeks. After that period, 63 percent of the people surveyed remembered the advertising. One month later, 32 percent recalled it. Two weeks after that, 21 percent remembered it. That means *79 percent forgot it.*
3. *Your competition isn't quitting.* People will spend money to

make purchases, and if you don't make them aware that you are selling something, they'll spend their money elsewhere.

4. *Marketing strengthens your identity.* When you quit marketing, you shortchange your reputation, reliability, and the confidence people have in you. When economic conditions turn sour, smart companies continue to advertise. The bond of communication is too precious to break capriciously.

5. *Marketing is essential to survival and growth.* With very few exceptions, people won't know you're there if you don't get the word out. And when you cease marketing, you're on the path to nonexistence. Just as you can't start a business without marketing, you can't maintain one without it.

6. *Marketing enables you to hold on to your old customers.* Many enterprises survive on repeat and referral business. Old customers are the key to both. When old customers don't hear from you or about you, they tend to forget you.

7. *Marketing maintains morale.* Your own morale is improved when you see your marketing at work, and especially when you see that it does, indeed, work. Your employees' morale is similarly uplifted. And cutting out marketing seems a signal of failure to those who actively follow your advertising. That won't be many people, but it will be some.

8. *Marketing gives you an advantage over competitors who have ceased marketing.* A troubled economy can be a superb advantage to a marketing-minded entrepreneur. It forces some competitors to stop marketing — giving you a chance to pull ahead of them and attract some of their customers. In all ugly economic situations, there are winners and losers.

9. *Marketing allows your business to continue operating.* You still have some overhead: telephone bills, yellow page ads, rent and/or equipment cost, possibly a payroll, your time. Marketing creates the air overhead breathes.

10. *You have invested money that you stand to lose.* If you quit marketing, all of the money you spent for ads, commercials, and advertising time and space becomes lost as the consumer awareness it purchased slowly dwindles away. Sure, you can buy it again. But you'll have to start from scratch. Unless you are planning to go out of business, it is rarely a good idea to cease marketing completely.

I hope I have talked you into living with your commitment to your marketing program. This in no way means that you are going to market your business successfully. A marketing plan is necessary, in fact crucial, for a company or an entrepreneur. But a marketing plan is a bit like a fancy, comfortable, powerful, great-looking car — without gas. The fuel that powers your vehicle is the advertising itself: what it says, how it looks, what it feels like. That's where the creative process comes into play in marketing. And that's when it's got to be used with style and power. There's a way of making sure those creative juices flow. I'll let you in on some of the secrets in the following pages.

5
Secrets of Developing a Creative Marketing Program

PROBABLY THE MOST ENJOYABLE part of the marketing process is the creative part. And if you want to succeed in making your small business big, you should realize that the creative part applies to every single aspect of the process. We'll start by going into ways you can make your advertising itself creative. Later, we'll explore how you can be creative in media selection, market planning, and public relations.

I'm not sure who first said it, but almost any marketing person worth his or her salt will tell you that *marketing is not creative unless it sells*. You can pretty much ensure that you'll end up with creative marketing if you start out by devising a *creative strategy*. Such a strategy is similar to a marketing plan, but limited to advertising only — and directed solely at the content of ads and/or commercials.

Creative strategy

If you think there's a simple formula for establishing such a strategy, you're absolutely right. Here, in the simplest terms possible, is a typical three-sentence creative strategy:

"The purpose of Mother Nature breakfast cereal advertising will be to convince our target audience, mothers of children twelve years of age and younger, that Mother Nature breakfast cereal is the most nutritious and healthful boxed cereal on the market. This will be accomplished by listing the vitamins and minerals in each serving of the cereal. The mood and tone of the advertising will be upbeat, natural, honest, and warm."

In this one paragraph we have listed the purpose of the advertising, the method by which the purpose can be achieved, and the personality the ads or commericals will have.

You've probably seen Miller beer advertising, showing men with exciting jobs drinking Miller beer at the end of their workday — a time referred to in the commercials and ads as "Miller time." The creative strategy for that type of marketing might have read:

"The purpose of Miller beer advertising will be to convince our target audience, beer-drinking males, that Miller beer is what macho-type men enjoy after a hard day's work. This will be accomplished by showing the men at work, then after work, enjoying mugs and bottles of Miller beer. The mood and tone of the advertising will be masculine, joyful, socially oriented, and blue collar."

The first step in developing a creative marketing program is writing a simple creative strategy. You can get a great deal of insight into writing one for yourself if you practice first by writing creative strategies for current advertisers. Pick a newspaper advertiser, a television advertiser, and a direct-mail advertiser and compose three-sentence creative strategies that apply to each of them. Do the same for your competitors: That will help you figure your own positioning and prevent you from becoming a me-too company.

Seven steps to advertising that works

After you've got your own strategy — one to which you have devoted much time and thought — you can embark upon a seven-step program to assure yourself of successful advertising. Let's check all seven steps.

1. *Find the inherent drama within your offering.* After all, you plan to make money by selling a product or a service or both. The reasons people will want to buy from you should give you a clue as to the inherent drama in your product or service. Something about your offering must be inherently interesting or you wouldn't be putting it up for sale. In Mother Nature breakfast cereal, it is the high concentration of vitamins and minerals.

2. *Translate that inherent drama into a meaningful benefit.* Always remember that people buy benefits, not features. Women do not buy shampoo; women buy beautiful or clean or manageable hair. Men do not buy skis; men buy speed, control, durability, and excitement. Mothers of young kids do not buy cereal; they buy nutrition. So find the major benefit of your offering and write it down. It should come directly from the inherently dramatic feature. And even though you have four or five benefits, stick with one or two — three at most.

3. *State your benefits as believably as possible.* There is a world of difference between honesty and believability. You can be 100 percent honest (as you should be) and people still may not believe you. You must go beyond honesty, beyond the barrier that advertising has erected by its tendency toward exaggeration, and state your benefit in such a way that it will be accepted beyond doubt. The company producing Mother Nature

breakfast cereal might say, "A bowl of Mother Nature breakfast cereal provides your child with almost as many vitamins as a multivitamin pill." This statement begins with the inherent drama, turns it into a benefit, and is worded believably. The world *almost* lends believability.

4. *Get people's attention.* People do not pay attention to advertising. They only pay attention to things that interest them. And sometimes they find those things in advertising. So you've just got to interest them. And while you're at it, be sure you *interest them in your product or service, not just your advertising.* I'm sure you're familiar with advertising that you remember for a product you do not remember. Many advertisers are guilty of creating advertising that's more interesting than whatever it is they are advertising. But you can prevent yourself from falling into that trap by memorizing this line: *Forget the ad; is the product or service interesting?* The Mother Nature company might put their point across by showing a picture of two hands breaking open a multivitamin capsule from which pour flakes that fall into an appetizing-looking bowl of cereal.

5. *Motivate your audience to do something.* Tell them to visit the store, as the Mother Nature company might do. Tell them to make a phone call, fill in a coupon, write for more information, ask for your product by name, take a test drive, or come in for a free demonstration. Don't stop short. To make guerrilla marketing work, you must tell people exactly what you want them to do.

6. *Be sure you are communicating clearly.* You may know what you're talking about, but do your readers or listeners? Recognize that people aren't really thinking about your business and that they'll only give about half their attention to your ad — even when they are paying attention. Knock yourself out making sure you are putting your message across. The Mother Nature company might show its ad to ten people and ask them what the main point is. If one person misunderstands, that means 10 percent of the audience will misunderstand. And if the ad goes out to 500,000 people, 50,000 will miss the main point. That's unacceptable. One hundred percent of the audience should get the main point. The company might accomplish this by stating in a headline or subhead, "Giving your kids Mother Nature breakfast cereal is like giving your kids vitamins — only tastier." Zero ambiguity is your goal.

7. *Measure your finished advertisement, commercial, letter, or*

brochure against your creative strategy. The strategy is your blueprint. If your ad fails to fulfill the strategy, it's a lousy ad, no matter how much you love it. Scrap it and start again. All along, you should be using your creative strategy to guide you, to give you hints as to the content of your ad. If you don't, you may end up being creative in a vacuum. And that's not being creative at all. If your ad is in line with your strategy, you may then judge its other elements.

The creative use of tools

The key to creative advertising is starting with a smart creative strategy. The test of creative advertising is sales. If what you want to sell doesn't sell, you are not truly being creative. And creativity doesn't end with the creation of your advertising. Once you have highly creative marketing tools — in the form of ads, commercials, signs, circulars, store decor, whatever — you must be creative in the way you use them. I know of a deodorant company that did a lot of TV advertising to introduce its product during the winter. Why the winter, when people are not buying as much deodorant? Because this company lacked the funds to go head-to-head with the big guys. So instead of vying for public attention during the summer, when their competition would be shooting the big guns, this company attracted attention during the winter, when no other deodorant companies were advertising and it had the stage to itself.

There are other ways to be creative. You can be creative in the use of personal letters by having them hand delivered or by sending them via Express Mail or some other out-of-the-ordinary delivery service. You can canvass creatively by wearing a unique outfit and handing a small gift to each prospect. You can be creative in your use of signs by putting them in unusual places, such as in the hands of paid picketers (one of the most unique advertising vehicles I know). Show creativity in the yellow pages by the size of your ad, its message, and its graphic treatment. Be creative in the use of newspaper advertising by running six small ads in one issue, rather than one large one.

As you can see, there are limitless ways to exercise creativity in all facets of marketing. In an earlier book of mine, *Earning Money Without a Job,* I told of a couple who got married in their boutique, after informing the local newspapers and TV station about the wedding. Naturally, they received a lot of free coverage. (I hope they didn't get married simply to get free publicity.)

A former boss of mine used to remind his staff that you can be creative by coming downstairs with your socks in your mouth — but what's the point? There should be a reason for your creativity. And it should never detract from your message.

When practicing guerrilla marketing, you must be more creative than your competition in every single aspect of marketing. Merely doing it by the numbers isn't enough. You've got to do it properly, do it intelligently, do it clearly, do it creatively, and do it consistently to assure yourself of successfully marketing your product or service. You don't have to know how to write or draw to be creative. All you've got to do is supply the creative idea. You can always hire a person to write or draw for you. But it's not easy to hire a person to be creative about your business for you. That task should fall to you. And you should revel in it.

Now let's look at a few examples of creativity in action:

Creativity is action

Example A: A CPA wanted to increase his business, so he wrote a tax newsletter and sent it, free of charge, every three months, to a large list of prospects. By doing this, he established himself as an authority and dramatically improved his business. Not an earthshaking act of creativity, but it worked like crazy for the CPA.

Example B: A waterbed retail store wanted to rid itself of the counterculture identity associated with waterbeds, so it relocated in an elegant shopping center, required its staff to dress to the teeth, and hired a man with a voice like God to serve as the announcer on its radio commercials. Great results all around.

Example C: A jeweler wanted to attract attention to himself every Christmas, so he invented outlandishly expensive Christmas gift ideas. One was a Frisbee with a diamond in the center. Price: $5000. One was a miniature hourglass with real diamonds instead of sand. Price: $10,000. One was a jewel-encrusted backgammon set with a price tag of $50,000. The jeweler sold hardly any of these items. But he attracted national publicity and his December sales soared.

Notice that in none of these examples did I talk about the creativity one usually associates with ads themselves. That's the obvious place to be creative. But these examples show how you can be creative in your prospecting, store decor, employee attire, methods of gaining free publicity, and many other ways. If you train yourself to think that the opposite of creativity is mediocrity whenever you engage in marketing, you'll start forcing yourself to use marketing tools in the most creative manner possible.

In case you're wondering where creativity starts, I'll tell you. It **The source** starts with *knowledge*. You need knowledge of your own product or service, knowledge of your competition, knowledge of your target audience, knowledge of your marketing area, knowledge of the economy, knowledge of current events, and knowledge of the trends of the time. From this knowledge, you'll not only develop a creative marketing program but you'll also be able to produce creative marketing materials.

I find that I can glean a lot of knowledge by keeping abreast of world events in the usual manner. I read one weekly news magazine and twelve monthly special-interest magazines. I watch the late TV news most nights. And I read one daily newspaper. Some people are far more attuned to world happenings than that. But that's enough for me. It lets me in on the world situation, the local situation, and up-to-the-minute trends. It also allows me to get a look at the marketing of others — especially my own competition. If you're not keeping up, you're falling behind. And guerrillas just can't afford to fall behind.

Armed with all of this knowledge, you are able to do what many people define as the essence of creativity: You can combine two or more elements that have never before been combined. For instance, when 7-Up wanted to boost its sales up there with Coca-Cola and Pepsi-Cola, it referred to itself as "The Uncola." This put it in the category of the colas, yet proudly proclaimed that it was different. By combining the prefix *un*, which means "not," with the word *cola*, 7-Up exercised great creativity. The advertising person who dreamed up the concept used his knowledge of the art scene at the time by employing psychedelic art in advertisements both in print and on television. His knowledge of his product, his competition, his target audience, and the trends of the day resulted in exceptionally creative advertising. And the proof of that creativity was in the increased sales enjoyed by 7-Up. Where did it all start? It started with basic knowledge.

The Marlboro cigarette company exercised creativity when it combined the ideas of a cowboy and a cigarette. The telephone company used creativity when it combined the ideas of an emotionally charged situation and a telephone ("Reach out and touch someone"). Avis Rent-a-Car showed creativity when it capitalized on being the second largest, rather than the largest, and flatly stated, "We try harder." In all of these cases, plus thousands more, creativity started with plain and simple knowledge.

Thinking backward   As a guerrilla, you are obligated to become knowledgeable about a broad range of topics. Guerrillas are generalists, not specialists. Guerrillas know that to remove the mystique from the creative process, they must *think backward*. They must start by picturing the mind of their customer at the moment that customer makes a decision to purchase. What led to that decision? What were the thought processes? What made them take place? What were the customer's buttons and what did you do to push them? Thinking backward takes you to the needs and desires that are crucial to motivation.

Let's take a moment to examine marketing in the light of psychology. "Freudian marketing" would dictate that you change people's attitudes about things so that they eventually buy. This is possible. This is practiced. This is commonplace. But this is changing to a more direct type of marketing. "Skinnerian marketing" would dictate that you modify behavior. This means saying, showing, or doing something that causes a customer to change his or her behavior so as to act in the way you want that customer to act. You gently nudge the customer to buy, to call, to visit, to compare, to clip a coupon, to follow your command.

Freudian marketing is addressed to the unconscious — the most powerful part of a person's mind. Skinnerian marketing is addressed to the conscious — less powerful, but more easily activated.

Guerrilla marketing is addressed to both the unconscious and the conscious. It changes attitudes while modifying behavior. It comes at the customer from all directions. It persuades, coerces, tempts, compels, romances, and orders the customer to do your bidding. It leaves little to chance. It is the essence of precise planning.

6
Secrets of Selecting Marketing Methods

IF YOU ARE CONSCIENTIOUS, you can create a dynamite marketing plan, even a brilliant creative strategy. Still, there are many places you can go wrong. One way is to run the right advertising in the wrong media. But how do you tell the right from the wrong?

The marketing spectrum

Every method of marketing has its own particular strength. Radio is the most *intimate* of the media, allowing you to spend chunks of time in one-on-one situations with your audience. Sometimes the listeners will be in crowded restaurants. But other times they'll be in cars or in their homes — alone.

The newspaper is a prime medium for disseminating the *news*. And that strength can become your strength. Advertising in the newspaper, other than in the classified section, should be newsy, interruptive, and to the point.

Magazines are media with which readers become more *involved*. Whether they buy or subscribe to magazines, they generally take a good, long time to read them. So you can attempt to capture the editorial "mood" of the magazine in your ads. You can put forth more information because readers will be willing to take more time reading a magazine ad than a newspaper ad.

Television is the most comprehensive of the media. It enables you to convince your prospects by means of actual *demonstrations*. Such powerful selling devices as demonstrations are not possible by any other means — except for seminars, fairs, and live contacts with audiences. Television allows you to combine words with pictures and music, and to get into the minds of your potential customers in more ways than any other medium. Television advertising is also very costly and must be done properly or not at all. This is not a medium with which to dabble.

Direct mail allows you to take *the most careful aim* at your target audience. When created skillfully, direct-mail advertising enables you to go through the entire selling process — from the securing of your prospects' attention to the actual obtaining of sales by means of coupons that can be completed and toll-free phone numbers that can be called. Like TV, direct mail can be very costly when misused. And it's quite easy to misuse.

Signs and billboards are superb at *reminding* people of your existence and your reason for being. They do not work well all by themselves, except in rare instances. But they work well in combination with other marketing methods.

Canvassing takes more time than any other method of marketing, but it is highly effective. It has few limitations and gives you *personal contact*. In many cases, it is difficult to handle the canvassing yourself. But you can delegate the job to a professional salesperson or a high school student, depending upon the complexity of your sales presentation. Canvassing is greatly strengthened by mass-marketing methods, which help remove you from the category of complete stranger.

Yellow pages marketing and classified advertisements hit the *very hottest of prospects*. These people are taking the time to look up information such as that you're offering, so you don't have to expend much energy getting their attention or selling the general benefits of your product or service. This advertising also places you in direct confrontation with your competition. Just knowing that should enable you to be more precise with your message.

Brochures offer the greatest opportunity for you to go into *great detail* about your product or service. People expect a lot of information from a brochure, so you should feel encouraged to give it to them. This is not an invitation to be boring, but it is a hint that you can be very informative.

Telephone marketing allows you to be even more intimate than you can be in radio advertising — the most intimate type of advertising among the mass media. This type of marketing provides you with *great flexibility*. It can be used as an adjunct to direct mail or any other marketing method. It can stand alone. It can take a person from total apathy about your product or service to complete readiness to purchase. And you can take orders if your prospects have credit cards.

Tiny signs on bulletin boards serve to make you *part of the community*, increasing the amount of confidence people have in you. They are also extremely inexpensive, and if your product or service can fill unanswered needs, such signs frequently prove to be the most fruitful of all marketing methods. Like yellow page ads and classified ads, signs on bulletin boards tend to attract serious browsers. Such is not the case with, say, television advertising.

Advertising specialties, T-shirts, and calendar advertising work like billboards and signs to *remind people of your existence*, but they can't do the entire selling job. They can, however, pave the way to acceptance of your offering when used in conjunction with other marketing vehicles. The same goes for the sponsorship of teams and events.

Many businesses get a terrific shot in the sales curve by marketing at trade shows and exhibits. They find the opportunity there to *make contacts with purchase-minded people* who are thinking about the primary topic of the show or exhibit. The ability to reach people who have this type of mindset is a great advantage. There are fewer barriers preventing completed sales. Some companies and entrepreneurs obtain all the business they need by this one method of marketing. If you fall into that category, your life will be simpler.

Public relations, encompassing community relations, publicity, and even the joining of clubs and organizations, is another marketing method that should always be considered. It fits in well with virtually all other methods and often is the key to success. Involvement in community relations — meaning service to your community — helps you make powerful contacts, especially if you work your butt off for the community and not merely to serve your business needs. Publicity adds a great deal to your *credibility*, and at worst puts your name in the public eye. Joining clubs and organizations seems also to do what community service does — put you in contact with people who can help you. It seems a bit self-serving to join with that purpose in mind, but many do. And it serves their purposes well.

With all of these marketing methods available, which does a guerrilla choose? The answer should be obvious: *as many as you can do well*.

The marketing calendar   Once you have selected the marketing vehicles that can propel you to your goal, be sure you use them in an orderly, logical manner. This can best be accomplished by using a *marketing calendar*. A marketing calendar will help make all the elements in your program mesh. It enables you to plan your budget and helps you avoid unforeseen expenditures. It prevents you from engaging in hit-or-miss marketing. It protects you from marketing lapses. It precludes surprises. It aids enormously in planning, buying, and staffing.

Most marketing calendars address themselves to the weeks of the year, to the marketing vehicles that will be employed during those weeks, to the specific promotions or events in which you will be engaged, to the length of each promotion, and, when applicable, to whether or not co-op funds from manufacturers will be available to help pay the tab. In addition, some calendars include the cost of the marketing for each promotion.

Armed with such a calendar, as all guerrillas should be, you can see far into the future. The marketing process will come into clearer focus for you. And you will find it considerably simpler to be committed to your marketing program, to see it as the investment it is, and to recognize the consistency that is built into it.

A moment ago, I told you that a guerrilla makes use of as many marketing vehicles as he can implement effectively. A marketing calendar lets you know whether or not you *can* use these methods properly, because it forces you to come to terms with the costs and realities of utilizing the media you have selected.

Let's examine the marketing calendar on page 40 to get a better line on what it looks like. Note that the calendar runs a full fifty-two weeks so that the owner of this small retail store can see well ahead what ads to run, what products to have in inventory, what costs to project, what sales to plan.

The calendar utilizes the *Chronicle* newspaper every single week, but staggers the monthly use of the *Sun*, the *News*, the *Independent-Journal*, and the *Gazette*. It also allows for a testing of the *Times* and the *Reporter*. This seems like a lot of newspapers, but it is clear that the *Chronicle* will be the marketing flagship.

Lengths of the marketing activities vary from one to five weeks, with a healthy balance of long, short, and medium-length events. This prevents the marketing from being too predictable. Radio is used, but not every single week. With such a calendar, Video Vanguard is following a well-conceived plan. Promotions and sales are balanced with periods with no special sales.

Just as you shouldn't run just one week's worth of TV commercials or join a club with no intention of coming to meetings, you should not employ a marketing vehicle unless you are going to use it like a pro. And that means putting time, energy, money, and talent into it. It also means selecting marketing tools that are compatible with your business.

The compatibility factor

All of the compatible marketing methods that you can possibly employ with skill, and on a regular basis, should be put to work for you. In chapter 4, we saw that the entrepreneur billing himself as

Computer Tutor became committed to using fourteen methods of marketing. And that didn't even include decor, attire, and location. Computer Tutor has the option of being a single individual or a multi-employee company, yet its marketing plan calls for the utilization of personal letters, circulars, brochures (we'll get into the difference between these in chapter 12), signs on bulletin boards,

Video Vanguard Marketing Calendar

Weeks of	Marketing Thrust	Length	Co-opable	Radio	Newspapers	Cost Per Promotion
9/13	Giant Screen TV	1 wk	Yes	Yes	Chron/Sun	$615
9/20–10/4	New TV Set	3 wks	Yes	Yes-2	Chron/News	$1750
10/11–10/18	Video Experience	2 wks	No	No	Chron/IJ	$984
10/25–11/15	Names to Drop	4 wks	Yes	Yes-2	Chron/Gaz	$2044
11/22	Thanksgiving Sale	1 wk	Yes	Yes	Chron/Sun	$615
11/29	VCR Promotion	1 wk	Yes	No	Chron/News	$450
12/6–12/20	Xmas Promotion	3 wks	Yes	Yes	Chron/IJ	$2076
12/27	Last Week to Save	1 wk	Yes	Yes	Chron/Gaz	$611
1/3–1/17	TV Rut	3 wks	No	No	Chron/Sun	$1245
1/24–2/7	Trade-in Time	2 wks	No	No	Chron/News	$900
2/14–2/21	Clearance Sale	2 wks	Yes	Yes	Chron/IJ	$1384
2/28–3/28	Solve TV Problems	5 wks	No	Yes-2	Chron/Gaz	$2455
4/4–4/18	Giant Screen TV	3 wks	Yes	Yes-2	Chron/Times	$2044
4/25–5/2	People Who Love TV	2 wks	No	No	Chron/News	$900
5/9–5/16	Component TV	2 wks	Yes	No	Chron/IJ	$984
5/23	Memorial Day Sale	1 wk	Yes	Yes	Chron/Gaz	$611
5/30–6/13	Credit Is Easy	3 wks	No	Yes-1	Chron/Sun	$1445
6/20–6/27	VCR Promotion	2 wks	Yes	No	Chron/Rep	$976
7/4–7/11	Video Experience	2 wks	No	No	Chron/IJ	$984
7/18–7/25	Videotape Rentals	2 wks	No	Yes	Chron/Gaz	$1222
8/1–8/8	Free Home Demo	2 wks	No	No	Chron/Sun	$830
8/15–8/29	Giant Screen TV	3 wks	Yes	Yes-2	Chron/News	$1750
9/5	Satellite TV	1 wk	No	No	Chron/IJ	$492
9/12	Video Experience	1 wk	No	No	Chron/Gaz	$411

classified ads in local newspapers, display ads in local newspapers, magazine advertising, radio advertising, direct-mail advertising, advertising specialties, free seminars, sampling, and publicity — in newspapers, on radio, and on television. Sounds like this is going to cost Computer Tutor a huge sum of money. But it won't. You don't have to spend a double bundle to market like a guerrilla. In fact, you may be doing it wrong if you do spend too much money. Mind you, you won't get all that marketing for free. You'll have to pay, or, rather, invest. But it is possible to engage in a large number of marketing methods and save money with each.

Naturally, you start the process of selecting marketing methods by first identifying your target audience. The more exactly you know who your prospects are, the easier it will be to attain accuracy with your marketing plans. Kids don't read newspapers. Teen-age girls rarely read business magazines. Adult males hardly ever subscribe to *True Romance*. Those are the realities of the marketplace, and you have to tailor your selection of marketing methods to them. Select as many methods as you can. Select only the ones you will be able to do right. And select the ones that will be read, seen, or heard by your target audience.

Although marketing budgets are as unique as snowflakes, you might get a better bead on your target if you study the budgets of three fictitious companies. One is a small contracting company, Let George Do It, one year old, located in a town of 40,000, but within a marketing area of 150,000. The second is a two-person computer education organization, Computer Tutor, three years old, outside a city of 500,000, in a market area composed of 600,000 people. The third is a retail stereo store, Sounds Great, five years in business, smack dab within a city of one million people.

Let's suppose that Let George Do It grosses $4000 monthly in sales. The owner is willing to spend 7.5 percent of his sales dollars for marketing — a total of $300 per month, or $3600 per year. Computer Tutor takes in $20,000 in monthly sales and invests 10 percent of that in marketing: $2000 monthly, or $24,000 per year. Sounds Great grosses an average of $50,000 in monthly sales. An aggressive 12.5 percent is put back into marketing, permitting $6250 for marketing each month, $75,000 per year.

Because these companies are not brand-new, they do not have to invest extra heavily in advertising to get public attention. They already have a logotype; they have business cards, stationery, and invoice forms. They've even invested from $500 (Let George Do It) to $5000 (Sounds Great) for professional marketing consultation before they got started in marketing. So they each have a marketing plan, a creative strategy, and a media strategy. Their investment with the consultants has also netted them advertising themes, clear identities, and a visual format. Incidentally, the only way Let George Do It obtained such a large amount of consultation for such a low price was by building a sun deck for the marketing consultant as part of a barter arrangement. Computer Tutor and Sounds Great worked some similar agreement, if I know my guerrillas.

Here are the ways these guerrillas would apportion their funds:

Let George Do It ($300 monthly)

Marketing Method	Monthly Cost	Comments
Canvassing	$0	Main investment is time
Personal Letters	$0	Main investment is time
Circulars	$20	Cost of $240 yearly, amortized
Brochures	$50	Cost of $600 yearly, amortized
Signs on Bulletin Boards	$0	Posts his own circulars
Classified Ads	$40	Runs ads in two newspapers, once weekly
Yellow Pages	$20	Small listing, one directory
Newspaper Display Ads	$100	Runs ads in one newspaper, once weekly
Direct Mail	$10	Postage only, since he mails his circulars
Free Seminars	$0	Distributes his brochures at these
Trade-Show Booth	$10	Built booth himself, one-time cost amortized
Public Relations	$20	Cost of materials only, handles his own publicity
Production	$30	Amortized over one year, traded for a painting by George

George has selected many marketing methods, as you can see. His primary marketing medium is newspapers, yet he obtains quite a bit of business through his signs posted on bulletin boards and his free seminars. Neither cost him any extra money, and both are successful, according to George, because of his newspaper advertising. George installed a skylight for a graphic artist, who in return gave him nearly $1000 in artwork: layouts, illustrations, even type and a finished mechanical, all ready for the printer. George set up his trade-show booth at the Home Improvement Show, where he distributed his circulars freely and established a mailing list. George's $300 monthly investment in marketing runs 7.5 percent of his sales this year. He projects that next year that same $300 will represent only 5 percent of his sales. That is how much he expects his sales to increase as a result of his consistent marketing program.

Now, let's take a look at Computer Tutor's marketing budget:

Computer Tutor ($2000 monthly)

Marketing Method	Monthly Cost	Comments
Personal Letters	$0	Uses these to gain corporate jobs
Circulars	$30	Cost of $360 yearly, amortized
Brochures	$80	Cost of $960 yearly, amortized
Signs on Bulletin Boards	$30	Monthly fee to have company's flier posted
Classified Ads	$40	Uses one newspaper twice a week
Yellow Pages	$30	Medium listing, one directory
Newspaper Display Ads	$940	One ad weekly, two newspapers
Magazine Ad (One Time)	$100	One full-page ad in *Time*, amortized over one year
Radio Spots	$400	Spends $100 weekly; on one FM station
Direct Mail	$100	Postage only, since company mails circulars
Advertising Specialties	$30	Cost of computer-oriented calendars
Free Seminars	$0	Distributes brochures at these
Sampling	$0	Offered to corporations
Public Relations	$20	Amortized for one publicity push yearly
Production	$200	Amortized over one year — all production of circulars, brochures, ads, commercials

Computer Tutor gets a lot of referral business. The brochures spur word-of-mouth recommendations. The company's newspaper ads sell people completely, cause people to phone Computer Tutor, where they receive even more of a sales pitch, and motivate people to send for a free brochure. The radio spots direct people to make a phone call. Although Computer Tutor spends nil for telephone marketing per se, it engages in quite a bit of it as a result of responses to the newspaper and radio advertising. Computer Tutor would love to demonstrate its proficiency on TV, but simply cannot afford it. Each year, a publicity stunt such as free computer lessons for city-hall employees results in TV coverage. The 10 percent of sales invested in marketing will drop to 7.5 percent next year because of an increase in sales. Actual marketing outlays will remain the same.

The marketing expenditures for Sounds Great are even more ambitious:

Sounds Great ($6250 monthly)

Marketing Method	Monthly Cost	Comments
Brochures	$200	General brochures with no prices
Point-of-Purchase Signs	$205	One-time cost, amortized over one year
Yellow Pages	$200	One large listing in two directories
Newspaper Display Ads	$2800	Two large ads weekly, two newspapers
Radio Spots	$1400	Consistently run on three FM stations
Television Spots	$500	Two one-week TV splashes, amortized
Direct Mail	$300	Three yearly mailings, amortized
Free Seminars	$0	Held at store, sales made afterward
Searchlight	$20	For one yearly promotion, amortized
Production	$625	Amortized over one year

It's interesting to note that Sounds Great, which has the largest of the three budgets examined here, utilizes the fewest marketing methods. However, two methods are used very seriously: radio and newspaper advertising. The radio rates are very low, since spots are purchased through the company's internal ad agency (more about that in chapter 7) at a very favorable one-year contractual rate. The newspaper ads are also available at one-year contract rates, at a substantial discount. Television advertising is used with force, but only two times a year. The cost for the TV time is $3000 for each week.

Like other guerrillas, Sounds Great is now spending a large amount — 12.5 percent — on marketing. This tactic has eliminated several competitors who spent less boldly. Although they were larger than Sounds Great, their marketing did not reflect this. Sounds Great, like all smart guerrilla marketers, plans to spend the same amount in marketing next year, but figures this will represent only 10 percent of sales. The year after, that same amount should represent 7.5 percent of sales. The plan is to spend no less than 7.5 percent on marketing, because the stereo business is highly competitive.

When advertisers discuss media, they talk of *reach* and *frequency*. *Reach* refers to the number of people who will be exposed to the message. *Frequency* refers to the number of times each person will be exposed. Although in some endeavors you should strive for reach, in most, frequency will help you even more. Remember, familiarity breeds confidence, and confidence serves as the springboard to sales.

Reach and frequency

Before you select any method of reaching the people you wish to reach, think these thoughts: It is not necessary to say everything to everybody, nor is it possible. If you try to say everything to everybody, you'll end up saying everything to nobody or nothing to everybody. Instead, you should strive to say something to somebody. Your marketing message is the "something." Your target audience is the "somebody." Just as you take care in selecting what you will say, you should take equal care in selecting to whom it will be said. Saying the right thing to the wrong people is not acceptable guerrilla marketing. I know that advertising on television does wonders for your ego, but if your prospective customers don't watch much television, it is folly.

I suggest that you set out with the idea that you will employ absolutely every marketing method listed in this chapter, maybe even more. Then, start cutting down the list on the basis of who your audience is, whether you can utilize the method properly yourself, and whether you can afford it. With those methods that are left on your list, go to glory. Plunge into each as if it is your only. When you combine two marketing methods with two other marketing methods, the total is more than two plus two. A synergistic effect is created whereby two plus two starts to equal five and six and seven. And when you combine five marketing methods with five others, your possibilities for success are increased many fold. The more methods of marketing you employ, and the greater your skill at employing and selecting them, the larger the size of your bank balance. That's the guerrilla truth.

7
Secrets of Saving Marketing Money

SAVING MONEY IS IMPORTANT to everyone. To consumers. To large companies. And to entrepreneurs — *especially* to entrepreneurs. Don't forget, entrepreneurs for the most part are suffering from resource poverty. So not a penny can be wasted. And all money should pull more than its own weight. But is this possible? Bright entrepreneurs *make* it possible. This chapter suggests several ways to stretch your marketing dollars without decreasing their effectiveness one iota.

Dollar stretching

First of all, don't feel that you must constantly change your ads. This costs unnecessary production money and dilutes the overall effect of your advertising. Stick with one ad until it loses its pulling power. That's hard to do for most advertisers. In the beginning, most people will like your ad. Then, you'll become bored with it. Next, your friends and family will get tired of it. Soon, your fellow workers and associates will feel ho-hum about it. And you'll be tempted to change the ad.

Don't do it! Let your accountant tell you when to change ads. That's right, your accountant — the person who takes long looks at your profit picture. You can be sure your accountant won't get tired of an ad that is still pulling in business. The important thing is the public's reaction to an ad. It takes a long, long time for the public to get tired of advertising run on a scale that can be afforded by most small businesspeople. By remembering this, you will stretch your media money and save production dollars.

Barter

Another way to save impressive sums is to make use of the concept of barter. Maybe your local radio station or newspaper doesn't want what you are selling. But they do want *something*. In all likelihood, you'll be able to trade with someone who has that something they want. When that happens, you'll get your media ads for a fraction of their usual cost, since you'll be paying with your own services or goods *at their full retail price*.

Example: A stereo dealer wanted radio commercials but felt he couldn't afford the cost. He offered to trade recording equipment, but the station just wasn't interested. The station was interested, however, in constructing a new lobby. The stereo dealer found a contractor who wanted new stereo equipment. Result: The contractor received $5000 worth of stereo and television equipment; the radio station got its new lobby; the stereo dealer received $5000 worth of radio time. Yet the dealer's cost was only $2500 in equipment. In fact, his cost was even less than that, because he traded discontinued merchandise that would have had to be discounted.

There are many barter houses in the United States that specialize in setting up such trades. Find them in the yellow pages in large metropolitan areas, listed under "Barter Services." At least 500 magazines will trade ad space for whatever it is they need. But policies vary at these publications, and trades must be individually negotiated. Just remember that everyone needs something. By learning what your selected media need, you might put yourself in a position to set up a money-saving trade.

Co-op advertising   You can also save money by getting access to cooperative advertising funds. Many large advertisers pay cash fees to small advertisers who mention the name of the large advertiser in their ads. I know a woman who owns a small furniture store. When she mentions the name of a large mattress company in her ads, she receives a small sum of money from that company. Naturally, most of her ads mention the name of some large manufacturer that offers these co-op ad funds. Worth looking into. It not only helps save money for entrepreneurs but also lends credibility to their offerings by mentioning the name of a nationally known company. Some companies that offer these co-op funds insist they be the only company mentioned. Others don't care, just as long as you spell their name right. Still others demand that you include their theme line or logo in your ad. A smart entrepreneur, interested in saving lots of marketing money, will include the names of several co-op–oriented companies, thereby saving a large percentage of the ad cost — frequently more than 50 percent. This takes research and prearranging, but if you're interested in saving money, it's worth it. You can obtain free co-op literature from the Co-op Resource Center, P.O. Box 2243, 515 N. Front St., Mankato, Minnesota 56002.

P.I./P.O.   I suggest you put forth the effort to set up a P.I. or P.O. arrangement with an advertising medium. This is a rather common method entrepreneurs employ to save and make money. P.I. stands for "per inquiry" and P.O. stands for "per order." Here's how it works. You contact, say, a television station to see if it is interested in a P.I. or P.O. arrangement with you. That means that it gives you television time, and in return, you give it a preagreed sum of money per inquiry or per order.

Suppose you want to sell books for $10 apiece by mail. You strike up a deal with a TV station whereby the station gives you commercial time and you give the station, say, $3 per order. At this point, no money has changed hands. Okay. Now, the TV station provides you with the equipment to produce a commercial heralding your book. Normally, it might charge $100 to run a one-minute commercial, but it gives you the time for free. Then the commercial runs and fifty people order the book. That means the TV station receives $150 (at its $3 per order), which is a good deal for the station. You also come out very well, because you receive fifty orders ($500) and risk no marketing costs. Now, if you can make that same arrangement with one hundred other TV stations, you can clearly achieve very attractive profits without risking marketing outlay.

P.I. and P.O. arrangements are available with many magazines, radio stations, and television stations. I have never heard of this kind of deal being available with newspapers, but I imagine some far-sighted publishers would welcome the idea. All it takes is a letter to the medium of your choice, outlining the arrangement you're proposing. If the medium feels it can make money on your offer, you're in business. In this way, you can engage in quite a bit of high-level marketing with virtually no out-front costs to you, other than minimal production costs. Of course a TV station might put your commercial in a time slot after midnight, a time slot that couldn't be sold to another advertiser. But you can bet that the TV station wants to make money on the arrangement. Therefore, it will go all out. And if it makes money, you make money.

So you can understand why many an entrepreneur has made many a dollar with this little-known method of saving marketing dollars. A client of mine recently sold $3000 worth of his newsletters through a P.I. arrangement with a magazine publisher. The publisher gave free ad space (a full-page ad usually sold for $900) in return for a $50 cut of a $100 subscription price. Thirty subscribers signed up. Result: $1500 for the publisher and $1500 for my client — the first year. Renewals will increase his profits.

Free research

People enjoy being asked about themselves, enjoy talking about themselves. Take advantage of this human characteristic by asking questions of your customers. This can provide you with expensive research data for free. Prepare a questionnaire asking your customers all sorts of questions. Some will toss your questionnaire right in the wastebasket. Others will complete every question and provide you with a wealth of information. This research, if obtained through standard research-company channels, would cost you a fortune. But when obtained the way I've just described, this same information costs very little. More about this in the next chapter.

Gang runs   If you are a patient sort, you can save money, lots of it, by taking advantage of "gang runs." Large printing companies often run huge amounts of full-color printing on large presses all at once. Sometimes they have an opportunity to run a bit more printing than is scheduled. If you are about to have something printed and wish to save money, let a large printer know that you are interested in being included in a gang run and are patient enough to wait until it happens. Then furnish the printer with the press-ready materials and the paper, and sit back and wait. Eventually, the printer will have that gang run and you will be the happy recipient of a mass of your full-color brochures, obtained at a fraction of the normal price. And all you had to do to take advantage of this money-saving opportunity was to be patient. I've seen clients too impatient to wait for gang runs. They paid five times the price they could have enjoyed if only they hadn't been in a hurry. And the sad thing is that often their rush was unnecessary.

Being in a rush is a deterrent to good marketing and to inexpensive marketing as well. If you wish to gain the maximum effect from your marketing and to save money at the same time, avoid rushes like the plague. With a solid marketing calendar, a program that is planned ahead for a year, it will be quite easy to avoid them.

TV and radio rate-card fiction   You can also save considerable sums of money if you realize that radio and television rate cards can be likened to tales by the brothers Grimm, or charming stories by Aesop. In short, they are fiction and not to be taken seriously. If *anything* is negotiable, it is the cost of radio and TV time. Of course, prime time or drive time is hard to buy, therefore hard to negotiate. But understand that if radio or TV time is unsold, it is wasted forever. Therefore, stations will usually accept prices far below their normal rate-card prices.

To entice new advertisers — that is, entrepreneurs — TV stations will ordinarily offer even more attractive prices. Just knowing this will save you money. Large advertisers do know that rate cards are works of fiction. But small advertisers often believe what they read on rate cards. Don't you believe it. Remember that you can save media money by making an offer you *can* afford. You'll be surprised at how many radio and TV stations will accept your offer.

While we're on the subject of radio and television and saving money, let me emphasize that a vast amount of research has proven that you can accomplish almost as much with a thirty-second commercial as you can with a sixty-second commercial. So save money by cutting the verbiage and saying your message in half a minute. You can save money by applying this same truism to your print efforts. Unless it is necessary for you to look important by running large, expensive newspaper or magazine ads, you can attract business just as well by running small, inexpensive, but consistently run newspaper or magazine ads. You may not look as important as the purchasers of full-page ads, but you'll end up making more money. Don't forget: As I emphasized in chapter 3, consistency is the most important factor in marketing. And you can gain that consistency with small ads as well as large ones. Largeness does not produce the consumer confidence that comes with consistency — a truth that can save you impressive sums.

Ad size

It is axiomatic that shoddy production gives you a shoddy image. Therefore, when running print ads, especially newspaper ads, it is usually silly to save money on production by having the newspaper or other medium design your ads. Instead, you should have a professional do that work.

Professional production

There are two types of professionals: expensive and inexpensive. To save the most money and gain the best identity, hire an expensive designer to lay out your first ad and create a visual format for you. Then hire an inexpensive designer to do all of your follow-up ads, telling him or her to follow the format created in the original ad. This will not infuriate the inexpensive designer, who will probably be thrilled with the business. And it will not anger the expensive designer, who got a fair sum for the talent expended. The result will be that you will always have sharp-looking ads, even though you paid through the nose only one time. You get the best of two worlds: a classy look and format throughout the life of your marketing campaign, and a low price for the production of all the ads except the first. You shouldn't have to spend high production fees more than one time, but believe me, it is well worth it that one time. Ask any entrepreneur who has employed this tactic.

Have you ever heard of remnant space? Probably not, unless you're in the marketing business. Many national magazines publish

Remnant space

regional editions. When doing so, they sell advertising space to regional advertisers. Because of the way magazines are put together, publishers think in terms of four-page units, since it takes one large piece of paper folded in half to make four pages that fit comfortably into a magazine format. Often a magazine will have sold three of its four pages when publication date is right around the corner. What does the publisher do with that one extra page — that remnant space? Sells it at an astounding discount to a local advertiser, that's what. If you wish to be that local advertiser, just contact the publication well in advance of the date you wish your ad to appear, or get in touch with Media Networks, Inc., a company devoted to selling remnant space to local advertisers. The company is national, and its headquarters are at 600 Third Avenue, New York, New York 10016. The telephone number is 212-661-4800. This company will be able to put your ad in most national magazines, in the regional issues, at a far lower cost than you may think. For example, although in 1981 it cost $49,335 for a full-page, black and white ad in *Time* magazine, Media Networks, Inc., could sell you a full-page black and white ad in *Time* magazine in Tucson or El Paso or Wilmington for a mere $625 — a $48,710 savings. Some difference!

You are the advertising agency

While we're on the subject of the cost of advertising time and space, we should take a look at one of the most efficient money-saving strategies in all of marketing — establishing a house advertising agency for yourself. Normal advertising agencies earn their money by receiving a 15 percent discount from publications and broadcast stations where they place advertising. If an ad or commercial costs an advertiser $1000, that same ad space or commercial time costs an advertising agency only $850. This is known as an agency discount, and in my opinion, advertising agencies are entitled to every cent of it. The advertiser would have to spend $1000 anyhow. So by utilizing an ad agency, the advertiser receives professional help at no extra cost, since the advertisement will cost $1000 with or without an agency. And the ad agency picks up $150 for its efforts.

But what if you're too small to require an advertising agency? What if you just plain don't want an advertising agency? You should establish your own in-house ad agency. To do this, you usually need do no more than tell the advertising medium that you are an in-house or internal agency for your business. In some cases, the medium may require that you have a checking account in your agency's name (ten dollars in an account will do nicely). And you may need agency stationery. Again, this is no problem. If your business is called Atlantic Manufacturing, just call your agency Atlantic Advertising on inexpensive stationery you have ordered in the minimum amount.

With this checking account and stationery, you are now ready to be your own in-house advertising agency. And you can save 15 percent on almost all the advertising you place for yourself. You can save on virtually everything but newspaper advertising, where you pay only the retail rate, which is low to begin with. It's so easy to set up an internal agency that I'm surprised more entrepreneurs don't do it. But you can. You can save a considerable sum of money after you do. And your $625 *Time* ad will then cost only $531.25.

If you ever do use local television, start out with tight, well-planned scripts. Have a rehearsal session or two prior to the shooting date, then try to shoot three or four commercials in one session. Although the average thirty-second TV commercial costs around $70,000 to produce, you can get that cost down to $300 if you shoot several spots at once, work with thought-out scripts, and avoid paying high talent fees to actors and actresses. Once again, some difference! The difference is due to a variety of things. For one thing, full-scale TV productions usually involve large crews for lighting, props, make-up, hairstyling, and moving the camera around. That ordinarily involves unions and inflated costs. Guerrillas work with skeleton crews and do not work with unions unless absolutely necessary.

TV production on a shoestring

One of the highest costs in TV production, especially with videotape, is editing. With very well-planned scripts, you will need very little editing.

Some advertisers feel that they must have a celebrity to hawk their wares. This adds from $5000 to $50,000 to the tab. Guerrillas rely on the power of an *idea* and save the cash.

Expensive production devices such as complex scenery, special effects, and ornate sets make commercials cost more than they should. Because many people are involved in the actual shooting, each scene may be shot four or five different ways, to stroke four or five different egos. Guerrillas shoot each scene one way and get their ego kicks by making sizable bank deposits.

In addition, TV professionals tend to shoot commercials to suit their own tastes and needs. They can spot flaws that most viewers would never see. So they reshoot and reshoot and reshoot. Guerrillas accept minor flaws and get on with the commercial.

All this adds up to a whale of a difference in money — *but not in quality*. I have a reel of commercials, each costing under $500. TV pros who have seen them have estimated that the cost of each spot was $10,000 or more. In my opinion, unnecessary TV production costs are murdering many large-company production budgets. The amazing thing is that they are *easy to avoid*. So avoid them.

In the final analysis, there are two kinds of advertising: expensive and inexpensive. The expensive kind of advertising is the kind that doesn't work. The inexpensive kind of advertising is the kind that does work — regardless of cost. This chapter has suggested additional ways to save money with your marketing. But you'll save the most if you always make sure to run inexpensive advertising — the kind that gives you the results you want. And that has more to do with quality than cost.

8
Secrets of Obtaining Free Research

IT'S NOT DIFFICULT to turn up a marketing pro who will tell you that the three most important things to do to market anything successfully are to test, test, and test. That is pretty good advice. But it is unrealistic for those with resource poverty, who cannot shell out big bucks for sophisticated research.

The big secret is that you need not shell out any money to learn about your market. If you know what to look for and where to find it, you can obtain crucial information for nary a cent. Let's examine some of the things you might want to find out.

1. What should you market — your goods, your services, or both?
2. Should your marketing feature some sort of price advantage?
3. Should you emphasize yourself, your quality offerings, your selection, your service, or merely the existence of your business?
4. Should you take on your competition or ignore all competitors?
5. Exactly who are your competitors?
6. Who are your best prospects?
7. What income groups do they represent?
8. What motivates them to buy?
9. Where do they live?
10. What do they read or watch or listen to in the way of media?

Ten crucial questions

The right answers to these questions can prove invaluable to a marketing effort. The wrong answers, or no answers, can prove disastrous. Do what you must to get the right answers.

In most cases, great advertising is preceded by great research. There are three prime ways for you to engage in research that will provide you with the information that can make the difference be-

The free money library

tween success and failure, yet not cost you much, if anything. The first is to go to your local library. The reference librarian will be able to steer you to just the books and other publications that contain a raft of money-making information for you. Some of these publications have market studies of your area, conducted by companies that paid impressive sums for the data. Others contain studies of products or services such as yours, and indicate the level of their acceptance by the public. Still others include census reports, research reports, industry studies, and more. Whenever I write a book, I find myself in libraries ferreting out information. And I am always dazzled by the expertise of the reference librarians, who not only know where to find information but also seem to delight in the finding. And all the information to which they lead you is free for the asking.

The customer knows

A second, and commonly overlooked, way to obtain information is to ask your own customers. If you have a new business, I strongly suggest that you prepare a lengthy questionnaire for them. On it, ask them everything under the sun.

Large corporations that enclose brief questionnaires with their manufactured items such as TV sets, electric razors, or blow dryers report that fewer than half the questionnaires are returned. These questionnaires consist of five or six questions, even fewer. On the other hand, I had a client who gave each of his customers a fifteen-question questionnaire. Seventy-eight percent of the forms distributed were completed and returned. It seems that many people enjoy providing personal information, just as long as they can remain anonymous.

Suppose you wanted to establish a company that provided auto mechanical services at people's homes rather than in a garage. You might prepare and hand out a questionnaire that asks the following of your prospects — namely, motorists:

> *We are establishing an automotive service that makes "house calls." To help us serve you most effectively, please provide the following information:*
>
> What type of car do you drive? _____
> What year is it?_____ What model? _____
> How long have you owned it? _____
> Who usually performs mechanical services for your car? _____
> _____
> Would you want these services to be performed where you live? _____

List the three main reasons you would want "house calls" made to service your car:

_____

_____

_____

Would you pay more to have "house calls" for your car? _____
What is your sex? _____ Your age? _____ Your household income? _____
What newspapers do you read? _____
What radio stations do you listen to? _____
What TV shows do you watch? _____
Which magazines do you read? _____
What type of work do you do? _____
Would you purchase products as well as service from a traveling automotive service? _____
Who do you consider to be our competition? _____
Where would you expect us to advertise? _____
Do you have any other comments? _____

In this game of twenty questions, you always emerge the winner. By studying the *questions only*, you can easily see how much you can learn. Just think of how informed you'd be by studying the *answers!* This kind of questionnaire should be distributed for a number of months, and the answers should be studied each month, so trends can be spotted after the business has been established. Notice that the questionnaire did not ask the name or address of the customer, so anonymity was preserved, enabling you to ask many personal questions.

Analysis of the completed questionnaires will show you the kind of people your prospects are, how to reach them through the media, how to appeal to them, and what kind of cars they drive. You can analyze the questionnaires by grouping the responses to each question. Perhaps you'll learn that the majority of people interested in patronizing your business drive foreign cars. That would alert you to the possibility of doing a mailing to foreign-car owners. Their names are available from mailing-list brokers. It might be that your customers are owners of older cars. Again, you can reach these people with a targeted mailing. Also, the questionnaire will help you focus your advertising on the right people.

From the questionnaire, you can learn who your competition is by learning who usually performs mechanical services for your prospects. You can determine what it is you offer that is most enticing to your customers — again helping you choose the proper emphasis for your advertising. You'll discover the sex and age of your customers, and you'll learn exactly how and where to communicate with them, once you ascertain the newspapers, radio stations, TV shows, and magazines that interest them. If your customers are primarily white-collar workers, this questionnaire will inform you of that fact, and you'll be able to tailor your media selection to that reality. You can find out which marketing vehicles will work most effectively for you. And you can obtain a report on your own service.

It is very simple to make this analysis, very useful in helping you determine your marketing thrust, yet extremely inexpensive for you. This information can be used to update or revise your marketing plan. And just think, the only cost was for duplicating the questionnaire — well under $100. This is free research at its best, and frankly, you're nuts if you don't take advantage of it.

The third way to take advantage of inexpensive research is to prepare a questionnaire similar to the preceding one, and hand it to people using the kind of services you provide. That way, you'll be researching serious, rather than potential, prospects. You'll receive fewer returns than the 78 percent my client enjoyed, but you'll learn something — which is a lot more valuable than knowing nothing. Naturally, you won't hand your questionnaire to motorists if you are selling computer education. If that's your business, you'll want your questionnaires in the hands of people entering or departing computer stores. If you are a traveling hairstylist who makes house calls, hand your questionnaires to people leaving beauty salons or barbershops. Whatever your business, you can find prospective customers somewhere: with their kids at the kiddie playground; at the beach; in the park; downtown; coming out of the hardware store; leaving the ballpark. Chances are, you've already got a line on where they are. All you've got to do is go there and hand them your long list of questions.

How do you ensure that the prospective customers will return your questionnaires? Well, you can furnish them with stamped envelopes. You can tempt them with offers of free (but inexpensive) gifts. You can offer discounts to them if they complete and return your questionnaire. And you can use pure honesty by telling them, atop the questionnaire, exactly why you are asking so many questions. Just be sure to include your address, so that the questionnaires will be mailed (or brought) to the right place.

It helps if you have an introductory paragraph atop your question-naire. It should say something like, "We're trying to learn as much as possible from motorists in the community, so that we can offer them the best possible service. We apologize for asking you so many questions in this questionnaire, but we're doing it so that you can benefit in the long run. We promise that your answers will remain anonymous (notice we are not asking for your name). And we also promise that we'll use the information to help you enjoy better automotive service." Such an honest introduction serves to disarm those people who resent being asked so many questions; and it does explain exactly why you are doing it.

Once again, you end up with valuable information. Once again, it costs you hardly anything. A true guerrilla will try *all three methods* of obtaining such free research. Then, he or she will put the information to work to create a first-rate marketing plan, using reli-able data that can aid in the selection of marketing methods, the evaluation of the competition, and the framing of the creative mes-sage.

When questioning your target audience, it might help to list some **The basic needs**
of the basic needs people have, and ask them to make check marks by those that pushed their particular buttons. Most people will react to one or more of the following basic needs (known as "appeals" in advertising lingo):

    Convenience
    Comfort •
    Love
    Friendship
    ⌐ Security
    ✓ Style •
    ⌐ Social approval (status) •
    Health and well-being
    ⌐ Profit
    ⌐ Savings or economy •

If you have had the feeling that people patronize you because you offer convenience and economy, you may be surprised to learn, via your questionnaires, that they really give you their business because your work adds to their sense of security.

You can engage in more free research by conscientiously studying the other advertising that is going on in your community — not only that of your competitors but that of everyone else as well. Have frank conversations with your customers. Talk with your competitors. Talk with other businesspeople in your community. You'll find that these sources will provide you with useful information and won't charge you one cent for it. Research can help you save a lot of money and earn a lot of money. Free research can help you save and earn even more.

II
Mini-Media Marketing

IT IS IN MINI-MEDIA MARKETING that practitioners of guerrilla marketing have their chance to shine. For standard marketers rarely, if ever, resort to such teeny-tiny marketing methods as canvassing, writing personal letters, marketing by telephone, distributing circulars, posting signs on bulletin boards, running classified ads, using signs other than billboards, and putting the yellow pages to work. Fortunately, because the titans do not practice mini-media marketing, you'll come across very little competition in these arenas — except from fellow guerrillas.

Your mini-media marketing must still adhere to your marketing plan. It must still be accomplished with talent and style. It must still follow many of the fundamentals. But it gets to break many of the rules, too. For instance, you can make letters highly personalized. You can post one-of-a-kind signs. You can take advantage of the smallness of your business when making telephone calls. Make them personal, friendly, informal, yet professional.

I urge you to utilize as many media as you can possibly use correctly. And I especially urge you to use the mini-media to the max. Big companies don't. This will rarely put a strain on your budget. Production costs will be small. You'll have an opportunity to star in the mini-media more than in the maxi-media, where you can be outspent even if you're not being outthought. In the mini-media, your size will be an advantage, not a disadvantage. So I hope you'll put the following marketing methods to work while you're still small.

9
Canvassing: Marketing on an Eye-to-Eye Basis

CANVASSING CAN BE the most inexpensive marketing method of all. In fact, it can be free, except for the time you devote to it. And if you're just starting out, time is something you have a great deal of in your inventory. After all, canvassing is merely asking prospective customers for business. During a canvass, which the dictionary defines as "a soliciting of sales," you should engage in three separate steps.

The first step, called the *contact*, is when you first meet your prospect. That first impression counts like crazy. So make your contact friendly, upbeat, customer-oriented, honest, and warm. *Try to establish a relationship*. You need not talk about business if you don't want to. You can talk about matters personal, about the weather, about a current event — probably about your prospective customer.

Three steps to successful canvassing

The second step of a canvass is called the *presentation*. It usually takes longer than the other steps, yet it need take no longer than one minute. During the presentation, you outline the features of your offering and the benefits to be gained from buying from you. Some pro canvassers say, "The more you tell, the more you sell." I'm not sure about that. Depends upon what you are selling. If it is a home security system, your presentation might take fifteen minutes. If it is an offer to wash your prospect's car, the presentation might take one minute or less.

The third step of a canvass is the most important part. It's called the *close*, and it is that magical moment when you complete the sale. That happens when your prospect says "Yes" or signs on the dotted line or reaches for his or her wallet or merely nods affirmatively. If you are a poor closer, it doesn't really matter how good you are at the contact and the presentation. You've got to be a good closer to make canvassing work at all.

Before there were any other methods of marketing, canvassing existed. In fact, the very first sale in history probably occurred when one caveman asked another, "Want to trade me an animal skin for this fruit I picked?" No advertising was necessary. No marketing plan, either. Life has become far better since then. But far more complicated, too.

If you think that canvassing is like door-to-door selling, you're right only if you want to do it that way. You can canvass by going from door to door. You can do it in residential neighborhoods, and you can do it in commercial neighborhoods. Or, you can presell your canvass by first calling or writing the people you intend to canvass. You have a choice of telling them you'll be coming around so that they'll expect you sometime, or actually setting up an appointment. When that happens, it's more like making a sales presentation than canvassing. For most guerrillas, canvassing is something done with little or no advance warning. Sure, it helps if you advertise so that the prospective customers have heard of you when you come calling. But you don't have to advertise. If you make a good contact, a crisp presentation, and a dynamite close, and if you are offering a good value, canvassing may be the only marketing tool you ever need.

The clever canvasser

I mentioned that canvassing can be free, and I wasn't kidding. But canvassing improves when you do invest a bit of money in it. Where to invest? For one thing, you want to look good so as to inspire confidence. That means you should wear clean, neat clothes. If you are canvassing store owners with the idea of getting them to sign up for your window-washing business, you need not wear a coat and tie. But it helps if you're wearing spotless work clothes, and even if you have a clean rag dangling from your rear pocket.

The investment increases a bit more if you offer a business card to the person you are canvassing. The card establishes that you are for real and enables a person to give you business later, if not now. It also helps your referral business — if you do a good job. Your investment will be even greater if you decide to canvass using a brochure or circular. If you do produce such materials, either use them as sales aids while you are making your presentation or give them away after you have closed the sale. Don't expect a person to read your sales literature and listen to your sales talk at the same time. Generally I frown on giving out a circular during this contact, since it gives your prospect an opportunity to avoid buying by telling you he or she will "study" your circular, then get back to you. If they don't buy now, figure that they won't buy later. Most of the time, they won't. Some entrepreneurs give free demonstrations or samples while they canvass. Although this adds to your investment, it is often a smart addition.

Once you learn the best way to accomplish your canvassing, you will be confronted with several choices. First, will you want to continue using this method of marketing? Second, are you doing it as well as it can be done? Third, should you be delegating the canvassing job to someone else or to several other people? The advantages of canvassing are readily apparent. It doesn't cost much, if anything. It is a great way to get a brand-new business going. It strengthens your contacts, because looking a person directly in the eye is more personal by a long shot than writing a letter, making a phone call, or attracting attention with an ad. Canvassing is also a good way to learn the objections, if any, to your offering. It provides instant results and can be instituted instantly as well. And it lets you be sure that your message is being heard. Like television advertising, it enables you to demonstrate. Like radio advertising, it enables you to be intimate. Like newspaper advertising, it allows you to be newsy. And like magazine advertising, it allows you to involve your prospect.

The success of canvassing depends upon you and you alone. You can't blame the media if you mess up. And if you succeed, you deserve to get all of the credit. Furthermore, canvassing is very accountable, meaning that you know darned well whether it's working or not. Results aren't always so accountable once you get into the more sophisticated media.

Let's say you have a brand-spanking-new home security company. You sell and install burglar alarms and smoke alarms. You've named your company Always Alert, and you've printed up business cards, nothing else. Your marketing plan calls for you to spend the first two months canvassing for business. The first month, you'll canvass commercial establishments. The second month, you'll canvass homes. Then you'll decide whether to concentrate on businesses or homes, and you'll decide whether or not to continue canvassing for new business. Let's assume you're so short of cash that you cannot afford to run even one ad. I hope that is never the case, but right now, let's stack the deck against you.

The canvassing campaign

Okay, you're ready to make your detailed canvassing plans. What to wear? I'd suggest a dark business suit, whether you are male or female. The dark colors — navy blue, black, deep gray, or charcoal — lend authority to what you say. The suit itself implies professionalism. I'd stay away from any accessories that detract from the professional look you wish to convey. I'd also be sure that my hair was neat and my hands were clean, and that I had a handsome case to carry either samples or sales literature provided by the manufacturer.

Once you're properly attired, the next step is to decide what you'll say during the contact, that first precious moment. It is probably best to make a comment first about the store you are visiting: "I like your window display. It seems just right for this location. My name is Tim Winston. My company is Always Alert. We offer security systems to businesses such as yours. What type of security system do you have now?"

During this contact, you have complimented the prospect on his or her window display, thereby showing that you noticed it in the first place. I hope you were smiling as you announced your name and the name of your company. Finally, you qualified your prospect with one single question. By "qualified," I mean you determined your prospect's need for your product. If the prospect has a security system and tells you that it consists of both a burglar alarm and a smoke alarm, you can save time by making no presentation whatsoever, and go ahead on your way after first thanking the person for the information imparted. You might inquire if the person is happy with the current security system, and even leave your card behind just in case he or she wishes to make a change later. But you'd be best off keeping the time spent with nonprospects down to a minimum. Once your prospect indicates that he or she already has what you're selling, you should save time for both of you.

At the next store, following a similar contact, the prospect may tell you that they have no security system. That's your cue to make your presentation. While giving it, remember that *whenever you mention a feature, follow it with a benefit.* For instance, "Always Alert features security systems that run on solar power. So they never need batteries. They use up no expensive electrical power. And they are maintenance free." The feature is the solar power. The benefits are freedom from purchasing batteries, from spending money for electrical power, and from taking up time maintaining the devices.

Continue your presentation, making it as long as it must be, yet as short as it can be. After all, both you and your prospect have other things to do. While presenting, be constantly on the lookout for closing signs. It may be that you have already made the sale and that the prospect wants to buy. But if you don't look for signs that you've said enough, you might end up losing the sale. As the topnotch salespeople say, A-B-C — *Always be closing.*

After you have made your presentation, try to close with a question that requires more than a yes or no answer. Such a question might be, "Well, that about does it. Will it be better for me to install your alarm system Wednesday or Thursday?" Another closing question might be, "Do you intend to pay for your alarm system at the time of installation, or should I bill you?"

Many excellent books on salesmanship carefully dissect the sale, examining the contact, the presentation, and the close. Canvassing requires salesmanship. It requires a contact, a presentation, and a close. Furthermore, it requires just as much quality in that salesmanship as is needed for the sale of an expensive car or an item of furniture. And it requires far greater salesmanship in terms of quantity. A great car salesman may make ten contacts, presentations, and closes in one good day. You may make ten in one good *hour*. To succeed at canvassing, you must have enthusiasm about your product, an honest enjoyment of people, and a load of determination.

But if you're to succeed as an entrepreneur, if you're to build your small business into a large one, you'll have to move beyond canvassing, even though it may continue to be part of your marketing mix. The disadvantages of canvassing are that it takes too much of your time, that you can't reach enough prospects even in one high-energy day, and that it is limited in scope geographically. Some of those disadvantages disappear when you start delegating the canvassing to others. But if you succeed at canvassing, you'll soon become itchy to reach more people.

Before we go into ways you can do that, let's try to make you the best canvasser possible. To do that, let's examine the contact, the presentation, and the close in a bit more detail.

First, realize that *somebody* is going to close a sale with your customer. It might be a competitor of yours. It might be a friend of the customer. But it *will be somebody*. That somebody can be someone else or you. While your customer is with you, you have a lot of control over who will close — the most control you will ever have. After you've left your customer, you have very little control, if any. So *while your customer is with you is the best time to close*. And remember: Closing is really the name of the canvassing game. So even though you will need to make a contact and a presentation, you should be thinking "close close close" all along. By doing that, you'll be gradually closing all the time you're with your customer. And that's good. Still, in spite of the importance of closing, it is crucial that while you are making your contact, you think of *that* as the most important part. If you mess up on it, you may not have a chance to

Who will close the sale?

move on to the close. Do the contact well, and you may breeze right through to the actual close. That's how important the initial contact is.

If your contact comes from a "cold" call, and your prospect is a complete stranger, take steps to make that prospect a new acquaintance. If your contact comes from a lead — a recommendation from a friend, an answer to an ad you ran, or some other reason to make you believe the prospect can be converted into a customer — refer to that relationship, that bond between you. It will help break the barriers that much faster. Here are a few tactics canvassing pros use:

Tips on making a good contact

- Greet your prospect warmly and sincerely, using eye contact.
- Allow your prospect some time to get acclimated to being with you, some time to talk. Don't come on too strong. But don't waste your prospect's time, either.
- Engage in casual conversation at first — especially about anything pertinent to what you are about to discuss. Make it friendly and not one-sided. Be a good listener. But let the prospect know that your time is precious. You are there to sell, not to talk.
- Ask relevant questions. Listen carefully to the answers.
- Qualify the prospect. Determine whether or not this is the specific person to whom you should be talking, the person with the authority to give you the go-ahead, to buy. Try to learn, during the contact, what to emphasize in your presentation.
- Try to learn of your prospect's attitude toward your type of offering. Tune in on his or her fears, expectations, feelings — so that you can tailor your presentation to them.
- Learn something about the person to whom your contact is directed, so that he or she will feel like a *person* rather than a *prospect*. Make your prospect *like* you, for people enjoy doing business with people they like. But don't be phony. Don't be syrupy.
- Be brief, friendly, outgoing, and truly inquisitive. But be yourself.

Important elements of your contact are your smile, your attire, your posture, and your willingness to listen and look directly into the prospect's eyes. Your nonverbal communication is as important as your verbal communication. The impression you make will come as much from what you don't say as from what you do say.

It is often during the contact that the sale is cinched. This happens if your contact has truly opened up communications and convinced your prospect that you are honestly interested in helping him or her. During a successful contact, each party will have made a friend — and thereby paved the way to a sale, even continuing sales. The contact may be the shortest of the three phases of a canvass. But it does establish the basis for the presentation and the close.

When making your presentation, keep in mind that you are not talking by accident. You are there because of intent on your part. If your prospect is still with you and has not ended the canvass, there is intent on his or her part, too. And the intent is to buy. Either you will buy your prospect's story about why a sale cannot be made, or your prospect will buy whatever you are selling. It truly is up to you. And don't forget: People *do* enjoy being sold to. They do not like being pressured. They do like being persuaded by honest enthusiasm to buy. Here are some tips to make your presentations flow smoothly:

- List all the benefits of doing business with you, one by one. The more benefits a prospect knows about, the more likely a prospect will buy.

  **How to make
  your presentation**

- Emphasize the *unique* advantages of buying from you. You should be able to rattle these off with the same aplomb you can state your own name and address.
- If your prospect has no experience with what you are selling, stress the advantages of your *type* of offering, then of your specific offering. If you're selling security devices, talk of the value of owning them, then of the value of owning *yours*.
- Tailor your presentation to information learned during your contact.
- People do not like to be pioneers, so mention the acceptance of your products or services by others — especially people in their community. If you can mention names and be specific, by all means do so. The more specific you are, the more closes you'll make. But don't be boring.
- When you know enough about your prospect, you can present your product or service from his or her point of view. This ability will increase your number of closes dramatically.
- Emphasize what all of your product or service benefits can do for your prospect, not what they can do for the general population.
- Keep an eagle eye on your prospect's eyes, teeth, and hands. If

the prospect is looking around, rather than at you, you've got to say something to regain attention. If your prospect is not smiling, you are being too serious. Say something to earn a smile. Best of all, smile yourself. That will get your prospect to smile. If your prospect is wringing his or her hands, your prospect is bored. Say something to ease the boredom and spark more interest.

- A sales point made to the eye is ten times more effective than one made to the ear. So show as much as you can: photos, drawings, a circular, a product, *anything*. Just be sure it relates to your presentation.
- Sell the benefit along with the feature. If the feature is solar power, for instance, the benefit is economy.
- Mention your past successes so the prospect will feel that the key to success is in your hands and there is little chance of a rip-off.
- Be proud of your prices, proud of your benefits, proud of your offering. Convey your pride with facial expression, tone of voice, selection of words. Feel the pride and let it come shining through.
- Throughout your presentation, remain convinced that your prospect *will* buy from you. This optimism will be sensed by the prospect and can affect the close positively.

Despite the importance I have attached to the contact and the presentation, I still reiterate that all the marbles are in the close. Effective salespeople and canvassers are effective closers. Aim to be a dynamite closer and your income will reflect this. To close effectively, try to close immediately, rather than in a week or so. Also, remember these thoughts:

Closing like a pro
- Always assume that your prospective customer is going to do what you want, so you can close with a leading question such as, "Will it be better for you to take delivery this week or next week?"
- Summarize your main points and confidently end with a closing line such as, "Everything seems to be in order. Why don't I just write up your order now?"
- Ask the customer to make some kind of decision, then close on it. Typical points that must be agreed upon are delivery date, size of order, method of payment. A good closing would be: "I

can perform this service for you tomorrow, the eighth, or the fifteenth. The eighth would be best for me. Which would be best for you?"

- Begin to attempt the close as soon as possible by easing your prospect into it. If that doesn't work, try again, then again. Continue trying. If you don't, your prospect will spend his or her hard-earned money elsewhere — and with someone else. Count on that. Remember: People *like* to be sold to and *need* to have the deal closed. They won't make the close themselves. So you are performing a service when you sell and close.
- Always be on the alert for signs that the time is right to close. The prospect will hardly ever tell you when the time has come. You must look for hints in the prospect's words *and* actions. A mere shifting of weight from one foot to another may be a signal to close.
- Try to give your prospect a good reason to close *immediately*. It may be that you won't be back in the neighborhood for a long time, or that the prospect will wish to use your product or service as soon as possible, or that prices are expected to rise, or that you have the time and the inventory now but might not have them later.
- Let your prospect know of the success of your product or service with people *like* the prospect, with people *recently*, with people in the community — with people *with whom the prospect can easily relate*.
- Be specific with names, dates, costs, times, and benefits.
- If the prospect likes what you say, but won't close now, ask, "Why wait?" The prospect may then voice an objection. And you may close by saying, "That's great, and I understand." Then, you can solve the objection and close on it. In fact, one of the easiest ways to close is to search for an objection, then solve the problem and close on it.
- If you have not yet completed your presentation but feel the time may be right to close, attempt to close on the most important sales point you have yet to state.
- Always remember that a person knows what you want him or her to do, that there is a reason for your meeting, that your offering does have merit, and that at that moment, your prospect has your offering on his or her mind. Just knowing all these things will make it easier for you to close.
- When a prospect says "Let me think it over," that means "no."

- If you do not close just after your presentation, chances are you have lost the sale. Few prospects have the guts to tell you they will definitely not buy from you. They search for excuses. So do everything you can to move them into a position where they will buy from you. If you don't, a better salesperson will.
- Tie the close in with the contact. Try to close on a personal note. Something like, "I think you'll feel more secure now with this new security system, and that's important. Shall I have your smoke alarm installed tomorrow or the next day?"

If you don't feel comfortable with A-B-C, "always be closing," at least learn to feel comfortable with A-T-C, which means "always *think* closing." If you think closing, your thoughts will carry over to your prospect. And you'll close more as a result. But eventually, you just may want to exercise your powers of selling on larger groups of people. One of the ways to do that is by writing personal letters. So we'll examine the art of creating them in the next chapter.

10
Personal Letters — Inexpensive and Effective

THE WRITING OF PERSONAL LETTERS — not direct mailings of large quantities of letters and brochures, but simple, personal letters — is one of the most effective, easy, inexpensive, and overlooked methods of marketing. Certainly the large corporations don't consider using this type of communication, because it doesn't reach enough people to enrich their coffers. But it's just the ticket for many an individual businessperson. If you can write clear English, spell properly, and keep your message short enough, you ought to be able to develop enough business through this mode of marketing so that you need not employ many other methods. Even if you're a dismal grammarian, professional typists can usually help put your ideas into acceptable form on the printed page.

The primary value of a personal letter is that it enables you to convey a truly personal feeling and reach a special place in the mind of the reader. You can say specific things in personal letters that are just not practical in any other medium except for certain kinds of telephone marketing.

The personal touch

For example, you can say, "Mrs. Forman, your gardenias and carnations look wonderful this year. But your roses look as though they can use a bit of help. I can provide that help and bring your roses back to glowing health." That sure has more going for it than, "Dear Gardener, perhaps your garden isn't as beautiful this year as usual. We offer a full range of garden supplies and expertise to aid you."

The point is that in a personal letter you can, should, and must include as much personal data as possible. Mention the person's name, of course. But also mention things about the person's life, business, car, home, or — if you're in the gardening business — the person's garden. By doing so, you will be whispering into someone's ear rather than shouting through a distant megaphone. Naturally, you can't mention personal things unless you know them. So do your homework and learn about your prospective customers: their working and living habits, their hopes and goals, their problems. You can get much of this information from your chamber of commerce. You can get more by conducting your own informal research with the aid of a simple questionnaire, or by personal observation. Include in your letter these findings, and you'll be dazzled at the effect the letter has.

The follow-up   No matter how motivating your personal letter may be, you can double its effectiveness if you do one of two things — or preferably both: (1) Write another personal letter within two weeks; (2) Call the prospect on the telephone.

When you do the repeat mailing, your letter can be brief and for the most part a reminder of your original letter. However, it should also have in it new information, more reasons to do business with you.

When you make the follow-up telephone call, refer to your letters. Ask if the person read them. Talk about the high points. Take advantage of the fact that your letter has broken the "stranger barrier" and you are now on speaking terms with your prospect. Use the phone to develop a relationship. The stronger that relationship, the likelier the person is to do business with you. That relationship will intensify if your letter includes a number of personal references. That will prove beyond doubt that you have sent a personal letter and not a clever mass-mailed flier.

Multiple mailings   These days, with more and more advertising pieces being mailed, people are literally bombarded with letters. One way to make your letter stand out is by making it part of a two- three- or four-letter campaign. Such multiple mailing campaigns are more expensive than single letters, but incredibly effective. Study after study confirms that people patronize businesses with which they are *familiar*. When asked in a study what factors influenced a buyer's purchase decision, 5000 respondents indicated that *confidence* ranked first, *quality* second, *selection* third, *service* fourth, and *price* fifth. So much for offering the lowest price. Only 14 percent of the respondents listed price as their primary reason for making a purchase or selecting a business to patronize. By engaging in multiple mailings of personal letters, you are building up that customer confidence through familiarity, paving your way to a relationship and a sale. Only an entrepreneur with a carefully targeted market can afford this type of luxury. A large company has too many prospects to engage in personal letter campaigns.

Understand that there is a difference between a *personal* letter and a *personalized* letter. The latter type is really a rather impersonal letter with a person's name in the salutation and within the body of the letter, along with some personal references if desired. The personalization is accomplished by means of a sophisticated word processing machine. A personal letter, on the other hand, is extremely personal. It is directed to one person and contains so many specific personal references and so much personal information that it cannot possibly be meant to be read by anyone but the person to whom it is addressed. Naturally, it has a greater effect on a reader than a mere personalized letter.

Personal is not personalized

One fascinating way to do a personal mailing is to *make it unnecessary for your prospect to respond.* Oh, your letter might have an address or phone number, but in this case it should not ask for a written reply or a phone call. It should not include a means for responding. It should whet the reader's appetite. However, it should also tell the reader that you will be telephoning within a week to set up an appointment or firm up a sale. This accomplishes several things. It forces the reader to think about your offer — because it tells the reader that you'll be talking with him or her about it soon. It separates you from the many letter writers who leave everything to the discretion of the reader. It leaves the reader hanging, requiring you to provide the missing information. And it prepares the reader for your phone call. When you do call, you will not be a stranger but an expected caller.

This luxury of not including a response mechanism in your letter cannot be practiced by big firms, because it is too inefficient on a large scale. But it is the essence of guerrilla marketing, for it gives you an edge over mass marketers. And it goes to a unique extreme to gain attention.

Levels of the personal

The tone of your letter should incorporate business matters and personal feeling and should appeal to the reader's self-image. If written to the president of a company, for example, your letter should mention the responsibilities of a president, the importance of the job, and the problems encountered, and it should be well written and employ a relatively sophisticated vocabulary.

How long should a typical personal letter be? One page. But don't worry about going longer than that if necessary. Be sure to convey all the information you feel you must convey, but do it as briefly as possible. A good rule is to make your personal letter short unless it must be long. And when I say short, I mean one full page of warm, personal, motivating, enticing copy. Because it is a personal letter, it need not have a brochure or circular enclosed (although it may).

Your letter should give the reader relevant information, data that he or she might otherwise not have known. Occasionally, I will remind a prospective advertising client of an upcoming event or a promotion that worked well for another client. A gardener might alert a prospect to a coming season that is right for the planting of certain species. A tutor might talk of new advances in education. What it comes down to is giving something to the reader rather than merely asking for something or selling something. The information you impart freely might impress a reader with your intelligence, insight, or personality. It might also be utilized by the prospect with no recognition to you. But the rewards are usually worth the risks.

You are not the customer
It is crucial to remember that the letter should not be about you but about the reader. It should be in the *reader's* terms, about the *reader's* life or business. The letter should be loaded with potential benefits for the reader. The greater the number of benefits, the better. The classic advice about such letters is to remember the opera *Aida*. That's a memory crutch to remind you to get *a*ttention first, then *i*nterest the reader, then create a *d*esire, and finally make a call to *a*ction. But perhaps it's simpler just to remember to secure the reader's attention first, then state the benefits of doing business with you, and finally tell exactly what action the reader must take — make a phone call, write a letter, read page 5 of the Sunday paper, expect a phone call, anything, just as long as you say exactly what you want the reader to do.

From a purely technical standpoint, I offer these gems of personal-letter wisdom:

- Keep your letter to one page.
- Make your paragraphs short, five or six lines each.
- Indent your paragraphs.
- Don't overdo underlining, capital letters, or writing in margins.
- Do everything you can to keep the letter from looking like a printed piece.
- Sign your letter in a different-colored ink than it is typed.
- Include a P.S. — and have it contain your most important point.

P.S.
It seems that when people receive personal, and even printed, letters, they read the salutation first and the P.S. next. So your P.S. should contain your most attractive benefit, or your invitation to

action, or anything that inspires a feeling of urgency. There is an art to writing a P.S., and you should not sell such a brief comment short. Some personal letters contain handwritten P.S. messages. I recommend this. A handwritten P.S. proves beyond doubt that you have created a one-of-a-kind letter, that it is not a mailing piece that went out to thousands of people.

As with a great advertisement, a great personal letter should tell a person what you are about to say, then tell what you want to say, and finally tell what you just said. This may seem repetitious, but believe me, it's practical in these days of mailboxes filled with direct mail.

I have written myriad personal letters. Probably five in ten get ignored completely. Probably one in ten results in business. But the business from that one is usually so profitable that I can easily overlook the nine rejections. Ten percent is a great response rate compared with the 2 percent rate aimed for by many mass mailings. To give you some insight into how I create a personal letter, consider this one. I mailed it twelve times with zero business to me, then a thirteenth time that resulted in enough business to keep me grinning for months.

November 6, 1981

H. H. Thomas
Pacific Telephone & Telegraph
1313 53rd Street,
Berkeley, CA 94705

Dear Mr. Thomas:

The dollar bill attached here symbolizes the thousands of dollars Pacific Telephone & Telegraph may be wasting by not utilizing the services of a prime quality free-lance writer.

During this year alone, I have accomplished writing projects for VISA, Crocker Bank, Pacific Plan, Gallo, Bank of America, the University of California, and the Public Broadcasting System. Although these companies do not ordinarily work with free-lancers, they did work with me.

In each case, the projects were completed successfully. In each case, I was given more assignments. There must be a reason why.

If you want to provide Pacific Telephone & Telegraph with the best free-lance writing available for any type of project — or if you have a seemingly impossible deadline — I hope you will give me a call.

I have enclosed a description of my background — just to inform you that I have won major writing awards in all the media and that I have served as a Vice-President and Creative Director at

J. Walter Thompson, America's largest advertising agency. I guarantee you, however, that I am far more interested in winning sales than winning awards.

By your company settling for mere competent writing, or by having your writing assignments handled by traditional sources, you just might be wasting Pacific Telephone & Telegraph's money. A good number of the *Fortune* 500 companies have already figured that out.

Now, I look forward to hearing from you.

Very truly yours,
Jay Levinson

P.S. If you are not the person who assigns work to free-lancers, I would appreciate it if you would pass this letter (and this dollar) on to the person who does. Thank you very much.

It usually helps if you include a unique or informal enclosure with your letter. A newspaper article, a trade magazine article (especially in your prospect's trade), or a copy of your prospect's ad or a competitive ad helps a great deal, because the reader probably wants to read such material and will appreciate your sending it. In my case, the one-dollar enclosure served to separate my letter from the many others sent to the addressee.

Timing   Timing is also important. Be careful you don't mail when everyone else is mailing. Try to time your mailing to coincide with a particular season or the advent of a new competitor, or when you hear word that your prospect may be in trouble and in the market for whatever it is you're offering.

Do the necessary research by studying the appropriate directory at your library, so that you mail your letter to *the exact person* who ought to be reading it. The president of a company will either be that person or see to it that the right person does read it. You can be sure that if the president asks a subordinate to read something, it gets read.

The use of word processing equipment will allow you to send out several hundred letters, or more, all of which appear to be personal letters; for all are typed, and all can accommodate the insertion of personal comments within the body of the copy. Worth looking into, believe me, and quite inexpensive.

The personal letter is one more tool that favors the entrepreneur more than the huge corporation. So take advantage of it if you can. Doing so is practicing guerrilla marketing with maximum skill.

11
Telephone Marketing: Dialing for Dollars

AMONG THE MANY NEW FORMS of marketing is telephone marketing, which is now practiced by more and more companies — and by entrepreneurs. In fact, *Forbes* magazine has heralded telephone marketing as the marketing force of the 1980s.

Currently, there are three ways you can engage in telephone marketing. The first way, and the way upon which we'll concentrate here, is individual phone calls made by you or a member of your company. The second way is mass telephone marketing, which is carried out by firms specializing in it and is directed at thousands of potential customers at a time. The third way is by computer. Computerized calling machines actually call prospects, deliver tape-recorded sales pitches, and even pause during their messages so that prospects can answer questions and place orders. This method may be a bit impersonal, and many consider it an invasion of privacy, but it is commonly practiced. And for many a company, it works.

A telephone call takes less time than a canvass, is more personal than a letter, costs less than both (unless it's long distance), and provides you with fairly close personal contact with your prospect. It is hardest to say no to a person's face. It is less hard to say no to a person's voice. And it is least hard to say no to a person's letter.

As with advertising, telephone marketing should be part of an overall marketing program. And it should be a *continuing* effort. One phone call isn't enough. If a member of your company makes the phone calls, certain incentive policies should be instituted. For instance, you should always pay your designated callers both by the completed call and by the completed sale. Even if you use a salaried employee, add incentive bonuses to the salary.

No matter who does the calling, proper voice training for telephone sales is a good idea. Talk clearly. Use short sentences. Talk loud enough, but not directly into the mouthpiece of the phone; talking across the mouthpiece makes for the most effective voice

Maximizing telephone sales power

transmission. Your voice should project authority and warmth while instilling trust. Your message should be stated as concisely as possible. Whatever you do, don't read from a script. Don't even memorize a script — though it's always a good idea to memorize an outline, or "thought flow." The more naturally conversant you sound, the more sales you'll make. And that takes practice.

Notice how your friends, and probably even you yourself, assume different voice personalities when speaking on the phone. This is subtle, but it's there. Try to eliminate that telephone personality and bring out your most conversational qualities by actually practicing on the phone — talking to a tape recorder or to a friend. If you're going to do a good amount of telephone marketing, engage in role-playing, with you as the customer and a friend or associate as you. Then switch roles. Role-playing gives you a lot of insight into your offering and your message. Keep doing this until you are completely satisfied with your presentation.

Handling the objection
Many telephone solicitations crumble when objections are made. These objections are really opportunities in disguise. Many successful telephone salespeople (and nontelephone salespeople) are able to close sales when handling objections. In fact, "close on the objection" is a sales credo for many pro sellers. One way to handle an objection is to rephrase it. Merely by doing that, you can sometimes dissipate it. "We're already buying from someone else," says the person at the other end. "Oh, you're completely satisfied with the price, quality, and service you're currently receiving and feel there's no room for improvement?" By rephrasing the objection, you not only defuse it but create an opportunity for yourself.

The script
You must use an outline to structure your phone presentation. If your outline is longer than one page, there is probably too much in it and you should try to streamline it. An outline not only creates a structure for your thoughts and ideas but also helps keep the call on track when the person at the other end redirects it. Although you should not work from a script, or, as already mentioned, memorize one, it's still a good idea for you to write the script of a phone call. Once you have written the script, you should do three things with it: (1) Record it. See what it sounds like. After all, you'll be using "ear" words that are heard, rather than "eye" words that are seen. There's a big, big difference. (2) Make sure the recorded script sounds like a conversation and not like an ad. Leave room for the person being called to respond. (3) Make it a point not to restate the script but to rephrase it. State the same selling points. Present them in the same

order. But use different words, your own words. Your telephone outline should be able to accommodate several situations. After all, if your prospect decides to buy just after you've started, you should be prepared to close the sale and end the conversation.

When calling a potential customer, try to establish a real relationship with that person. You may not ever speak to him or her again, but you should try to create a bond between the two of you. Do it with a couple of personal questions or observations. Ask the person about some non-job-related subject. Relate as human beings before you relate as salesperson and prospect. You probably have some interests in common. Meet on that common ground if possible. Even though the two of you should relate as people, make no mistake: Your purpose in making the phone call is *to make a sale*. So go for it. As with the standard canvass or sales presentation, think in terms of contact, presentation, and close. **How to call**

Remember, your contact should be brief and warm. Your presentation should be concise, yet loaded with references to benefits. And your close should be clear and definite. Don't pussyfoot. There is nothing wrong in most instances with asking for the sale. Just don't do it in such a way that a yes or no answer can be given. Close by saying something like, "What will be the most convenient way for you to pay for this, check or credit card?"

A telephone outline/script that has been successfully used is shown here. It is not the perfect outline/script, but it's a good one. It shows you the basics. And you can learn from it: **The call**

> Hello, Mr. ———? This is ———. I'm calling for the Wilford Hotel in Los Angeles. Have you ever been to the Wilford? When was the last time you were in Los Angeles? Recently, we sent you an invitation. Did you receive it? Are you the person who makes out-of-town meeting arrangements for your firm, or is it someone else? Do you plan to take us up on our special offer now, or do you plan to request more information?
>
> As you may recall, we're offering special prices and complimentary services to companies that hold meetings at the Wilford between April first and June thirtieth. Will your company be holding a meeting in Los Angeles during that time? Did you like the special offer made to you? Do you have any questions about it? Do you usually have meetings in hotels such as the Wilford? What size meetings? Where do you ordinarily meet? I think you might be interested in holding a meeting at the Wilford. Don't forget, during the period from April first to June thirtieth, we're offering:

- Special room rates
- Complimentary meeting room
- Complimentary wine with dinner
- One free room for every 15 booked
- A complimentary coffee break daily
- Discounts on audio-visual equipment
- Preregistration for your people
- A suite for the meeting planner

Doesn't all that sound good? You get all these benefits with a minimum of only fifteen guest rooms.

Anything else we might offer you? When do you plan to hold your next meeting? When would be the best time to arrange a reservation for your group at the Wilford? Would you like to make the arrangements right now or later? When? Is there any other person at your company that you suggest I contact?

Thanks very much for taking this time to speak with me. Good-bye.

As you can see, a good phone script calls for lots of questions, so that the person called will feel he or she is part of the process and will not feel "talked at." Whatever you say on the phone should be part of your overall marketing and creative plans, so measure your scripts against your marketing strategies.

The preceding script is clearly from a telephone marketing program that was used in conjunction with a direct-mail program. That makes for a potent combination. These days, with direct-mail advertising growing so rapidly, it makes a lot of sense to follow up a mailing with a phone call. In this instance, the mailing was followed two weeks later by a phone call. A week later, another call was made. The program worked.

You'll have to use similar grit. You'll have to combine marketing methods and stick with them until you hit pay dirt. Often, your direct mailing can set up the phone call so that it is expected and the way is paved for a sale. Direct mailings also improve the performance of telephone salespeople. They help establish a relationship that becomes intensified by the phone call. Telephone calls also minimize cancellations of sales.

You've got to be prepared for massive amounts of rejection when you embark upon a telephone marketing program. For this reason, employee turnover in telephone marketing firms is tremendous. On the other hand, telephone marketing is so instantly effective for some **The boiler room** companies that they set up what are known as boiler-room operations. In these operations, several people gather in one large room, which is often partitioned. Each has a phone. And each can see the others. Each person makes call after call, trying to make as many sales, in as short a time, as possible. When a sale is made, a signal is given, such as an upraised fist. Seeing this signal, the other phoners give a reciprocal signal to show that they recognize the success. This seems to give a lift to the group morale and helps the telephone salespeople deal with the horribly high number of rejections. It also seems to nourish enthusiasm.

You can set up your own boiler-room operation. Or you can hire one. Many telephone marketing firms exist — more now than ever, because just a decade ago none existed. These firms are permanent boiler-room operations. They operate from their own facilities, using their own scripts, tailored for your needs, and their own telephone sales pros. They charge by the hour and by the call. And many companies find them well worth the expense. If you ever consider establishing your own boiler-room setup, first look into the economics of hiring an outside firm with a going operation. These firms can put their facilities to work for you or they can set up an operation for you, training your people to be masters at telephone selling.

One of the great advantages of telephone marketing is that you can obtain an *instant response* to your offer. You can deal with objections and overcome them. You can, by using a boiler-room operation, talk to literally thousands of people per day. In doing so, you can categorize the people you have called as customers, near customers, and noncustomers. In rare instances, you can accomplish all of your marketing by phone. Some companies do.

To succeed with this marketing method, you will have to know which benefits turn on your prospective customers. Give prime emphasis to those benefits you feel have the most impact. Be sure you are speaking with the right person. Be sure you have a specific offer in mind — and probably a special offer, one not available to all people at all times.

How to make the telephone work for you

The greater the number of people you call, the more sales you'll close. Of every twenty people you *call*, you'll probably make contact with only about five on your first try. The others will be busy, sick, away, on the phone, or otherwise indisposed. Of every twenty people you *reach*, you may close a sale with only one right there on the phone. So you can see that you'll have to make about eighty calls to close one sale. That might sound like a lot, but to a true-blue telephone marketing pro it means that a mere eight hundred phone calls will result in ten sales. Figuring an average of three minutes per call (some will take up to ten minutes, but most will take less than one minute), this means that forty hours of calling will result in ten sales.

This also means that you'll either spend one full work week on the phone or you'll hire someone to be on that phone for you. If your profit per sale is great enough, you should give serious consideration to marketing this way. If ten sales aren't nearly enough, perhaps you should think about using other marketing methods. For some entrepreneurs, ten sales in one week means joy, wealth, and fulfillment. If that's you, and you feel telephone marketing makes sense for your offering, utilize it before your competitors discover its powerful capabilities. It is still a relatively unknown selling force. That means it is very appropriate for a guerrilla.

12
Circulars and Brochures — How, Where, and When

LET'S GET THIS STRAIGHT at the outset: There is not much difference between a circular, a flier, and a brochure. To me, circulars and fliers are the same, and a brochure is longer and more detailed than either. My dictionaries don't shed much more light on the subject, so we'll have to live with my distinctions.

There are several ways to distribute circulars and brochures. They may be mailed alone, mailed as part of a mailing package, placed in mailboxes, slipped under doors, slipped under windshield wipers, handed out at street corners, handed out at trade shows, handed out wherever lots of prospects congregate, handed out to prospects and/or customers, placed in racks that say "Take One," placed on counters for general distribution, or dropped from airplanes. I don't recommend the latter. If you're going to distribute many of these, make them circulars, because circulars are less expensive per piece. If your plans for disseminating them are relatively limited, you might opt for the more expensive brochures.

Distribution

The simplest form of one of these printed pieces is a single sheet of paper, printed on one side. Printing on both sides makes matters a tad more complex. Printing on both sides of two pieces of paper — each folded in half — makes a booklet, which I call a brochure. Some brochures run as long as twenty-four pages. When planning to produce such materials, remember that when you fold a sheet of paper in two, you have a total of four pages (two on each side). So generally you must think in terms of four-page units. Brochures are ordinarily four or eight or twelve pages. Some brochures have panels that fold rather than pages that turn. Usually, these are six-panel brochures — three panels on each side.

Content and format

The format isn't nearly as important as the content. And the content must be factual information, enlivened with a touch of style and romance. Unlike ads, which must flag a person's attention, a brochure — or circular — already has that attention. So its primary job is to inform with the intention of *selling*. Most brochures, and some circulars, use artwork. Sometimes this is intended to keep the piece visually interesting. But most of the time, its purpose is to explain, inform, and sell.

When writing a circular, think first of the basic idea you wish to express. Then, try to marry a picture (art or photograph) to a set of words. After you've stated your idea as briefly as possible, try to explain more fully what you are offering. Always be sure to include information about how to get in touch with you: address, phone number, place to find you.

George's flier   I know an entrepreneurial-minded contractor named George. He markets his services well, and decided he'd improve business even more by distributing a circular or a brochure. Here's the way he proceeded. Being no dummy, George started out with a circular, to see how this marketing vehicle would work for him. If it worked well, he might upgrade it to a brochure. On the circular, he had a drawing done of a man (George) doing five tasks at the same time, in front of a house. Above the drawing, he listed his company name, which, incidentally, made a dandy headline for his circular: Let George Do It. Beneath that headline and picture, he briefly stated his offering:

George builds sun decks and patios.
George installs skylights and hot tubs.
George paints and puts up wallpaper.
George does masonry and electrical work.
George also designs and makes building plans.

LET GEORGE DO IT!

Call George at 555-5656 any time any day.

All work guaranteed. Contractor's License #54-45673.

Not very fancy, but quite explicit. The cost for George to write this circular was nil. An art student did the illustration for $50. And the cost to produce about 5000 of the circulars, including paper, was another $100. So George ended up spending about $150, which comes to three cents per circular. Even if printing costs had been higher, George would have spent less than a nickel per circular. And without paying for color, George was able to get a colorful circular by the ingenious use of colored ink on a colored paper stock — dark blue ink on light tan stock.

George then distributed his circulars by several methods: He mailed 1000; he placed 1000 on auto windshields (he had a high school student do some of this for him); he distributed 1000 more at a home show in his area; he handed out 1000 more at a local flea market; and he held on to 1000 to give to satisfied customers to pass on to their friends and neighbors. Being bright as a penny when it comes to saving money, the enterprising George also asked each of his customers where they had heard of him. When they said, "I saw your flier," George asked where they got it. This way, he learned which of the five methods of circular distribution were most effective.

Now that's guerrilla marketing. Not expensive whatsoever. But very effective. One job could recoup for George his entire marketing budget for circulars. And since 5000 circulars were distributed, you have to believe that George got more than one job.

Perhaps George will decide to put out a brochure someday. As a first step in planning a good one, he'd think in terms of photography, so that he could show actual pictures of work he has accomplished. **George's brochure** And because he has such a comprehensive offering, he'd figure that an eight-page brochure was needed to do the trick. He'd use a simple $8\frac{1}{2}$ x $5\frac{1}{2}$ size, which is half the size of a standard $8\frac{1}{2}$ x 11 sheet of paper. Unless the brochure was full-color — a good idea — all type and photos would be in black ink. The paper stock, either glossy or not, would be white or some other light color.

He'd plan to use the same drawing on the cover that he used with his circular. After all, if it worked once, it ought to work again. So his cover would show his drawing, list his company name (which fortunately doubles as a headline and a brochure title), and maybe, but not definitely, list the other copy points from his circular. Let's say he does list them, since he wants to impart as much information as possible. *Repetition in marketing is far more of a good thing than a bad thing.*

Following his cover page, page one, his second page might list a bit about George. It would indicate his experience, his training, and jobs he has accomplished, and would list his skills and offerings. It might even include a photo of him. It would lead up to the other things he is about to say.

Page three would show photos of a sun deck and a patio, and would give a description, about five sentences long, of George's capabilities in this area. Page four would show photos of a skylight and a hot tub that George installed. Again, five or six sentences would indicate his expertise.

Page five would show photos of a room that George painted and another room that George papered. It would also include a bit of copy attesting to George's talent at painting and papering. Page six would feature photos of houses with masonry by George and electrical work by George. One would be an exterior shot and the other an interior shot. Again, copy would describe the work accomplished. Each of these pages, by the way, would repeat the short copy lines from the cover. For example, the seventh page, showing a gorgeous room addition designed and built by George, would have as its headline, "George also designs and makes building plans." A few sentences of copy would follow the photo. The copy would not have to be brief. Don't forget, the purpose of the brochure is to inform.

Finally, George's eighth page, the back cover, would give the name of his company, his phone number, his contractor's license number, and probably a repeat of the best photo from the interior of the brochure. Such a brochure might cost George as much as one dollar per unit. But it would be worth it, when you consider George's profit per sale.

A solar-heating company for which I created a brochure had a special problem. They realized that a brochure would help their business, but the technology in their industry was changing so rapidly that they were reluctant to commit themselves to producing one. Solution: I created an eight-page brochure with a pocket inside the rear cover. Within the eight pages, the brochure dealt with all of the aspects of solar technology that were not changing: its economy, its cleanliness, its responsibility to the environment, its acceptance and success in all parts of the world. Within the pocket were inserted separate sheets dealing with specific equipment. These could be replaced at will. Price lists, also replaceable at a whim, could be put there as well. This enabled the company to have a brochure and have flexibility at the same time.

Let's look at another example. A jewelry-making firm manufactured beautiful but very inexpensive jewelry. To add an element of value, it produced a lavish brochure — full-color, glossy, and photographed in the most glamorous parts of San Francisco. Each two-page spread contained one gorgeous photo of the San Francisco area and one photo of an item of jewelry. This lent an air of value to each piece of jewelry that could not have been created with a single photo. A brochure was just the ticket.

One of my clients sent a photographer on a dream assignment: to visit Mexico and shoot photos of a wide variety of villas and condominiums that my client was renting to people for vacation use. These photos were later made the basis for a colorful brochure. Without the photos, the brochure could only have dealt with villa and condo vacations in a theoretical sense. The photos brought the theory to vibrant life. The brochure helped the company quadruple its sales. Without a vehicle to show the many villas and condos, complete with beaches, pools, balconies, lush living rooms, and spacious bedrooms, the company could not have made its point.

Still another company was able to grow from tiny to tremendous merely by the proper use of a brochure. The company owned the patent on a new product that replaced the old-fashioned blowtorch. But it couldn't communicate all of the advantages of its product with ads or letters or phone calls. Personal demonstrations were impractical because of logistics problems. A brochure was the answer. It was incredibly detailed, listing all of the advantages of the product and all of the famous-name companies using it, and showing several exciting shots of the product in use. The brochure included a pageful of testimonials from satisfied users, and it described the technical data in such detail that even the most nit-picking engineer would be impressed. In addition, it was very handsome. This inspired confidence in the company, and it grew like Topsy. To this day, the company's primary marketing tool is that brochure.

And so it is with a number of other companies. They have a story that does not translate well in advertising but becomes brilliantly clear when the details, both verbal and graphic, are communicated in a brochure. If yours is one of those companies, you *can* afford to spend a great deal of your marketing budget producing a knockout brochure. The cost, including everything, runs anywhere from $500 to $50,000. But don't let the $50,000 figure dazzle you. That's only $4166.67 per month, a lot less than many companies spend on media advertising alone. Perhaps you won't even need the mass media. Perhaps a brochure will do the trick for you.

Other tips

Although some businesses benefit almost every time they give away their brochure, there are times not to give one away. If you have a store and distribute brochures to your potential customers, that gives them an excuse not to buy. They can tell you that they want to look over your brochure before buying. I advise my clients not to give their brochures to shoppers — only to people who have purchased or to people who are on their way out anyhow.

I also advise people who run newspaper or magazine ads that contain a lot of information to consider using those ads as brochures.

Merely reprint them and add front and rear covers by printing on the back of the folded-in-half advertisement.

If you don't have the budget for large ads, you might consider running small ads offering your free brochure. I know a man who earns his entire income (a six-figure income, I might add) by running tiny ads in myriad publications, offering his free brochure in each ad. The people who request the brochure are serious prospects. They took the time to write for the brochure. They are interested in what he's offering. My friend's brochure does his entire selling job for him. It describes his offer, gives the details, and asks for the order. His ads and his brochures are his only marketing tools, and he is very successful as a one-man show. This demonstrates how important a brochure can be.

Guerrilla business cards

A final point, and a mighty important one: When printing your business cards, think of them as mini-brochures. On them print your name, address, phone number, and theme line, of course, but also include brief body copy — as much as you can fit. Some clever entrepreneurs hand out double-size business cards, folded in half. The outside of the cards has the standard business-card information. The inside has a headline, beneath which are listed several features and benefits. These cards look like business cards but work like brochures. And brochures work well.

13
Classified-Advertising Hints: Making Small Beautiful

WHEN YOU THINK OF CLASSIFIED advertising, you probably think in terms of finding a job, looking for a car, selling a sofa, buying a boat, or locating a house or apartment. Think again. Classified advertising can also be used to support a business. And many a flourishing enterprise exists primarily on the pulling power of classified ads.

Why, today alone, my local newspaper features classified ads for a ticket-selling firm, a number of attorneys, an advertising medium, a pregnancy consultation center, a credit association, a fortune teller, a job-finding service, several books, a game arcade, a psychic adviser, a rent-a-mailbox firm, a ghostwriter, several introduction services, a group of escort services, two full columns of massage businesses, one and a half columns of firms offering loans, unique telegram companies, hairstylists, barbers, moving companies, auto transport firms, travel agencies, calligraphers, gobs of home-service entrepreneurs, tropical fish stores, pawnbrokers, coin and stamp dealers, antique dealers, auctioneers, TV dealers, computer equipment stores, musical-instrument stores, a horse ranch, boat dealers, a flying school, two résumé-writing services, loads of schools, tutors, employment agencies, auto and truck dealers, motorcycle dealers, hotels, rooming houses, bed and breakfast places, rest homes, guest houses, realtors, business brokers, motels, and mobile-home dealers. And today is a weekday, not even a Sunday.

If all of these entrepreneurs and/or businesses use the classified section, it makes sense for you to consider it, too. I notice that many of these advertisers have had ads in the classified section *for more than ten years*. And I know that they wouldn't spend their money there if they weren't getting handsome returns.

In my files, I have magazines with far more classified ads than the newspaper just mentioned. And I'm sure you know of newspapers — many of them, and the number keeps rising — that consist of nothing but classified ads. Obviously, classified ads work as a marketing medium. And if you can see any advantage for your company in using this medium, a bit of investigation and investment on your part is worthwhile.

Where and why and how much

Generally, there are three places you can run classified ads: in a multitude of magazines, in daily newspapers, and in classified-ads newspapers. If your offering is one that requires proximity to your customers, forget the magazines. And if your offering is national in character, forget the newspapers. There is little likelihood that you'll want to run classified ads both in local newspapers and national magazines — unless the papers you select are in localities spread throughout the country, and you want to combine that advertising with national magazine advertising.

As you may have heard, it doesn't cost an arm and a leg to run a classified ad. And you'll usually be offered a frequency discount. This means that if your five-line classified ad costs you $10.00 to run one time, it will cost only, say, $9.00 per insertion if you run it three times, and only $7.50 per insertion if you run it five times. The more frequently you run it, the lower your cost per insertion. Classified ad charges are based upon the number of words, the number of lines, or the number of inches. Depends upon the publication.

Many people read the classified ads each day. Some read them to find specific bargains. Others read them merely to browse via the newspaper. And still others find them the most fascinating part of the newspaper. Check them yourself. See which ads draw your attention. Also notice which classified-ad categories catch your attention. By reading through the ads, you'll get a sense of whether or not your business can profit from this method of marketing. You'll also begin to learn, by osmosis, what to say in a classified ad and what not to say.

Classified information

Although classified ads are short, fraught with abbreviations, and devoid of illustrations, they are not as simple as they may seem. If you decide to give the classified-ad section a go, there are a few concepts that you should keep in mind. For one thing, keep your headline short — and be sure you do have a headline, printed in all capital letters. Don't use abbreviations unless you are sure that people will understand them. While living in England, my wife and I searched for an apartment by scanning the classified ads. Many said that the rental included CCF&F. At first, we were completely thrown by that. Do you know what it means? Later, we learned that it stands for "carpets, curtains, fixtures, and fittings." We also learned that most Britishers already know that.

Don't use esoteric terms in your ads unless you're sure that most of your readers (99 percent) know the meaning. Write in short sentences. Try to sound more like a human being than a want ad. And be sure you include a way to contact you. More than once I've seen an ad with no phone number or address.

In most instances, publications have people who can help you word your want ads. I suggest that you use these people as guides but do not slavishly follow their advice. If they were brilliant writers, they'd probably be paid for their writing and not for taking want ads. If you are a good writer, write your own classified-ad copy. If not, go to a pro. Don't rely on the person who takes the ads to write your copy.

Word your ad in such a way that it contrasts with other ads in the same section. And choose that section very, very carefully. Some newspapers have categories that do not appear in other papers. Such categories include: attorneys, announcements, Christmas items, computers, and so forth. Be sure that you advertise in the right category. Make that plural. You may want to place your ad in more than one category.

Strange as it may seem, classified ads often outdraw display ads. So don't think that just because an ad has no picture and doesn't cost much it's not going to be effective. Many companies run display ads and classified ads in the same newspapers on the same day. They claim that the ads reach different classes of consumers.

I've been earning about $500 per month for the past nine years **An ad that works** working about half an hour per month. I do it with a classified ad. I've been running the same ad, with minor changes in wording, all nine years. After I had been working for a few years as a free-lance writer, I'd learned quite a few important things about free-lancing, things nobody had ever told me, things that weren't written in books. So I wrote a book and published it myself. I called the book *Secrets of Successful Free-Lancing*. And although it had but forty-three pages (still does), I priced it at $10. The reason I charged $10 was because I sincerely felt the book was worth it. Still do. The book cost me about $1 to print, including type and binding. Advertising runs about $3.33 per book. So I figure that I make $5.67 per book. Here's a sample of the classified ad I've been running:

I EARN MORE AS A FREE-LANCER THAN I DID AS VP/CREATIVE DIRECTOR AT J. WALTER THOMPSON.

I loved my JWT days. But I love now more. I live where I want. I work only 3 days a week. I work from my home and take lots of vacations. To do the same, read my incisive book, *Secrets of Successful Free-Lancing*. Send $10 to Prosper Press, 123 Alto Street, San Rafael, CA 94902. $11 refund if you're not completely satisfied.

Notice how my ad uses standard language rather than want-ad language. When I've run other classified ads using "people talk," I've also had good results. A regularly worded ad appearing in a sea of want-ad-worded ads tends to stand out.

The cost of the ad was $36 for one inch in the publication in which it originally appeared. And the entire ad fit in one inch in the classified section. Today, that same ad in that same publication costs $71.50. Still, for every dollar I invest in the ad, I average three dollars in sales.

For me, the biggest challenge (and biggest problem) was to find enough places to run the ad. After all, everybody isn't a prospect for a book on free-lancing. So far, I've run the ad in three advertising-trade magazines, two art-director publications, two writers' magazines, and the *Wall Street Journal*. Some of these publications draw a great response every single time I run the ad — and I run it every three months. Others haven't pulled well for me, so I've discarded them from my schedule. But by sticking with the four publications that work, I am able to bring in around $500 per month in profits — after paying for the ads, the books, and the mailing. I have all of the orders mailed directly to a mail-order-fulfillment house that mails out the books on the day orders are received, puts the names of the people ordering into a computer, and sends me the checks weekly — coded so that I know which publications are working best.

By the way, although people in the mail-order book business tell me that a 5 percent request for refunds is about par for the course, my requests for refunds are 1.2 percent. And don't forget, I offer an $11 refund for a forty-three page $10 book.

The half-hour per month I spend on this business is used to keep tallies on the pulling power of the various magazines and to fill out deposit slips for my bank. Not a lot of money from this endeavor, to be sure. But $500 per half-hour isn't anything to complain about. And just think — my only method of marketing is classified advertising.

Many marketers use the classified ads only to check out products, claims, prices, copy, headlines, and appeals. It's an inexpensive way to gain valuable information. Once you have a proven winner, you can then put forth your message in display ads if you wish. But remember, classified ads sometimes pull better than display ads.

A friend who advertised his books in *Psychology Today* found that classified ads at 25 percent of the price of display ads pulled considerably better than display ads. The kind of classified ad he ran is called a *classified display ad*. This is an ad that appears in the classified section but has a box around it and features dark, large display type. It costs more than regular classifieds, less than regular display ads, and, depending upon the offering, pulls better than both in many instances. Worth checking into. **Classified display**

It is a false economy to keep your classified ad as short as possible. Don't use too many adjectives, but do use a lot of facts. Aim to be as clear in your message as you can. Remember that your classified ad is really your sales presentation. So don't hold back on features if your offering has features to boast about. You may end up spending several dollars more because your ad is longer, but if it pulls in sales, this will easily outweigh the extra cost. **Classified content**

When thinking about classified advertising, think first in terms of clarity, then in terms of reader interest. You've got to capture your readers' attention. Do it with a catchy word such as GHOSTWRITING! or with a zippy headline such as NEED EXTRA MONEY? Keep in mind that you have but a fleeting instant to gain attention. The way to get it is with your short headline. The rest of your copy should follow directly from the headline. The GHOSTWRITING! headline might be followed with this sentence: "A professional writer will write, rewrite, or edit your letter, essay, manuscript, or advertisement so that it sings." The NEED EXTRA MONEY? headline might be followed by copy that begins with: "Obtaining the extra cash you need is not as hard as you think."

The idea is to maintain the momentum created by the headline. Write copy as though you are talking to one human being and not to a mass audience. Although you should mention as many features and benefits in your ad as you can afford, you should also practice the *selective withholding of information*. Merely by omitting certain facts, you may generate phone calls, visits, or whatever type of response you desire. The information you withhold may be the price, the location, or some other data the reader needs to complete the picture.

A good exercise for classified-ad writing is to write your ad as though it were to be a display ad in a newspaper. Then, start cutting copy to make the ad shorter and shorter. Finally, you will be left with the bare-bones facts. But remember, shortness does not equate with quality. Pepper your facts with a few adjectives, with word pictures. "I can paint your house so that it gleams like the day it was built" sounds a whole lot more appealing than "House painting at reasonable prices."

Though classified ads need not be as short as possible, they must nonetheless motivate your prospective customers. They must create *a desire to buy*. One advertising agency that specializes in classified ads claims that the key to success in the classifieds is simplicity and tight copy. If you think that is easy to achieve, you are wrong. It's tough to be simple, tough to be brief. The writing of classified ads is a very special art. The ads must be well written or else they will not inspire confidence. Just because they're short does not mean they can be shabby.

Study the winners
To gain the greatest possible insight into writing successful classified ads, I suggest that you spend some library time. Look through current newspapers and magazines, perusing the classifieds. Then look at one-year-old versions of the same newspapers and magazines. Check to see which ads are in both the new and the year-old publications. Those must be winners, or the people running them would not be repeating them. By studying them, you can learn what it is that makes them so successful. Is it the headline? The offer? The price? The copy? Apply whatever you learn to your own business.

Many large businesses that run high-powered advertising and marketing programs, making use of TV, radio, magazines, and other publicity, still use the classified section. They recognize that there are some people who read classified ads when looking for, say, antiques or certain automobiles. So don't think classified ads are small potatoes. There are even advertising agencies that specialize in running classified ads. You give them your ad copy and they place the ad in 150 newspapers around the country. If you will be marketing a product or service nationally, consider not only national magazines but also newspapers in multiple markets.

If our friend George were to run a classified ad in a local newspaper, he'd probably run it in the "Home Services" section, and it would say something like:

> WANT A SUN DECK? PATIO? SKYLIGHT? HOT TUB? Let George do it! George can give you those things plus masonry work, electrical work, and building plans. Free estimates. Call 555-5656. All work is fully guaranteed.

In fact, a person with an offering similar to George's did run such an ad. After it appeared only six times, he had to withdraw it because he couldn't handle all the work. I wish you the same success.

Remember that classified ads in newspapers allow you to home in on a local audience. Classified ads in magazines allow you to home in on a more widespread audience. And all classified ads allow you to test the waters with your message and with the advertising media you are trying out.

If you feel that classified advertising might be your marketing mainstay, I heartily recommend that you get in touch with Morlock Advertising Agency at 188 W. Randolph Street, Chicago, Illinois 60601. Their phone number is 312-726-8336. Ask for their "Advertisers Guide Book" — the current edition. It's free. And it covers magazines, newspapers, trade papers, rates, circulations, closing dates, publication dates, and more. It shows that classified advertising can be big-time advertising even though it comes in short paragraphs consisting of short sentences. And it lists all the magazines that accept classified advertising. Whether or not you use the services of Morlock Advertising, you'll certainly want to have at ready reference the copious information in their free guide book. Although I consider myself a true expert on the use of classified advertising, I often turn to Morlock for advice.

So remember. Just because classified ads are small and inexpensive doesn't mean they're ineffective. A true guerrilla marketer tries to find ways to put the power of classified ads to work. Hardly any other medium enables you to talk to honest-to-goodness prospects and not just browsers. There's a huge difference between the two.

14
Signs — Big and Little

THINK OF SIGNS IN TWO WAYS: those that appeal to people outside of your place of business and those that appeal to people who are within the place where you do business. The first category consists of billboards, which we'll discuss in another chapter, small signs on bulletin boards, which are discussed in this chapter, window signs, store signs, banners, signs on trees, and poster-type signs. Category two is made up of interior signs, commonly called point-of-purchase (P-O-P) or point-of-sale signs.

Whichever you use, or if you use both, be certain that your signs tie in as directly as possible with your advertising. Your ads may have made an unconscious impression on your potential customers, and your signs may awaken the memory of that advertising and result in a sale. Many people will patronize your business because of your ads. Your signs must be consistent with your advertising message and identity or those people will be confused. If the signs are in keeping with your overall creative strategy, consumers' momentum to buy will be increased.

Most exterior signs are there to remind, to create a tiny impulse, to implant thoughts a wee bit deeper, to sharpen an identity, to state a very brief message. As a rule, exterior signs should be no more than six words long. Naturally, some successful signs have more than six words, but not many. Probably the most successful of all have just one to three words.

Sign language Right now, since we're talking about the power of words — few words — let's examine some of the strongest words in the English language. Many are used in headlines. Many are used in signs. Almost all are used in advertising.

Psychologists at Yale University tell us that the most persuasive words in the English language are:

you   easy
money   safety

save	love
new	discovery
results	proven
health	guarantee

To that list, I would hasten to add:

free	yes
sale	benefits
now	announcing

Now that you know these words, I'll bet you can come up with some dandy signs.

Frequently, motorists make abrupt decisions (and right turns) when they pass windows with huge banners proclaiming SALE! or FREE GIFTS! or SAVE 50%! As you probably know, it doesn't take many words to convince some people that they ought to buy from you — right now.

And many famous businesses were built with signs and signs alone. I instantly call to mind Burma-Shave (for whom I had the privilege of writing two signs that were actually "published," or shall I say "roadsided"), Harold's Club in Reno, and Wall Drug Store of South Dakota. These are nationally famous businesses. Many locally famous concerns marketed their wares the same way. You can be sure that the Burma-Shave people, Harold, and Mr. Wall were all pioneer guerrillas, for they blazed trails that led directly to the bank.

Other exterior signs that usually work well are those that say such things as VOTE FOR LEVINSON, GARAGE SALE, FLEA MARKET, PARK HERE, and GAS FOR LESS. Not a lot of creativity, to be sure. Nonetheless, they work.

Almost (but not quite) as important as the wording of the sign is **Good-looking** the overall look of the sign. By this I mean the picture or pictures, **signs** the lettering style, the colors, and the design of the sign. A powerful graphic lends more power to the words. A sign that says FRESH DONUTS can be made doubly effective if it shows donuts growing in a meadow like flowers. If the sign says DELICIOUS DONUTS, it can be more motivating if it shows a picture of a grinning little girl holding a donut with a giant bite taken from it.

Usually, it makes sense to use very light lettering against very dark background colors or very dark lettering against very light colors. Using one type of lettering makes for easier reading than using more than one type. The words on the sign should be as large as possible while leaving room for the picture.

Keep in mind that although your sign should only be expected to remind, and not to make an actual sale, it will be better if you do go for the jugular and try like crazy to make the sale from the sign. Large advertisers with humongous marketing budgets can use signs for reminding only. But guerrillas have to get more mileage from their money. So although they know deep down that signs remind, they also realize that it is possible to sell *some* people with a sign, and they go for the sale with the sign.

Consider also the "clutter factor." Are there many other signs nearby? If so, your sign should stand out. If not, you can approach the creation of your sign with a different mindset. In England, when designing an outdoor sign campaign for a product that promised economy, we took the clutter factor into account and introduced black and white signs that contrasted with the surrounding sea of color signs. Our black and white beauties not only won awards but, more important, won customers. Had we used color with the same words and pictures, we would not have enjoyed such a high level of success. Our uniqueness, which tied in directly with our promise of economy, helped us stand out and make our point.

A powerful visual image should be created if you are going to use many signs. The Marlboro cowboy comes to mind immediately. Because you want your sign to be instantly identifiable with you, a graphic identity is highly recommended. The look should be un-usual, connected with your company's identity, and suitable for being maintained over a long period of time. Consistency. Remember?

The only punctuation mark with which you need be concerned is the exclamation mark. It lends a tone of excitement. Question marks, while of use in print advertising, take too much reflection time to be utilized on signs. Stay away from them unless you have a good reason to break that rule. Commas and periods usually are not necessary with six-word messages. And long words are to be avoided whenever possible.

Making a sale with a visual image plus five or six words calls for a lot of thought, a lot of creativity. As with all other marketing devices, a great sign starts with a great *idea*. If you lack the idea, your words and pictures will probably end up plain vanilla. But with the right words and the right pictures, along with the right idea and the right location, a sale can be made.

Guerrillas must fight their battles with every single available weapon. And small signs on bulletin boards have proven to be extremely effective weapons for many an entrepreneur. I'm talking about signs on cards as small as 3 inches by 5 inches. Even business cards. A sign need not be big to attract customers. Little signs do the job, too.

Think small

What kind of businesses and individuals might avail themselves of this minor a medium? Tutors. Gardeners. Plumbers. Typists. Writers. Baby sitters. House sitters. Movers. Accountants. Room renters. Music teachers. Nurses. Answering services. Pet groomers. Cleaning people. Painters. Astrologers. Mechanics. Printers. Seamstresses. Decorators. Tree pruners. Entertainers. And a whole lot more.

If your business has any prospects who have occasion to see bulletin boards, perhaps you should use small signs on bulletin boards to promote your business. You'll find such bulletin boards, as do countless eager board readers, on campuses and in libraries, cafeterias, dormitories, company rest rooms, offices, supermarkets, Laundromats, locker rooms, bookstores, pet stores, sporting goods stores, barbershops, hairstyling salons, toy stores, and sundry other locations.

You can either post the signs yourself or you can hire companies that specialize in posting the signs for you. Our local company calls itself The Thumb Tack Bugle. It services eighty locations. In most instances, your sign must be replaced on a regular basis (monthly or weekly). But sometimes it can stay in place for years. In a few cases, you'll have to pay a tiny fee to post your sign, but often this method of marketing is free (if you do your own posting). The companies that post for you promise to place your sign on a guaranteed number of boards — a large number, I might add — and they'll also replace it on a regular basis. Unless you've got the time to check your signs, look into these posting services. You can find them listed in your yellow pages under "Signs" or "Bulletin Boards." If signs do work for you, consider allowing one of these companies to handle all of that work for you, so you can concentrate on your primary way of earning money.

A crucial point to remember is to keep the lettering on your sign very clear. Fancy lettering is a definite no-no. Typing is fine. But clear, handsome hand lettering is probably best. If you haven't the proper calligraphic skills, ask a friend to letter your sign for you. And remember to keep your copy short and to the point. Incidentally, it is

Format

okay to make copies of your signs. One original plus a slew of copies and enough thumbtacks, and you've got the marketing tools to make yourself a success.

If George of Let George Do It posted bulletin-board signs throughout his area, they'd be very similar in wording to his circular. In fact, a sign for George might say:

Let George Do It!
George builds sun decks and patios,
installs skylights and hot tubs,
does masonry and electrical work,
and designs building plans.
Call George at 555-5656 any time any day.
All work guaranteed. Contractor's License #54-45673.

George probably wouldn't even need a 3 x 5 sign. Instead, he could post his circular. Circulars have a charming way of doubling as small signs.

Amazingly, there are some businesses that need only promote via this wonderfully inexpensive method of marketing. Perhaps you can be one of them. Although guerrilla marketers should utilize as many marketing methods as they can do effectively, they should also save marketing money whenever they can do so intelligently. Promoting your business with 3 x 5 cards is a true saving of marketing money. In fact, if you do the lettering and the writing and the posting, it's free.

Graphics are generally not necessary when marketing with small signs. If you post on a regular basis, though, it's a good idea to change the wording — but not the basic message — of your sign periodically. It's also a good idea to use different-colored paper so that your sign stands out from the rest. But be careful that your paper color does not impair the clarity of your ink color. Green ink on green paper makes for a very green but very unreadable sign. If you use green paper, make it light green — and make your ink a very dark color. Don't forget: Your major purpose is to motivate prospective customers, and if they can't read your message, they can't be motivated.

Where and how   I suggest that you visit a few places where signs are posted in your region and notice the clever ways people are utilizing this unique marketing method. When I look at the galaxy of signs on bulletin boards, I get the feeling that many entrepreneurs are true guerrillas. Of course, that is not necessarily true. Merely using such a method does not make one a guerrilla marketer. But a guerrilla marketer does consider such a method seriously when developing an overall marketing plan. And a true guerrilla doesn't think it is at all silly to combine radio advertising, newspaper advertising, and bulletin-board advertising in his or her marketing strategy.

Be sure to make your headlines large. Make plenty of signs. In fact, it's a good idea to make about ten at a time and staple them together. Tack the whole packet to a bulletin board and carefully letter the words "Take One" atop your signs. This way, people can not only read your sign but the serious prospects can take one home with them for future reference.

If you place signs on ten different bulletin boards, be sure you engage in the same kind of research you would employ if you were testing any other type of marketing. Ask your customers, "Where did you learn of my business?" When they tell you that they saw your sign, ask, "Where did you see it?" This way, you'll be able to pinpoint your best sign-posting locations. The more you can home in on your most productive marketing methods — including such subtleties as wording, sign color, sign location, and lettering style — the more successful you'll be.

It won't hurt for you to call some of the people who have posted signs in your area, asking about their effectiveness. Ask how long they've been posting signs, where they post them, whether the one you saw was typical, which locations seem best, and what success stories they may have heard. People are surprisingly open with information like this, and many enjoy being singled out as experts.

Interior signs require far more creativity than exterior signs, and you are allowed to use far more words. In fact, you are encouraged to.

P-O-P   Point-of-purchase signs are considered by those who use them to be extremely effective because they create impulse sales. They also put forth extra selling energy and cross-merchandising opportunities. A person comes in to buy a pen, sees a sign that says briefcases are marked down, and buys a briefcase, too. That's cross-merchandising.

P-O-P signs make it easier for customers to locate and select products. They serve as silent salespeople, as aids to the actual salespeople. They demonstrate product features. P-O-P signs give customers product information, reinforce the ad campaign at the retail level, offer premiums and discounts, and actually generate sales all by themselves.

Many manufacturers offer free point-of-purchase materials to their customers. If you purchase from a manufacturer, you should ask if P-O-P materials are provided. If not, request some. Most manufacturers are happy to comply. They'll set you up with signs, brochures, display racks, window banners, display modules, counter cards, window cards, Plexiglas merchandisers, posters, display cases, stand-up signs, and more. Just ask.

Although *Forbes* magazine says that telephone marketing is the emerging marketing force of the 1980s, another publication claims that P-O-P is. The reason it gives for the popularity of P-O-P advertising is the high cost of television and radio advertising in large markets. This forces many advertisers away from TV and radio, and makes P-O-P a far more cost-effective marketing medium. To give you an indication of the size of the P-O-P advertising market, it is estimated by the Point-of-Purchase Advertising Institute that in 1981, $5.5 billion were spent making P-O-P materials. Some surveys indicate that P-O-P materials will make up 50 percent of many advertisers' budgets in the near future.

Plan the sale when planning the ad

The basic dictum in creating any advertising is: *Plan the sale when you plan the ad.* That means that you shouldn't think in terms of a person reading your ad or hearing your commercial. Instead, think of the person at the moment of purchase. Is your message designed to motivate the potential customer at that crucial moment? By nature, almost all P-O-P marketing materials are. P-O-P signs get to people when the getting is good. They are there. They are in a buying mood. They are thinking in terms of the type of merchandise or service you offer. P-O-P advertising gives them many reasons to buy, or at least it should.

Many a smart guerrilla has run an ad, then blown the ad up into a five-foot-high poster, mounted it, and used it as a sign — inside the place of business, outside the place of business, and in the window. This is a way to market intelligently while saving lots of money, and it ensures that the interior signs will tie in with the ads.

Interior signs can be used to encourage customers to touch your offering, try it out, and compare it with the competition, and also to explain complex points by means of clear graphics. The Point-of-Purchase Advertising Institute claims that 64.8 percent of all buying decisions are made right in the place of business. I don't blame them for pointing with pride at such a lofty number. But even if it were half that, it would be impressive. And it should cause any guerrilla to take the use of signs very, very seriously.

The Institute points out that today decisions to buy are less casual than they once were, and that people need to be convinced *right there*, at the point of sale. If your business is in a location where your customers will come to browse or buy, the Institute says you should consider your aisles to be your "trenches" — where the true battle for customer dollars takes place. Since many battles are won or lost in the trenches, your point-of-purchase materials should be as potent as possible.

While the other marketing methods and materials create in the customer a desire to buy, as well they should, point-of-purchase signs promise instant rewards. True guerrillas recognize that people patronize their businesses on purpose, not by accident. And they capitalize on the presence of prospects by using motivating, informative signs. Some have lengthy copy. Some have brief copy. Some go into detail about product features and benefits. Some contain lists of satisfied-customer testimonials. Some display ornate graphics. Some point out advantages of related merchandise. But each is there to move as much merchandise or sell as many services as possible.

You might want to walk the aisles of successful businesses in your area, to find out how they use point-of-purchase signs. And to learn even more about point-of-purchase signs, drop a line, requesting free information, to POPAI, 60 East Forty-second Street, New York, New York 10165.

Whenever possible, signs — outdoor and indoor — should be employed to pull the trigger on the gun already cocked by aggressive guerrilla marketing.

15
The Yellow Pages:
Making Them Turn to Gold

IF YOUR BUSINESS IS ALREADY off and running, you probably know quite a bit about the yellow pages, having learned it from the yellow pages sales representative. But if your business has not yet started, it's a great idea to name it something that will appear as the first listing in its category in the yellow pages. For example, a new storage company called itself Abaco Storage. Storage companies don't advertise, except in the yellow pages. Success came to the company that first year, and phone inquiries resulting from first listing in the yellow pages were clearly responsible.

The first thing to decide is whether or not your business is the type that can benefit from yellow page marketing. Do most people look there, as they do for storage companies, to find a product or service such as yours? If you are a retailer, chances are that people will consult the yellow page phone directory and find out about you. But if you're an artist or a consultant, people will probably find out about you through other sources.

Which directories give you direct business

Once you've decided you should be in the directory, determine which directory or directories. Will one be enough? Or, as is the case in large metropolitan areas, will you have to be in five or ten? The answer to that may be clearer after you've considered these findings by the Small Business Administration:

• The average independent store draws the majority of its customers from not more than a quarter of a mile away.
• The average chain store draws most of its customers from not more than three-quarters of a mile away.
• The average shopping center draws customers from as far away as four miles.

Some businesses draw customers from as far away as 100 miles — especially in wide-open areas such as North Dakota and Iowa.

Waterbed stores attract business from an average distance of eight miles away. One of my enterprises, Prosper Press, draws business from throughout the nation. How about your enterprise? If you think you should run yellow pages ads in a number of directories, decide whether these ads should be as large as your primary area ad or smaller. Decide whether you should have an advertisement or a listing. Decide whether the listing should be in dark, bold type or in regular type. My publishing business is listed in but one directory, in normal type. It is not the type of business that attracts yellow pages searchers. But some of my clients have large yellow page ads in three directories, small yellow page ads in five more directories, and bold-type listings in six other directories.

The cost for a large number of listings is assessed monthly, and it's steep. Find out the names of other companies in your business category and try to learn what percentage of their business each month comes from people who have located them through the yellow pages. I have some clients who obtain 6 percent of their business from people who first learned of them by consulting the yellow pages. Others obtain 50 percent of their business that way.

You must do the groundwork to see how, where, and whether you should make use of a strong yellow pages program. Now you know some questions to ask and answer. Here's another: In which categories in your yellow pages directory will you list yourself? For example, if you run a sleep shop in which you sell beds and bedroom furniture, should you list your shop under "Furniture," "Mattresses," or "Beds"? Can you do with one listing, or do you need to pay for several? Answer: You'll probably have to list where people look. And they look in all three categories.

Advantages

A prime advantage of listing in the yellow pages is that you can appear as big as your biggest competitor, as large as the largest business of your type in town, as well established as the oldest business of your type in town. Although directories differ from yellow pages publisher to yellow pages publisher (and there are several), usually the largest space unit you can purchase is a quarter of a page. Since that's also the largest ad space available to your competition, you can appear equal in size. And you can take advantage of this by running a more powerful ad than your competition.

Some bright entrepreneurs, who realize that a great deal of their business comes from people who consult the yellow pages, spend the majority of their marketing budgets on this medium. But here's a crucial truth: Unless you totally dominate your section of the yellow

**Never send them
to the yellow
pages**

pages — I mean run the only large ad and the only good ad — you
should *never*, in your advertising on radio and/or television, when
directing people to your store or phone number, say "You'll find us
in the yellow pages." If you do that, you will be spending your media
dollars turning people on to your direct competitors.

Believe me, many people innocently do that. They run a fine
radio commercial, tell listeners to find them in the yellow pages,
then sit back while nothing happens. Why? Because in the yellow
pages, the listeners learn of several other places they can buy the
product or service being advertised. Nope. If you don't appear as the
clear choice within your category of the yellow pages, steer people
away from the yellow pages. Tell people, "You'll find us in the *white
pages* of your phone directory." There, in the peace and quiet of the
noncompetitive white pages, listeners and viewers can learn your
phone number, your address, and even how you spell your name.
And they'll not be aimed in the direction of any of your competitors.

**Exploiting the
yellow pages**

Now that that's understood, let's talk about how you must think of
the yellow pages as a marketing vehicle, an advertising medium, an
opportunity to sell. Many people think the yellow pages are merely a
place to put their phone numbers in large type. Silly thinking. The
yellow pages are an arena for attracting the business of active prospects. They are a place to confront prospects on a one-to-one basis.
You are selling. Others are selling what you sell. The prospect is in a
buying mood. Understand that opportunity, and you'll be able to
create yellow pages ads that translate into sales.

More and more yellow pages directories are now giving you the
chance to use color in your ad. If you're springing for a large ad, do
it. Many directories also give you a chance to participate in coupon
promotions by placing coupons for discounts on your offering in the
back of the directory. Not enough results are in yet to evaluate that
type of yellow pages marketing. I'd suggest calling a few coupon
advertisers in your area and asking if the coupons work. Maybe it's a
hidden gold mine. Maybe it's a disaster area. A guerrilla would
check into it.

If you decide to run one large ad in the yellow pages directory for
your locality, you may decide to run smaller ads in outlying directories. So you may need a large ad and a small ad. Maybe even
more. At any rate, it's too expensive to run yellow pages ads that are
poorly written. And most of them are. By putting a bit of thinking
into the content of your ad, you can greatly increase your yellow
pages response rate.

I'm familiar with a local business that was attracting 2 percent of its sales with yellow page ads. Two percent isn't all that good, but it does represent a fair sum of money at the end of the month. So the business couldn't eliminate that particular marketing tool. Instead, it changed its ad copy. That's all. The result was a 600 percent increase in business from yellow page ads. The store now drew 12 percent of its sales from people who first learned of it via those pages of yellow.

The answer must always be yes

What accounted for this dramatic increase? This store, which carried a goodly selection of waterbeds, by no means the largest in the area, but big enough to enable it to promote its product seriously, understood the mindset of yellow pages readers. It realized that people who consult the yellow pages are actively looking to find specific information. But it also realized that you can usually motivate people more effectively if you get them to the point where they agree with what you are saying — *the point where they are saying yes to questions you are asking.*

The waterbed store asked a question to which the person looking in the waterbed section of the yellow pages directory would always answer yes. The question was, "Looking for a waterbed?" Naturally, the answer was yes, and the reader read on. Whatever buttons the reader had were pressed intentionally by the ad. The advertiser did not feel self-conscious about putting forth a lot of information. The advertiser also recognized the nature of the medium and actively sought the business of the prospective customers.

See the two-column by five-inch ad on page 109 as it appeared in the San Francisco yellow pages. That other advertisers in the same directory used the same space to list their names, phone numbers, and little else is a good indication that if your offering is suitable for yellow pages advertising, you have a splendid opportunity.

If you use the yellow pages:

The do's and don'ts

- Do list a whole lot of facts about yourself.
- Do make your ad look and "feel" classier.
- Do treat it like a personal communication, not a cold listing.
- Do let folks know if you accept credit cards or can finance.
- Do gain the reader's attention with a strong headline.
- Do let people know all the reasons they should buy from you.
- Don't let the yellow pages people write your ad.
- Don't run small ads if your competitors run big ads.
- Don't make your ad look or sound boring.
- Don't forget to use graphics to communicate handsomely.

- Don't list your business in too many directories or categories.
- Don't treat your ad less lightly than a full-page magazine ad.

Lucky for you, the yellow pages are a misunderstood advertising medium. Now for the first time, specialized yellow pages advertising companies are being formed to help businesspeople take advantage of the opportunities offered. The yellow pages deserve your careful attention. But there is absolutely no reason why you *must* advertise there. If in doubt, read the yellow pages where you live and see what your competitors think about the whole idea.

III
Maxi-Media Marketing

MAXI-MEDIA MARKETING refers to the mass-market media, such as newspapers, magazines, radio, TV, billboards, and direct mail. Mistakes cost dearly in this area. The competition may be able to outspend you dramatically. For instance, the average cost to produce a television commercial in 1982 was in the neighborhood of $70,000. That's for a thirty-second live action commercial. You've got to add to that the cost of running the commercial, and running it often enough.

Still, you should not think of maxi-media marketing as expensive. That is not the case. Expensive marketing is marketing that does not work. If you run one radio commercial on one local radio station and it costs you only $5, but nobody hears it or acts on it, you have engaged in expensive marketing. But if you've shelled out $10,000 to run one week's worth of advertising on a large metropolitan area radio station and you realize a profit that week of $20,000, you have engaged in inexpensive marketing. Cost has nothing to do with it. Effectiveness does.

When a guerrilla marketer uses the mass media, he or she does what is necessary to make them effective, therefore inexpensive. A guerrilla is not intimidated by the mass media but is fascinated by them, finds ways to use them with precision and carefully measures the results, makes them part of an overall marketing plan, and realizes that using them calls for a combination of science, art, intuition, and business acumen. A guerrilla knows what maxi-media marketing is all about: selling and creating a powerful desire to buy.

16
Newspapers: How to Use Them with Genius

WHETHER YOU'RE USING THE mini-media, the maxi-media, or no media, as a guerrilla you should be aware of the changes always taking place in the U.S. marketplace. Because of the baby boom from 1946 to 1964, the median age in the United States is moving steadily upward. Soon, it will exceed thirty-five. People are living longer as well. In fact, *Newsweek* magazine informs us that in 1990 the second biggest job opportunity will be in the field of geriatric social work (the biggest being industrial robot production). The population shift to the sunbelt — Texas, Florida, Arizona, and California — will continue. Immigrants will account for 25 percent to 33 percent of our population, with Hispanics superseding blacks as the largest minority group. Ten percent of the population will be Hispanic. More and more minorities will move to the suburbs.

Marketers must be aware of these trends as they begin to consider newspaper advertising. In most areas, a large number of newspapers are available. They all reach specific audiences. Which newspapers, which audiences, are best for you? Since there are metropolitan newspapers, national newspapers, local newspapers, shopper-oriented newspapers, classified-ad newspapers, campus newspapers, business newspapers, ethnic newspapers, and daily, weekly, and monthly newspapers to choose from, you can see that your work is cut out for you. You must make your selection skillfully.

By far the major marketing method used by small business is newspaper advertising. Of course your type of business may not benefit from newspaper advertising. But if you think it may, pay close attention.

Newspapers offer a high degree of flexibility in that you can decide to run an ad or make changes up to a couple of days before the ad is to run. Radio gives you even more flexibility in that regard, allowing you to make changes up to the day your spot is to run. Magazine and television marketing allow you the least leeway.

Test it in the right way

If you don't have a clear-cut favorite newspaper — favorite being defined as most local and most appropriate for your ads — there is a test you should use. Remember that there are most likely far more newspapers in your region than you ever imagined. Run an ad in as many of the newspapers in your area as you can — there may be as many as thirty. Use coupons in your ads. Let each coupon make a different offer, such as $5 off or a free book or a 15 percent discount or a free plant. In the ad, request that the customer bring the coupon when coming to your place of business, or mention the coupon when calling you.

By measuring the responses, you'll soon see which newspapers work, which newspapers don't work, and which newspapers work best of all. You don't have to run ads in all thirty newspapers to learn which is the best paper. Maybe you'll only have to test in three or five or ten papers. But you are nuts unless you test. And be sure to determine what generated the customer's response — the offer or the newspaper. You can do this by means of a second test. Make a different offer in the most effective paper. If it still pulls well, you've got a horse to ride.

Don't forget, we're talking about advertising in terms of a conservative investment. So don't waste your money advertising in a paper that you happen to read or that your friends happen to recommend or that has a supersalesperson selling ad space. The paper you eventually select will be the one in which you advertise consistently. That paper is the one to which you will commit your marketing program, your regularly placed ad, your money, your hopes. So select with the highest care possible. The paper must have proven itself in your coupon test. It should be the one read by prospective customers in your marketing area. A monthly paper is not preferable. Use it, but make sure your major newspaper is at least a weekly, if not a daily paper.

Make it look good

Marketing is part science and part art — and the art part is very subjective. The artistic end of marketing is not limited to words and pictures but also involves timing and media selection and ad size.

The importance of the appearance of your ad is not to be underestimated. Far more people will see your ad than will see you or your place of business, so their opinion of your business will be shaped by your ad. Don't let the newspaper people design your ad, and don't let them write the copy. If they do, it will end up looking and sounding like all of the other ads in the paper. Your competition is not just the other people in your business, but everybody who advertises. You're out there vying for the reader's attention with banks, airlines, car companies, cigarette companies, soft-drink companies, and who knows what else. So give your ad a distinct style. Hire a top-rate art director to establish the look for your ad. Later, you can ask the paper to follow the design guidelines set down by that art director. But at first, either you or a talented friend or a gifted art director should make your advertising identity follow your marketing plan — and do so in a unique manner. You won't win customers by boring them into buying. You've got to create a desire. And a good-looking ad helps immeasurably.

I must caution you that perhaps one in twenty-five newspapers has a first-class art department that can design ads with the best of the expensive graphics companies. Put another way, twenty-four out of twenty-five newspapers have art departments that can help you waste your marketing money by designing ordinary-looking ads. The same with copy. Newspapers will help write your copy — because they want you to advertise. Give your marketing money to charity instead. Or spend it on a great ad writer who can make your ad sing, motivate, cause people to sit up and say, "I want that." If you have a winning ad, your marketing money can be safely invested in newspapers with the expectation of a high return.

The type used in your ad should be selected for readability and clarity. Don't use any type size that is smaller than the type used by the paper. In fact, even type that size is too small. Make it easy for the reader to read your ad. If you decide to make your ad look different by having it appear in black with the type appearing in white (a process called reversing the type), be sure that the black ink doesn't spill over into the white letters, obliterating them. It happens every day. Don't let it happen to you. Newspapers are notorious for making good-looking ads come out faint and unreadable as a result of their particular printing process. Be sure you, or your art director, check your ad with the newspaper to see if they can suggest any ways you can ascertain that the ad will print well.

Make it read well

Then, there's the matter of size. Of course, a full-page ad is probably best. But you won't want to pay for a weekly full-page ad, so you must make do with something smaller. What size can you comfortably afford?

Newspapers charge you by the line or by the inch. There are fourteen lines to the inch. If the newspaper charges, say, $1 per line, you are paying $14 per inch. If you want your ad to be fifteen inches high and three columns wide, you multiply $14 by fifteen, coming

Make it the right size

out with $210, then multiply that by three, for a total ad cost of $630. If you run an ad that size weekly, it will cost $2709 per month. (I multiplied the $630 by 4.3, because that's the approximate number of weeks per month.) If that charge is too high, you can run a smaller ad, one you can afford. Some people can run a ten-inch ad (two columns by five inches) all year every year and enjoy a sales increase each year. Other people want more of an increase, so they run a larger ad and run it two times a week. A lot depends upon the cost of advertising in the particular paper.

Most full-sized newspapers are twenty-two inches high. If you can afford it, run an ad that is twelve inches high or higher. That way, you'll be sure your ad is above the fold. Most full-sized newspapers are six columns wide. So you can be certain of dominating the page with a four-column by twelve-inch ad.

That's a great tack, and if you use it you won't be wasting your money. But you can save a bit of money if you run a smaller ad with a powerful and unique border. An ad does not have to dominate a page to be seen. It merely has to interest the reader, then create a desire, then motivate the reader to do something you want him or her to do.

If you run your ad in a tabloid-size newspaper rather than a full-sized newspaper, you can save money by running a smaller ad. A ten-inch ad seems a bit buried in a large newspaper, but it stands out in a tabloid. Many Sunday newspapers have tabloid-sized sections, and you can save money by using them. But don't use them just for that reason. Be sure that your prospects read that paper and that section.

Run it on the right day
What are the best days to run your ads? It differs with different towns and different businesses. Ask your local newspaper's space salesperson for a recommendation. Generally, Sunday is the day that the most people read the paper and spend the most time with the paper. But can your business succeed by running ads on days your doors are closed? Some businesses can. If yours can, give a nod to Sunday.

Monday is a pretty good day if your offering is directed to males, since many males read the Monday papers carefully because of all the sports events that went on the preceding weekend. Saturday is also a fairly good day, since many advertisers shy away from it and you'll have less competition. Some papers make Wednesday or Thursday their food day, so the papers are loaded with food ads and grocery ads.

You'll have to observe the papers yourself, then ask the person who will be selling the ad space to you. That ad space comes a lot cheaper if you sign a contract for a given number of lines or inches per year. Ask about the discounts you can receive for volume usage. They are quite substantial — a fringe benefit of consistent advertising in the same paper.

In most cases, the best place to have your ad appear is as far to the front as possible, on a right-hand page, above the fold of the paper. But few, if any, papers will guarantee placement unless you sign a King Kong–sized contract. The main news section is also considered to be an optimum place for an ad, because of high readership by a large cross section of the paper's circulation.

Put it in the right place

Because of the nature of your product, you may want to run your ad in the business section, the sports section, or the entertainment section. Advice: Run your ad where competitors run theirs. If you have no competition, run your ad where services or merchandise similar to yours is being offered. Why? Because that's where readers are conditioned to look for offerings such as yours.

Incidentally, readers most likely will read your ad, because study after study shows that newspaper readers read the ads almost as intensively as they read the stories. Because of the power of graphics, some ads attract *more* attention than the actual news stories. Use graphics in your ad, but go easy. Generally, more than three or four pictures — whether art or photography — is too many. But that's a rule that is both useful to know and useful to break. I've broken it successfully more than once. I've also run very successful ads that have only one illustration or photo.

When selecting your newspaper, you of course want to know its circulation. And you also want to know if the paper's circulation is in your marketing area. Otherwise you'll be paying for wasted circulation. A good thing to keep in mind is that when you hear a circulation figure, you can multiply it by three and learn how many people are actually reading the paper. When a family has a subscription to the paper, and two adults and three kids read each issue, that only gets counted as one subscriber. When a woman buys a copy of the paper to read on the bus on her way home, and her husband reads it when she arrives home, that, too, gets counted as one reader, according to circulation statistics. So newspaper circulation figures are one of the few entities in marketing that are understated.

Know the newspaper

If you have a truly good ad — one that tells all the features and benefits of your offering — consider making multiple reprints of the

Reprint the ad

ad and using them as circulars, customer handouts, mailing pieces, or interior signs. They cost very little, and most of their cost was spent when you had the ad produced. And remember, you can blow up the ad and make it into a poster.

Remember that many people newspaper shop before they buy. That is, they scan the papers before going out to purchase. Keep that in mind when running your ads. If your product is aimed at a particular group of people, such as businesspeople, consider running your ad in a business paper rather than a metropolitan paper. If your offering is geared to discount hunters, run your ad in shopper-oriented papers. If it will appeal to college kids, advertise it in the campus paper. A finished newspaper marketing plan usually calls for ads in a number of papers, some primary, others secondary. The combination you choose can be the key to your fortune. You want to obtain exceptional results from both primary and secondary newspapers. Exceptional results mean many sales. And many sales come from many inquiries, be they in the form of phone calls, visits to your place of business, or even letters.

To increase the number of inquiries you receive through newspaper advertising, first and always remember to put your name and primary message continually in front of readers. In addition, put the following tips into action:

Tips for success with newspaper ads

1. Mention your offer in your headline.
2. Emphasize the word *free* and repeat it when possible.
3. Restate your offer in a subhead.
4. Show a picture of your product or service in action.
5. Include testimonials when applicable.
6. Do something to differentiate yourself from others who advertise in the newspaper. That means all others — not just your direct competitors.
7. Say something to add urgency to your offer. It can be a limited-time offer. It can be a limited-quantities offer. Get those sales *now*.
8. Put a border around your ad, if it is a small ad. Make it a unique border.
9. Be sure your ad contains a word or phrase set in huge type. Even a small ad can "act" big if you do so.
10. Always include your address, specific location, and phone number. Make it easy for readers to find you or talk with you.

11. Create a visual look that you can maintain every time you advertise. This clarifies your identity and increases consumer familiarity.
12. Experiment with different ad sizes, shapes, days run, and newspaper sections.
13. Consider free-standing inserts in your newspaper. These are increasingly popular and may be less expensive than you imagine.
14. Try adding a color to your ad. Red, blue, and brown work well. You can't do this with tiny ads, but it may be worth trying with a large ad.
15. Test several types of ads and offers in different publications until you have the optimum ad, offer, and ad size. Then run the ad with confidence.
16. Be careful with new newspapers. Wait until they prove themselves.
17. Do everything in your power to get your ad placed in the front section of the paper on a right-hand page above the fold. Merely asking isn't enough. You may have to pay personal visits. Be a squeaky wheel.
18. Don't be afraid of using lengthy copy. Although lengthy copy is best suited for magazines, many successful newspaper advertisers employ it.
19. Run your ad in the financial pages if you have a business offer, in the sports pages if you have a male-oriented offer, in the women's pages for household services and products, in the food pages for food products. The astrology page usually gets the best readership. But in general, the main news section is still the best.
20. Study the ads run by your competitors, especially their offers. Make yours more cogent, more concise, sweeter, different, better.
21. Keep close records of the results of your ads. Experimenting doesn't mean a thing if you don't keep track of the experiments.
22. Be sure your ad is in character with your intended market.
23. Be sure your ad is in character with your product or service.
24. Be sure your ad is in character with the newspaper in which you advertise.
25. Try to use short words, short sentences, short paragraphs.
26. Don't put your address on a coupon only. If you use a

coupon, have your address appear on it and outside of it, so that if the coupon gets clipped, your address will appear anyhow.

27. Use photos or illustrations that reproduce faithfully in newspapers.

28. Always put the name of your company somewhere at the bottom of your ad. Don't expect people to get the name from the copy, headline, picture of product, or picture of storefront. Still, putting you name into your headline is generally a good idea. At least put it in the subhead.

29. Say something timely in your ad. Remember, people read papers for news. So your message should tie in with the news when it can.

30. Ask *all* of your customers where they heard about you. If they do not mention the newspaper, ask them directly: "Did you see our newspaper ad?" Customer feedback will be invaluable for you.

17
Magazine Advertising —
Its Value to Entrepreneurs

WHOEVER HEARD OF A small-time entrepreneur advertising in national magazines? You have now. Magazine advertising has been the linchpin for many a successful small business. Remember, the single most important reason people patronize one business over another is confidence. And magazine advertisements breed confidence by instilling familiarity and giving credibility.

That consumer confidence will not necessarily be gained from one exposure to your magazine ad. But if you run the ad one time, you can use the reprints of that ad forever. One highly successful company ran a single regional ad in *Time* magazine, then used reprints of the ad (reprints are available at a fraction of a cent each) in its window and on its counter for *more than five years* after the ad had run. Now that's getting mileage out of magazine advertising. Other bright entrepreneurs have run an ad one time in a regional edition of a national magazine, then mailed out reprints in all future direct mailings — each time gaining for their products the confidence that prospects ordinarily placed in the magazine itself.

You see, that is the whole point of magazine advertising for small businesses. *It gives them a great deal of credibility*. And credibility equates with confidence. And sales. And profits. If people feel that *Time* magazine is reliable, credible, trustworthy, and solid, they will feel those same things about the companies that advertise in *Time*. So if you wish to gain instant credibility, advertise in magazines that can give it to you.

The credibility factor

Don't forget, I'm not talking about running your ad in the entire edition of the magazine, just in your regional edition. Not all magazines have regional editions, and unless you are running a classified ad you may as well forget those that don't, unless you have a large budget or a product or service with national appeal. But many magazines do have regional editions that can save you a fortune.

Remember that most people do not realize there are regional

editions at all. When they see your full-page (or smaller) ad in *Time* magazine, they'll be quite impressed that you are advertising in a respected national magazine. And they'll turn that state of being impressed into a state of confidence in your offering. Check your library for the latest issue of *Consumer Magazine and Farm Publication Rates and Data* (published by Standard Rate and Data Service, Inc. — known as SRDS), and you'll learn which magazines have regional editions, and how much they charge for advertising in them.

Split runs: Test as you go If you run a small display ad in a national publication for a mail-order venture, you should do as much testing as possible. An inexpensive method of testing is to avail yourself of the split runs offered by many magazines. By taking advantage of them, you can test two headlines. Send your two ads to the publication, being certain to code each ad for response so that you'll be able to tell which of the two headlines pulls better, and ask the publication to split-run the ads. One headline will run in half the magazines printed; the other headline will run in the other half.

For example, a manufacturer of exercise equipment once ran a split-run ad with a coupon. One headline said STRENGTHEN YOUR WRISTS FOR BETTER GOLF! and the other said STRENGTHEN YOUR WRISTS IN ONLY 2 MINUTES A DAY! The coupon in the first ad was addressed to Lion's Head, 7230 Paxton, Dept. G6A, Chicago, Illinois 60649, and the coupon in the second ad was addressed to **Coding tells all** Lion's Head, 7230 Paxton, Dept. G6B, Chicago, Illinois 60649. Even though the coupons looked alike, it was easy for the advertiser to tell that the appeal of two minutes a day was far stronger than the appeal of better golf, even though the advertiser had guessed ahead of time that the golf headline would attract the better response. How could the advertiser tell? Because the responses to G6B ran four times higher than those to G6A. Incidentally, the advertiser could also tell by referring to those responses that they came from *Golf* magazine (G) and that they were in answer to an ad run in June (6). So the code allowed the advertiser to tell three things: the publication, the month run, and which of the two ads drew the best response.

Coding can be even more complex so as to tell you the year, the ad size, and other information. And some publications allow you to do a triple split run and not just a double, enabling you to test three headlines rather than two. If you can test three headlines instead of two, do it. Let your audience make your judgments for you whenever possible. After you count up the coded responses, you will know which headline is best. And the cost of the test itself will have been minimal. The magazine's split-run capability will have saved money for you while giving you valuable information. Now, you can run the successful ad with boldness and confidence.

Cutting costs

Don't count yourself out of advertising in national publications because of the cost. You can cut down on that cost by establishing an in-house advertising agency, by purchasing remnant space or space in regional editions, and by purchasing a tiny space unit — say, one column by two inches. Or you can advertise in the classified section that is available in many national magazines. Also, many magazines offer enticing discounts to mail-order advertisers. And virtually all magazines offer impressive merchandising materials: easel-back cards, reprints, decals with the name of the magazine (for example, "as advertised in *Time*"), and mailing folders. The magazine's advertising sales representative will be happy to tell you about all of the merchandising aids offered. Be sure you take advantage of them. They will be useful at your place of business, in your window (if you have one), and in other advertising you do. Your business will be helped if you simply mention "You've probably seen our ad in *Good Housekeeping* magazine." And these materials can be used as enclosures in direct mailings, as enclosures with personal letters, as signs on bulletin boards, as counter cards, as display pieces at trade shows, exhibits, or fairs, and as part of a brochure or circular. The cost of these aids is ridiculously low, and they're sometimes even free, so use them to the fullest extent. Magazines can help you market your offering immediately and well into the years ahead. And it's the years-ahead part that's going to result in profitable business for you.

When the waterbed industry was in its infancy, growth was dramatically spurred when Chemelex, a manufacturer of waterbed heaters, ran full-page ads in *Time, Newsweek,* and *Sports Illustrated.* Chemelex then distributed reprints of the ads to retailers throughout the country. The retailers prominently displayed the ads throughout their showrooms, and the industry grew to the point where it turned from a hippie-image industry into a $2 billion per year furniture-image industry. Reason: the instant credibility gained by advertising in highly credible publications.

Target your market

Magazine advertising offers other attractive advantages. You can target your market much better with magazines than with newspapers. Instead of reaching a general circulation, you can reach people who have demonstrated an interest in skiing, gardening, do-ityourselfing, snowmobiling, or you name it. This results in very little waste circulation. Everyone who sees your ad is a prospect. And one of the basic tenets of guerrilla marketing is to talk primarily to *prospects* and not to browsers.

A good guerrilla marketer also considers advertising in magazines other than consumer magazines. There is a whole world of trade magazines out there. Almost every trade and profession has its own publication or, more likely, group of publications. Because you want to home in on prospects, you should consider advertising in some of these trade publications, because they are subscribed to and read cover to cover by large numbers of prospective customers. This is especially true if your product is at all business oriented. Go to your library, locate a copy of *Business Publication Rates and Data*, another directory published by SRDS, and look through it. Try to find publications in which you might advertise your products or services. If you find a couple of magazines (newspapers are also listed) that might be right, send away for sample copies. You may find entrepreneurs with whom you can connect for greater sales. You may realize that you ought to be advertising in some of these publications. And you may learn a lot of inside information about your own industry.

You really can't tell unless you check it out yourself. I predict that you'll be pleasantly surprised at the large number of marketing opportunities available to you in trade publications. Most likely, you'll want to subscribe to at least one trade magazine — just to keep abreast of your field, to learn of new developments. *Standard Rate and Data* publishes a host of directories that may be of interest to you. And while you're at it, be sure you take the time to look at their consumer-magazine directory.

While you're at the library looking through *Consumer Magazine and Farm Publication Rates and Data* (if you want to own a copy, write to Standard Rate and Data Service, Inc., 5201 Old Orchard Road, Skokie, Illinois 60077, or call them at 312-470-3100), look carefully through the directory for the names of other publications in which you might want to place your ad. You'll find many, many magazines you've never heard of, and quite a few may be read by prospective buyers of what you sell. I've always been amazed at the amount of information in SRDS — as it is called in the ad biz.

An important advantage of magazines is that they enable you to use color much more effectively than in newspapers. If your offering is oriented to color — if you are marketing fabrics, for instance — consider advertising in magazines just to show off the hues and tones. And magazines are better suited to lengthy copy than any other medium. The reason is that people buy magazines with the idea of spending time with them, unlike newspapers, which are read for news. Magazines *involve* their readers, and your ads may do the same.

It is primarily because of guerrilla marketers that magazines now publish so many regional editions. Now that you know this, look through your local issue of *Time,* or *TV Guide,* or *Better Homes and Gardens,* and notice how many regional advertisers are using those media, how many of them utilize color to show off their product, and how many of them run long-copy ads. Most important, remember that in all likelihood these advertisers could never afford a national ad in the same magazine. But the growth of the entrepreneurial spirit in America has necessitated an increase in regional editions. Advertisers in these regional editions know that by advertising in a major magazine, they are putting themselves in the big leagues. Their ad might run on the page next to an ad for General Motors or U.S. Steel or IBM. Not bad company for a guerrilla, wouldn't you say? But after all, guerrilla marketing enables you to play in the big leagues without first struggling through the minor leagues.

It is only during the past decade that many major magazines have been available to minor advertisers. Availing yourself of these major magazines and all of their merchandising aids is a key to successful marketing. For at the same time that it gives you credibility within your community, it gives you respect in the minds of your sales staff, your suppliers, and even your competitors.

If you're a thinking entrepreneur, you'll utilize magazines in several ways. You will advertise regularly in a magazine that hits your target audience right on the nose. You will advertise only one time in a prestige magazine, so as to use its merchandising aids. You will use the classified sections of national magazines if you are in the mail-order business. And you will use the display sections of national magazines if what you have to sell is too big for the classified sections.

If you are practicing guerrilla marketing to the hilt, you will mention your national magazine advertisements in the other media you use: on the radio, in your direct-mail advertisements, on your signs, in your yellow pages ads, in your personal letters, in your telephone marketing program — everywhere you can.

It may be that you want to advertise in a national magazine because of the prestige, the huge circulation, and the easily identified audience but do not have the money for a large-enough ad. No problem. In that case, use a two-step process.

Do the two-step   The first step is to have the magazine run a small display (or classified) ad that hits the high points of your offering, then tells readers to write for *free* information. When they respond, send them your brochure and a motivating sales letter as the second step. Follow- up with still another letter if they do not order. Consider selling or renting their names to mailing-list brokers. These people buy and sell or rent names and addresses of many different types of consumers. Find them in your yellow pages under "Mailing Lists." The two-step process outlined above enables you to tell your entire story but does not entail the high costs of large-space advertising. It also gives you a large number of salable names, and you can be sure these are valuable names for your own mailing list.

This two-step process worked for an entrepreneur friend of mine after the running of a large ad failed. In the classified section of *Psychology Today*, he ran a classified display ad telling readers that they could earn a legitimate college degree — B.A., M.A., or Ph.D. — right from their homes. Then he told them that they could secure free details about the offer by writing him. My friend later told me that he made a great deal of money with this two-step process, but that it was twice as much work as the one-step process that I was employing at the time to advertise the free-lancing book I had written and published myself. Soon he was able to employ someone to handle the detail work for him, and his two-step ads continue to run in *Psychology Today* as well as in twenty-nine other publications. It has been over eight years since the first ad ran.

I tell you this to emphasize that if you come up with a winning magazine ad, you may be able to run it in a multitude of magazines. The result of this can be a multitude of profits. You can run your proven moneymaker for years and years in a wide selection of publications. To a guerrilla, few marketing situations are as delightful.

Most small businesspeople never even consider advertising in magazines. That's because they don't know about regional editions, remnant space, in-house agency discounts, the two-step process, and valuable merchandising aids. Now that you do know about these lovely aspects of magazine advertising, give serious consideration to the medium.

The value of magazine advertising   But the prime reason for using magazines is the lasting value of the ad. I recall placing a full-page ad in *Newsweek* magazine for a client. After the ad was run, the client asked each customer where he or she had heard of his company. At the end of one week, only five people claimed to have seen his ad in *Newsweek*, where it had run only one time. At the end of one month, that number climbed to eighteen people. And after a full year, a total of sixty-three *customers* said they had first heard of the company through its ad in *Newsweek*. And that's not even the impressive part! The really significant aspect of this story is that the entrepreneur blew up a reprint of the ad to the size of an enormous poster — five feet high — then mounted it and placed it outside his place of business. Thousands of customers patronized his business because of that huge poster. *Newsweek* turned out to be his most effective advertising medium that year — and yet he placed but one ad there. To make matters even more wonderful, the *Newsweek* page was purchased at *less than half* the going rate, because it was remnant space. The magazine had sold three full-page ads to regional advertisers and had one page left over — a remnant. So my client was able to buy the space for a fraction of its original price. If you are interested in advertising in any particular magazine, call the local representative of the magazine and say that you are definitely a candidate for any remnant space and that you should be phoned when it is available. You may wait a bit, but it will be well worth the wait. Do Coca-Cola and AT&T practice this tactic? No. But do successful guerrilla marketing people practice this? You bet their bank balance they do!

18
Radio: It Costs a Lot Less Than You Think

UNLESS YOU HAVE A GOOD friend who owns a radio station, most of your radio marketing will be of the paid, rather than free, variety. It is possible to have stories or interviews about your product or service on the radio, and it may be that those will cost you nary a cent. In chapter 26, we'll go into ways of obtaining free publicity on the radio and in other maxi-media. But as far as this chapter is concerned, you'll have to pay for your radio marketing.

Although newspapers are the primary marketing media for most small businesses, radio does come in a strong second. Radio advertising can be used effectively by a company with a limited budget. And radio can help improve your aim when you're trying to reach your **The radio** target consumers. Radio helps you establish a very close relationship **relationship** with your prospects. Because of its intimate nature, it brings you even closer to them than newspapers do. The sound of an announcer's voice, the type of musical background, the sound effects you use to punctuate and enhance your message — all of these are ammunition in your radio marketing arsenal. All can help win customers and sales for you.

Although it is true that you can, if you try, pay $250 for a single radio commercial on a large, commercial radio station, you can also, if you try, pay $5 for a single radio commercial on a smaller, less popular station. You'll certainly talk to far more people with the $250 spot. But you'll be talking to more than a few people with your $5 commercial.

Now don't think that you can spend $5 and feel that you are involved in radio marketing. But if you spend $5 times five spots per day ($25), and you run your spots four days a week ($100), three weeks out of four, you may be able to say that for $300 a month you are adequately covering the listener profile in the community that particular radio station covers.

Because radio listeners are notorious button pushers and change stations a lot, you're probably going to have to run radio spots on more than one station. This is a rule to know and to break. But make sure you know it. One station does not a radio campaign make.

How many stations do you need? Well, you may really need only one. But you'll probably need three or four or five. It may also be that you have the type of offering that lends itself so well to radio that you'll need no other ad media and can dive headlong into advertising on ten stations. Some of my clients have. One of the advantages to being on so many stations is that by tracking your audience response — that is, learning which stations are bringing in the business — you can eliminate the losers and narrow your radio marketing down to proven winners. You can also use the coupon-type testing we explored in the chapter on newspapers. That means you pick, say, five stations and run commercials on all five. In each commercial, introduce a different offer — money off, free gift, 50 percent reduction — and ask listeners to mention the offer when they contact you. By keeping careful track of the offers mentioned by your customers, you'll know which stations to drop (maybe all of them) and which to continue with (maybe all of them).

Which stations and how many

Unless you keep careful track of all of your media responses, you are not a guerrilla. If you run your ads and keep selecting media on blind faith, you are closer to a gooney bird. You've got to make your marketing as scientific as possible. This is one of those rare instances where you can measure the effectiveness of your media scientifically. Avail yourself of it.

If you have salespeople, ask them to track responses. If you're the person taking orders from customers, then you must track responses. Ask the customers, "Where did you hear of us first?" If they say radio, ask, "Which station?" If they name a station that you don't use, ask "Which stations do you ordinarily listen to?" Do everything you can to learn which stations are pulling in customers and which are not. After you've been marketing seriously for a year or three, you can cut down on your media tracking, though I do not suggest that you do. If you start learning for sure which stations pull best, you may feel that you need no longer ask. But until you are certain, you must ask. Because stations and people change, it is a good idea to keep track constantly.

There are many types of radio stations: rock and roll, middle of the road, public, all news, talk show, dramatic, Spanish language, black, bubble-gum rock, jazz, oldies, intellectual, avant-garde, local interest, farm-oriented, progressive rock. Which are most likely to be

Radio categories

listened to by your audience? Although it is possible to divide radio stations into fifteen categories, as I have just done, it is first advisable to divide them into two categories — background stations and foreground stations.

Some radio stations play background programming. That means they play music that is generally a *background* sound. People talk, converse, work, play, iron, cook, and do myriad other things with background radio sounds. The music does not get in the way, does not command attention, does not distract. Unfortunately, because people are not actively listening, the commercials also are in the background. Oh, sure, when a person is driving home with the radio on, all alone, the commercials — and the music — move up from the background. But in general, all music stations are background radio stations.

All radio stations that are all news or all talk are *foreground* radio stations. They are in the foreground of people's consciousness. They command attention. They do distract. They are poor stations to have on during a conversation, during work, during situations that require your concentration. As a result, the commercials that are broadcast on them are likely to attract more active listeners. *These people pay closer attention to commercials because they are actively listening to the radio.* They don't have it on some back burner of their mind, as is the case with background radio. This is not to say that foreground radio is better than background radio. But I do want you to be aware of the difference between the two.

There are other differences as well. Talk radio is hosted by "personalities" more than music radio is. All music radio requires is a person to say what music just played and what music is about to play. Talk radio requires more listener rapport, more informal chatter, more personal asides.

The ad-lib ad   Here's a guerrilla tactic that works wonderfully well on foreground stations when it is appropriate. Suppose you have a new company that sells, say, computer instruction. Invite a talk radio personality to take a few lessons. Then buy time on that personality's station. Rather than give him a sixty- or thirty-second script for your commercial, which you might ordinarily do, give him a sixty- or thirty-second outline — and invite him to ad lib as much as he wants. The result is usually a sincere commercial, far longer than the commercial for which you have contracted, that has loads of credibility. If your product or service is worth raving about, you can count on most personalities to give it their all. You only have to pay for a sixty-second spot, but you may end up with a three-minute spot at no extra cost.

That is about the only instance in which I'd advise you to put your message into the hands of the radio station. In virtually all other instances, I suggest that you have the radio station play recorded commercials, which you can tape either at an independent facility or at the station itself. Don't make the mistake of furnishing scripts to the station. Although some of their announcers may do a great job of reading them, other announcers may make mincemeat out of them, reading them with no conviction, no enthusiasm, but with oodles of errors. Murphy's law has a way of asserting itself at radio stations: If the commercial can be messed up, it will be. Protect yourself by furnishing finished tapes only — unless you can get a personality to breathe true life into your script.

Just as it is bad business to let a newspaper write your newspaper ad copy it is also a grave error to let a radio station write your radio ad copy. Most stations will be all too willing to volunteer. Don't let them. They will have the script written by someone not quite good enough to be paid as a writer, who will, by force of habit, make your commercial sound just like everyone else's commercials. One of the most asinine methods of saving money is to let the station write your advertising.

If the station offers to produce your spot, that's a different story. Check out their equipment. Probably it is all right. Listen to their announcers. If you trust their equipment — as measured by the sound of finished commercials produced on it — and you like one or more of their announcers, let the station voice and produce the commercial on tape for you. Generally there is either no charge or just a tiny charge for this service. And in most cases, but not all cases, it is worth the price.

Should you run thirty-second spots or sixty-second spots? A thirty-second spot is usually far more than 50 percent of the cost of a sixty. But in most instances, you can say in thirty seconds what can also be expressed in sixty seconds. So go with the shorter spots even though they are not great values. In the long run, they'll give you more bang for your bucks. If, however, you have a complex product or service, you'll just have to run a full sixty-second spot. Some advertisers achieve superb results with two-minute commercials. So take as long as you must to state your message; but make it thirty seconds if possible.

A long-time radio pro once told me that if he had to cut 33

Designing an effective radio spot

Thirty or sixty?

Music hath charms

percent of his radio advertising budget, but could spend that 33 percent on a music track for his commercials, he'd gladly do it. He believes that the presence of music lends a powerful emotional over-tone to the commercial. And I agree. Music can convey what words frequently cannot. And music can be obtained very inexpensively. You can rent it from the station's music library. You can have a music track made by hungry musicians who will record a track for very little money, appreciating the exposure they will receive. Or you can purchase an expensive music track — made expressly for you — and use it so much that the amortized cost is mere peanuts.

I know an entrepreneur who made a deal with a composer who had recently released a record album. The entrepreneur, upon learning that the cost of the particular music he liked was $3000, said that he'd pay the composer $100 per month for a full year. If, at the end of that time, he was still in business and wanted the music, he would then pay $3000 in addition to the rental fees he had paid. If he had not made it in business, he would merely be out the rental fees and the composer would still have the music. It sounded like a fair deal for both parties, so the composer agreed. At the end of one year, the composer did receive his $3000, in addition to the $1200 he had earned for renting out his music. His total gain was $4200. The entrepreneur, who at the time could barely afford the $100 rental, later could easily afford the $3000. Result: Everyone came out a winner.

If you have to use announcers and musicians who are members of the various unions (Screen Actors' Guild and/or American Federa-tion of Television and Radio Actors), be wary. Union costs and paperwork are overwhelming, and you might be better off doing all in your power to avoid unions. I only work with unions when I absolutely must. And when I do, I have all the paperwork handled by an independent party. Unions and guerrillas mix like gasoline and fire.

As music adds new dimensions to your selling message, so too do sound effects. Use them when you can, and remember that radio stations (and most production facilities) have libraries of them and rent them at nominal costs. Just be careful you don't get carried away with their use.

Three crucial seconds

When writing your commercials, keep in mind that you have but three seconds to catch and hold the attention of the listener. So be interesting during those first three seconds and say what you have to say, lest the listener's attention stray elsewhere. Be sure you use "ear" words rather than "eye" words, and, whatever you do, repeat your main selling point. Also, repeat your company name as many times as you comfortably can.

A successful way of putting together radio commercials is to put the president of the company into a recording booth and interview him or her. Let the interview go on for twenty or thirty minutes, or even longer. Then, use small sections of the interview as ingredients in future commercials. You might use only three-second lines and ten-second lines from the interview, alternating with comments by an announcer. It sounds different, believable, and allows the president of the company (you?) to go out on a limb publicly — a good idea.

The following script is reprinted not because it won Radio Commercial of the Year honors in Chicago, but because it successfully sold dog food at a not very generous savings. It is a sixty-second spot and cost very little to produce.

Bright spots

ANNOUNCER:	Ladies and gentlemen! The makers of Perk dog food — the rich, meaty, energy-giving, delicious dog food — now bring you one minute of rich, energy-giving, delicious . . . *silence.*
SOUND:	(*Five seconds of silence*)
MAN:	(*Whisper*) Aren't you going to say anything about the big Perk sale?
ANNOUNCER:	(*Whisper*) Shhh! This is supposed to be *silence!*
SOUND:	(*Four seconds of silence*)
MAN:	(*Whisper*) Won't you even remind people that if they buy three cans of Perk dog food during the sale, they get five cents off?
ANNOUNCER:	(*Whisper*) Quiet!
SOUND:	(*Four seconds of silence*)
MAN:	(*Whisper*) But this is important! Aren't you —
ANNOUNCER:	(*Whisper*) Will you be quiet!!
MAN:	(*Whisper*) Yes, but —
ANNOUNCER:	(*Whisper*) I mean *now!*
MAN:	(*Whisper*) Yes, but the big Perk *sale!* You've got to say *something* about how now is the time to stock up on Perk because people can get five cents off when they buy three cans!
ANNOUNCER:	(*Whisper*) I'm not going to say a word! Now quiet!
MAN:	(*Whisper*) Then I'm going to say something —
ANNOUNCER:	(*Loud whisper*) Keep away from that microphone!
MAN:	(*Loud whisper*) Listen, everyone . . . (*Louder*) Perk is having a big sale, and —
SOUND:	(*Scuffling and fighting sounds.* Man yells "*Oof!*")

That was a humorous commercial and the humor worked to gain attention. In a more serious vein, here's a straightforward spot as it might be broadcast, in thirty seconds, for a service-oriented entrepreneur:

> MALE VOICE: (*Over music*) If you dislike the inconvenience of driving your car to a mechanic, you'll like the convenience of having the Mobile Mechanic drive to your car and fix it while you're relaxing at home. If you're not happy with the price of having your car tuned up at a garage, you'll be very happy with the bargain price of having your car tuned up at home by the Mobile Mechanic. Keep you car in top shape, conveniently and economically. Call the Mobile Mechanic. Find him in the white pages of your local phone directory. The Mobile Mechanic. Call him.

Although most announcers can easily fit seventy words into a thirty-second spot, studies indicate that people listen more attentively if the announcer talks faster and crams more words into a short space. Thank Columbia University for making that study and giving speed talk a shot in the arm, and remember it when making your commercials.

A couple of radio hints for guerrillas:

• Save money by running ads three weeks out of every four, not all four.
• Concentrate your spots during a few days of the week, such as Wednesday through Sunday.
• The best time to run radio advertising is during afternoon drive time, when people are heading home. They're in more of a buying mood than during morning drive time, when work is on their minds.
• When listening to the radio commercials you have just produced, be sure you listen to them on a car-radio-type speaker, not on a fancy high-fidelity speaker like those production studios use. Many an advertiser, dazzled after hearing his commercial on an expensive speaker system, has become depressed when hearing what the commercials *really* sound like on the type of sound system most people have in their cars.
• Consider radio rate cards to be pure fiction. They are highly negotiable.

• Study the audiences of all the radio stations in your marketing area. Then, match your typical prospect with the appropriate stations. It's not difficult.

Unless you simply cannot see your way to using radio, do give it a try. You'll appreciate its flexibility, its ability to allow you to make last-minute changes, and the way you can home in on your prospects on the basis of station format, time of day, and day of the week.

I have a client, very successful, who owns a furniture store. Although he uses many marketing media — newspapers, yellow pages, billboards, point-of-purchase signs, and direct mail — he spends 90 percent of his marketing money on radio advertising. With such a high concentration of dollars in just one medium, does he qualify as a true guerrilla? He sure does! He has learned through the years that radio reaches his exact audience and motivates them to come into his store. He runs his commercials on anywhere from six to ten stations, and he often runs the same commercial fifteen times in one day. What's more, he's *never* off the radio, using it fifty-two weeks per year. Because he has learned how to use this medium to the benefit of his bottom line, he is a true guerrilla marketer. After *experimenting* with all kinds of marketing mixes, he finally decided that radio was the medium for him. He uses it a lot. He uses it with music. He uses it consistently. And he makes so much money that he is now able to live a luxurious life in Hawaii while his business, located in the Midwest, continues to flourish. Although many factors are responsible for his success, he gives most of the credit to radio advertising. This is living proof that you can prosper in style even as a one-medium guerrilla. But things rarely work out that way.

Radio only?

19
Television: How to Use It, How Not to Abuse It

ALTHOUGH TELEVISION IS THE MOST EFFECTIVE of all marketing vehicles, it is also the most elusive and easiest to misuse. It is elusive because it is not as simple as it seems, because it requires many talents, because it is not normally associated with small businesspeople, and because it is dominated by giants who give entrepreneurs a mistaken impression of how it should be used. Just remember: you cannot use TV as Coca-Cola and McDonald's use it unless you have their money. But you can use it. It is easy to misuse because it does seem straightforward, because almost anyone can afford to run one or two television commercials, because it is readily available, because it is the medium that strokes the entrepreneur's ego the most tantalizingly, and because it requires a whole new discipline. Television is not, as some believe, radio with pictures.

How much is enough?
Television can only be effective if you use it enough. And enough is a lot. Enough is expensive. How much is enough? Many experts say you can measure how much enough is by understanding rating points. A GRP, or Gross Rating Point, is calculated on the basis of one percent of the TV sets in the TV marketing area. If one million TV sets are in the area, one rating point equals 10,000 sets. The cost of TV advertising is determined by the size of each GRP in the marketing area, and advertisers pay for a given number of GRPs when they buy advertising time. The experts advise, and I do agree, that you should not consider TV advertising unless you can afford to pay for 150 GRPs per month. Those can come in the form of 75 GRPs per week every other week, or 50 GRPs for three weeks out of four, or even 150 GRPs for one week per month. How much a single rating point costs in your area depends upon the size of area, the competitive situation, and the time of year. Points tend to cost more around Christmas shopping time — October through late December. They tend to cost less during the summer when reruns are being shown. GRPs in small towns cost far less than GRPs in big cities.

The price ranges from about $5 per GRP in a small town to about $500 per GRP in a big city.

Can you start small in TV and then build up? Only if you start out by buying 150 GRPs for one month and have the funds and emotional endurance to hang in there for a minimum of three months. If you can't do that, don't fool around with TV. But if you can afford to pay for the proper number of rating points — and you can if you live in a low-cost TV marketing area such as those found in many rural sections of the United States, or if you are well funded — you'll find that TV can do many things the other media cannot. It allows you to demonstrate, to act, to dance, to sing, to put on playlets, to show cause and effect, to create a lively identity, to be dramatic, to reach large numbers of people, to home in on your specific audience, to prove your points visually and verbally — all at the same time. No other medium provides so many advantages to the advertiser at one time.

What TV can do

Of the various times you can advertise on the tube, steer clear of prime time — the 8:00 P.M. to 11:00 P.M. period when so many people are watching. You can realize better values — more viewers per dollar — by using fringe time, the time before and after prime time. You might also look into daytime TV, which attracts many women viewers. The audience size is smaller and so is the cost. The time period past midnight, when few people are watching, is very inexpensive and can prove a springboard to success. Some postmidnight shows have ratings so low they are unmeasurable. That also means, happily, that they are inexpensive.

If you truly want to advertise on television, find out what shows your prospects watch, then run commercials on those shows. For example, when the waterbed industry was in its infancy, aggressive marketing people soon learned that the same people who watch *Star Trek* tend to buy waterbeds. They also learned that the women who watch afternoon movies, not soaps, have a proclivity toward waterbeds. Some waterbed retailers went to the bank as a result of that fascinating information. Even though *Star Trek* was in its tenth series of reruns, it still proved to be a marvelous and inexpensive vehicle for waterbed marketers. Talk shows, which frequently attract an older audience, were determined to be poison for waterbed retailers. Their product simply did not appeal to seniors.

Which shows

To get the most out of TV, keep in mind that TV rate cards, like radio rate cards, are established as the basis for negotiation and are not to be taken as gospel. In fact, if you're going to go on to television, you should retain a media-buying service to make your plans and buys for you. They'll charge about 5 percent of the total for their services, but they'll save you more than 5 percent. Many small businesspeople make their own buys, thinking they are getting good deals. But the media-buying services, who purchase millions of dollars' worth of TV time monthly, obtain bargains that would shock the small businessperson.

You are not the commercial   TV salespeople have a wonderful way of putting the egos of their clients to work for them. Some convince an advertiser that he or she would be a terrific spokesman or spokeswoman. The advertiser, enjoying the strokes to his or her ego, then goes on TV and presents the commercial in person. Sometimes, but rarely, this is effective. Generally, the advertiser loses as many sales as he or she gains. Frequently the advertiser becomes a laughingstock but continues presenting the ads because his or her salespeople wouldn't dream of telling the truth. Don't let your ego get in the way of your TV marketing when it comes to buying the time or presenting the information. If you've watched enough TV, I'm sure you get the gist of what I'm saying.

I do suggest that you look into cable TV. It just may be that you can afford to market your offerings on television because of a new cable outlet. They are springing up all over the place, making TV more and more affordable to more and more small businesses. So continue checking cable. As I write this, TV is in a state of flux. Satellite networks are coming on strong. Keep your eye on them. I sure am.

Also, Videocassette recorder sales are skyrocketing, giving audiences access to postmidnight programming for viewing any time the next day. As cable, cassette, and satellite TV are burgeoning, network TV is gradually losing its audience to these other TV outlets. Stay tuned. These are very interesting times from the standpoint of television, especially if there is a chance you'll market your products or services on it.

How to produce a TV spot   If you do decide to invest in television marketing, there are many methods by which you can cut down drastically on the cost of producing TV commercials, which currently cost an estimated $70,000 for a thirty-second spot. Truth is, you can turn out a very good thirty-second ad for about $500. And even that figure can be reduced as you increase your TV savvy.

First of all, let your TV station provide all the production assistance. Not the writing. The *production*. Let *them* put up the equipment and furnish the camera people, the lighting experts, the director. Don't let them write the spot. If you do, it will look like all their other homegrown ads. Instead, either you or a talented individual you coerce, beg, or hire should write a tight script. The left side of the sheet of paper upon which the script is written is reserved for video instructions. On that side, describe every single action the viewers will see, numbering each one. The right side of the script paper is for the audio portion. These are the sounds the viewers will hear. Again, number each audio section, matching it up with the appropriate video section so that the audio and video make a team.

If necessary, and it usually is not necessary, make a storyboard. A storyboard is a pictorial representation of your script. It consists of perhaps ten "frames," or pictures. Each frame contains a picture of what the viewers will see, a description of what will be happening, and the message that will be heard while the action is taking place. Storyboards tend to be taken too literally, however, and do not allow you the leeway to make changes during production. Those little changes are often the difference between an ordinary and an extraordinary commercial. Most people have the imagination to understand a commercial from a script alone. If they don't, you just may have to resort to a storyboard. Artists charge $10 to $25 per frame, so you can see how utilizing storyboards will make costs go up.

While working in major ad agencies, I had to prepare a storyboard for every commercial I wrote. And I know that I wrote over a thousand. Many art directors were engaged in gainful employment because of my active typewriter and the traditions of advertising agencies, which called for storyboards. Since I've been working on my own, I have written well over a thousand commercials, and only five or six required storyboards. Yet the commercials were no less successful than those I made using storyboards that upped the budget.

You can also save money by having intense preproduction meetings with all who will be involved in the production of your commercial. Meet with the actors, actresses, director, lighting person, prop person, everyone. Make sure everyone knows what is expected and understands the script. Make sure the timing is on the button and not one detail is unexplored. Then, hold at least one tightly timed rehearsal. Have the people involved go through the motions before the cameras are running. By doing so, you'll be able to produce two commercials in the time usually necessary to produce one. You'll even be able to fit three commercials into the same production time, if you're good enough. When you are paying $1000 per day for equipment and crew, that comes to $333.33 per commercial when you do three commercials at once. A far cry from $70,000.

To keep the cost down, you will have to avoid expensive union talent and crew when possible (in some union cities such as Los Angeles and San Francisco, this is not easily possible), get everything right the first time as a result of well-planned rehearsals and preproduction meetings, and plan the editing when you plan the spot. Editing videotape can be very expensive — $250 per hour and up. So plan your shooting so that little editing will be necessary.

Whether you shoot with film or tape does not make much difference to the cost. Film allows you to use more special effects, has more of a magical quality because it has less "presence" than tape, and allows for less expensive editing. But with film you have no instant feedback. If someone goofed, you won't know it till the film is processed. With tape, you can replay what you have shot immediately, and if anything is wrong, you can redo it. No processing is necessary. As to which is better, there is no correct answer. Both can be ideal, depending upon the circumstances. But if you are planning to have the station help with production, better plan on videotape. Stations don't usually film for you.

What makes a great TV commercial? Well, Procter & Gamble, the most sophisticated advertiser in the United States, frequently uses "slice of life" commercials, which are little playlets, the type that seem boring and commonplace. But with the big bucks P&G puts behind them, they work extremely well. So don't knock them if you are considering TV as a marketing vehicle. You can learn plenty from P&G. I certainly did.

TV commercial guidelines

There are a few guidelines that will help you regardless of the type of commercials you wish to produce:

Remember always that television is a *visual medium with audio enhancement*. Many ill-informed advertisers look upon it as the opposite. A guerrilla marketer knows that a great TV commercial starts with a great idea. Try to express that idea visually, then add the words, music, and sound effects to make it clearer and stronger. Try viewing your commercial with no sound. If it is a winner, it will make its point with pictures only.

Again, go with thirty-second spots rather than sixties, and if you are using TV for direct response, such as for ordering by toll-free number, try two-minute spots. They're very effective.

Keep in mind that, as with radio, you have three seconds to attract viewers' attention. If you haven't hooked them right up front, you've probably lost them. So say what you have to say in a captivating manner at the outset. Say it again, in different words, in the middle of your spot. Say it a final time, again in different words (or maybe even in the same words), at the end. Don't fall into the trap of making your commercial more interesting than your product. Don't allow anyone to remember your commercial without remembering your name. There are bushels of sob stories of commercials that won all sorts of awards while the products they were promoting died horrible deaths. You want sales, not awards, praise, or laughs.

When you can, show your product or service in action. People's memories improve 68 percent when they have a visual element to recall. So say what you have to say verbally and visually, especially visually.

The following thirty-second commercial not only won first prize at the Venice TV Film Festival but caused the advertiser to withdraw it from the air because he was unable to keep up with the demand for his product. The basic idea to be conveyed in the commercial is that this particular cookie, known as "Sports" and manufactured by an English company called Carr's of Carlisle, has more chocolate on it than any similar cookie (known as "biscuit" in the U.K.). Simple enough? Here's the script:

VIDEO	AUDIO
1. OPEN WITH TWO SLAPSTICK CHARACTERS FACING THE CAMERA. ONE IS TALL AND ONE IS SHORT. TALL ONE SPEAKS.	1. (*Tall man*) Good evening. Sidney and I would like to prove that Carr's Sports have the most chocolate — by showing you two ways to make chocolate biscuits.
2. SHORT MAN SMILES WHEN HIS NAME IS MENTIONED, BUT LOSES THE SMILE WHEN HE HEARS THAT HE IS A BISCUIT.	2. Imagine Sidney here is a biscuit.
3. TALL MAN LIFTS HUGE CONTAINER MARKED "CHOCOLATE" AND POURS REAL CHOCOLATE FLUID ONTO SHORT MAN.	3. Now take your biscuit. Cover it with chocolate.

4. CAMERA TILTS DOWN TO SHOW POOL OF CHOCOLATE AT SHORT MAN'S FEET.	4. Effective, but not much stays on. Carr's makes Sports a better way.
5. CUT TO THE TWO MEN. TALL MAN NOW CARRIES SHORT MAN, HOLDS HIM ABOVE A TUB MARKED "CHOCOLATE." TALL MAN THEN DROPS SIDNEY INTO THE TUB.	5. Pop the biscuit in chocolate.
6. CUT TO SHORT MAN'S HEAD SURFACING FROM THE CHOCOLATE. AS IT SURFACES, MORE CHOCOLATE IS POURED ON IT.	6. Top it up, and when it's set . . .
7. DISSOLVE TO SHORT MAN NOW ENCASED IN CHOCOLATE AS HE IS LYING DOWN. TALL MAN STANDS PROUDLY ABOVE HIM.	7. . . . you have your biscuit with *all* your chocolate on it.
8. TALL MAN HOLDS OUT A CARR'S SPORT PACKAGE AS CAMERA ZOOMS TO CLOSE-UP OF IT.	8. That's how Carr's makes Sports.
9. HAND SETS PACKAGE DOWN NEXT TO SHORT MAN, STILL ENCASED IN CHOCOLATE. MAN LOOKS AT PACKAGE.	9. Carr's Sports — the bar of chocolate with the biscuit in the middle. Right, Sidney?

The commercial, which cost about $1500 to produce, including everything, states the premise right up front. In the beginning the two characters are whimsical, so the viewer's attention is caught. The commercial is very funny. But the product is always the star. All the talk is about the product. The theme is chocolate. And the viewer makes a clear connection between Carr's Sports and chocolate, which was the basic idea all along. Viewers are told in frame one that the product has the most chocolate. In frame seven, the point is made again. In frame nine, it is made one more time. Even if there were no words, viewers could tell what the commercial is all about and could understand the connection made between Sports and chocolate.

The commercial uses no music, has ninety-three words instead of the pedestrian sixty-five, and employs humor to make its point. Humor, often referred to as the most dangerous weapon in advertising because it is so frequently misused, works well here, selling a product that retails for about a quarter. And the spot makes full use of television's ability to demonstrate product advantages. Best of all, the commercial is so much fun to watch that viewers could watch it over and over without becoming bored with it. They must also have remembered the name of the product, in view of the sales that resulted.

This just goes to show that you don't need a huge budget and a fancy jingle to make a successful commercial. As a marketing man, I am far more proud of the sales than the awards won by this commercial.

20
Outdoor Advertising —
What It Can and Cannot Do

OUTDOOR ADVERTISING CONSISTS of billboards, bus ads, taxi signs, painted walls, and outdoor signs. Let's deal with billboards first. Rare is the entrepreneur who can survive on billboard advertising alone — although it can be done. We have already chronicled the successes of Harold's Club, Wall Drugs, and Burma-Shave, but these enterprises really used outdoor signs, not billboards. Billboard advertising — and to use the term *advertising* is somewhat of an overstatement — is really reminder advertising, for the most part. It works best when combined with advertising through other media.

Each year, an Iowa entrepreneur I know runs a month-long one-cent-sale promotion on the radio and in the newspapers. He supports the radio and newspaper advertising for a month each year with billboards, too. His sales rise an average of 18 percent. With billboards alone, this would never happen. But the billboards add an important ingredient to his marketing mix. He uses them only once a year to promote his furniture business. And they work wonderfully.

Two magic words

But billboard advertising doesn't have to be strictly reminder advertising. In some instances it can lead directly to sales. In regard to this, let me stop right here and tell you the two most important words you can use on a billboard. They are not at all like the high-motivation words we discussed several pages back — not at all that obvious. The two magic words that can spell instant success for you if used on a billboard are *next exit*. If you can use them on your billboard, it may do a full-blown job of marketing for you. For example, a new store in the San Francisco Bay Area that did not have enough money for most marketing could afford one billboard. And that billboard, fortunately, was able to display the words *next exit*. Success came rapidly and overwhelmingly. Of course, the store had to do everything else right to succeed, and it did. But the billboard must get the prime credit.

Most of the time, you cannot buy just one billboard. Usually you've got to rent ten or twenty billboards at once. Some are in winning locations. Some are sure-fire losers. You must take the bad with the good. But sometimes, through cogent arguing or through some loophole in the billboard firm's policies, you can lease just one beautifully located billboard. If ever you can, do it. Otherwise, be careful. Consider using billboards if you have a restaurant, tourist attraction, garage, gas station, motel, or hotel. But look with disdain upon billboard advertising if you've got a business that will not have instant appeal to motorists. If you have a car wash that really is at the next exit, a billboard might just be the ticket. If you have a computer-education firm, forget it. A billboard can, however, help you maintain your identity — if your identity is already established.

Location is all

The Marlboro cigarette company is able to maintain its cowboy identity with billboards. It wouldn't even have to use any words, though it does. But if you are thinking about using billboards simply as reminders and haven't invested a lot in your identity, as Marlboro has, scratch that idea from your marketing plan.

To ascertain whether or not you want even one billboard, find out how many cars pass the billboard site each day. This is known in the business as the traffic count. Billboard firms have that data at their fingertips. Find out also the type of traffic passing by. Trucks won't be able to patronize your car wash. On the other hand, homeward-bound affluent suburbanites may be interested in your take-home restaurant.

When planning a billboard, keep the rules for outdoor signs in mind. Rarely use more than six words. Remember that people are probably driving around fifty five miles per hour when they glance, if they glance at all, at your billboard. Keep it simple for them. Give them one large graphic upon which they can concentrate. Be sure the type is clear. Be sure the words are large. If the traffic count remains more or less the same at night, be sure your board is illuminated. That costs more than a nonilluminated board but may be worth the extra bucks.

Six words only

Billboard companies are open to price negotiation, although they may not appreciate my putting that down in print. They are also amenable to location negotiation. Once I wanted a specific location and was told that in order to get it, I'd have to rent nine other billboards — all in dismal locations. I said I was not interested. A couple of weeks later, I was offered the billboard along with only four other locations, also dismal. Again, I said no. Finally, I received a call from the sales rep saying I could have the one location I wanted, but the price would be significantly higher than originally quoted. It would have been a good deal, and I wished I could have said yes. But by this time, my client's monies had been committed. So we all lost out. Too bad the rep hadn't made me the same offer in the beginning. I could have used "next exit" on the billboard and had one more success story to report here.

In addition to attracting direct sales on occasion, billboards help guerrillas in three other instances:

1. When you are new to an area and want to make your presence known
2. When you want to tie in with a unique advertising campaign or promotion
3. When you have an idea that translates ideally onto a billboard, and you can rent just one board

An example of the third instance is a roadside cider stand that sells cherry cider grown from trees visible from the highway. A gutsy entrepreneur might display a billboard with the entire center section cut out so that motorists can see right through the billboard to the cherry trees. A simple line of copy at the top (or bottom) might say: CHERRY CIDER FROM THESE TREES — NEXT EXIT. I know it is seven words long, but it's okay to break the rules occasionally, just as long as you know them and have a good reason for breaking them when you do.

One of the more attractive aspects of billboard advertising is that if you supply the design, the billboard company will produce the billboard for you. That means the company will handle blowing the artwork up to a size that will fit on the billboard. Billboard sizes are measured in sheets, with one sheet approximating the size of a large poster. Whatever you do, make sure your billboard fits in with the rest of your advertising campaign. The Iowa man was able to present his message in six words on his immensely successful billboard only because the message had been explained more fully elsewhere. A guerrilla uses billboards like darts. A guerrilla either says "next exit," or ties his or her billboard in directly with a strong campaign, or uses a single billboard with surgical precision. No guerrilla uses a "next exit" billboard for the usual one month or three months. After testing the merits of a billboard, a guerrilla signs a one-year, three-year, or five-year contract for such a board. A guerrilla contracts with a billboard company to erect a billboard in a place where "next exit" can be used, if one does not yet exist. And a guerrilla still realizes that a great billboard isn't much more than a great reminder.

I would suggest that you avoid the use of billboards unless there is a compelling reason to use them. Drive around your community and carefully note the local companies that use billboards. Then talk to the owners of those companies and find out if the billboards work. Unless you are in a business that competes with theirs, you'll probably get a straight answer.

Research those billboards

Sometimes a guerrilla can get several fellow guerrillas to collaborate on a billboard. This brings the cost of the board down considerably and puts it within range of many an entrepreneur. If two or three companies share a board, the cost may be low enough to enable each of them to use the board on a full-time basis, as part of their overall marketing plan.

Call the billboard representatives in your area and listen to their sales pitches. Perhaps they can enlighten you as to special opportunities, new boards to be erected, chances to go in on billboards with other companies. Chances are, you won't be persuaded to put even the tiniest billboard into your marketing plan. But you've nothing to lose by talking with them. So do it. Better yet, listen to them. If you have a well-known theme, billboards might be for you. As with many other marketing media, it may be worth your while to test their efficacy. Different towns respond in different ways to billboards. Maybe you live in a town that gets motivated by billboards. Maybe you are located near a street that is ideal for a billboard. If that's the case, I recommend testing. If you test a billboard for a month or two and nothing happens, you're not out all that much money. But if you never give it a try, and then your biggest competitor tries billboards and goes to glory with them, you'll kick yourself from now till Sunday.

Billboard marketing is, almost without exception, *share-of-mind* advertising. Share-of-mind advertising is advertising that attempts to win sales down the road by implanting a thought or establishing an identity. It tries to win for you a constantly increasing share of the minds of the people in your marketing area. It does not normally prove effective in a hurry, cannot be translated into results, and is only profitable in the long run, if ever. *Share-of-market* advertising, on the other hand, is advertising that attempts to win instant sales. It tries to win for you a constantly increasing share of whatever market your offering belongs to. Share-of-market advertising is the kind of advertising that is the most effective, the most instantly translated

Share of mind

into results, and the most profitable in the short run. Most entrepreneurs are a bit too concerned with cash flow to worry about shares of minds. They want increased shares of markets, and they want them right now. So consider using billboards, but don't expect to attract highly motivated prospects through them.

Moving images   You can expect about the same, perhaps a little more, from bus signs, both interior and exterior, and exterior taxi signs. These may be employed as part of a marketing plan that calls for the use of signs in urban areas. These moving signs are seen by many people, a lot of whom may be serious prospects. Taxi signs are seen by people throughout the metropolitan area. Bus signs are usually seen by the same people — bus riders and people who live along the route. Of course buses don't always travel the same routes taxis do. But this should be kept in mind if you're thinking about using both bus signs and taxi signs.

A client of mine enjoyed a great deal of success attracting temporary office workers with signs placed inside buses. The client was an agency that provided these workers to large employers, and the signs were designed to appeal to both the workers and the employers. If your product or service is located near a bus line, you should consider placing signs on that particular bus line — on the exterior of the buses. Such signs will not serve as a complete marketing plan, but they can be an effective part of one.

Learning where your prospects go will help you determine the best location for outdoor advertising, whether it be placed on a billboard, a bus, a painted wall, or a sign on a barn. For example, you sell a new type of tanning oil and a paintable wall is available near a sunbathers' beach, grab it. If you market agricultural products or services and a paintable roof is available on a well-traveled country road, rent the space and paint it with your message. Give serious thought to placing a sign outside your own place of business. A good sign often results in good business. A poor sign invites disaster.

What makes a bad sign? Lack of clarity. Lack of uniqueness. Fancy lettering. Bland colors. Tiny words. Improper placement. What makes a good sign? Readability. Warmth. Uniqueness. An identity that matches that of your business. Clarity from afar, from moving vehicles, on dark nights. Good colors. Make certain that your sign communicates what your business is all about. For instance, "Moore's" tells us a lot less than "Moore's Stationery." To gain community acceptance, try to have your sign designed in such a manner that it fits in with the character of the community. Garish signs may be dandy in some locations and horrid in others. Conservative signs may be just the ticket on some streets, and a ticket to doom on others. Be sensitive to the tastes of your community.

Always be on the lookout for potential sign locations. I know a guerrilla marketer who could not secure a billboard near his place of business. But he was able to persuade the owner of a drive-in located within one mile of his business to sell him space on the back of the drive-in screen. It's no accident that the back of the drive-in screen faced a heavily traveled freeway.

Always look for sign locations

Don't allow yourself to be hemmed in by a small imagination. But remember that advertising seen by speeding motorists has less impact than advertising seen by relaxed prospects — the type that might take the time to read a direct mailing from you.

21
Direct-Mail Marketing: Pinpointing Your Prospects

ATTENTION ALL GUERRILLAS! Direct marketing is where it's at. Direct marketing is the name of your game. Direct marketing has a built-in mirror that reflects the true effectiveness of your advertising message. All other forms of marketing have much to be said for them, but direct marketing has more. All other forms of marketing can help you immensely, but direct marketing can help you more.

Direct marketing refers to direct-mail, mail-order, or coupon advertising, or telephone marketing, or any method of marketing that attempts to make a sale right then and there. It does not require a middleman. It does not require a store. It only requires a seller and a buyer. And because of that, much unnecessary game playing is removed from the marketing process, leaving only accountable results. Let me repeat that word: *accountable*. When you run a radio commercial or a newspaper ad, you do all in your power to make sure that it works, but you don't really know if it does. But when you engage in direct-mail advertising, the form of direct marketing upon which we will concentrate in this chapter, you'll know clearly whether or not your mailing worked. Either it did or it didn't. If it worked, you'll know how well it worked. And if it failed, you'll know how dismally it failed.

Direct mail is the least expensive method of marketing — on a per-sale basis. The overall cost may be high, but if it works for you, it is inexpensive marketing. There are many books, many articles, many chapters devoted to enlightening marketers as to the intricacies of direct-mail marketing. Read them. Keep reading. For a guerrilla, marketing is part art and part science. Direct mail is more science than art. This is not to downplay the art of creating a successful direct-mail package. But for now, let's focus on the science, the things we already know.

For instance, we know that the three most important things to do if you are to succeed at direct marketing are to test, test, and test. If you know that and do that, you are on the right road. If you play it by ear, you will probably fall on your ear. Direct marketing is growing faster than any other type of marketing. More and more people trust it. More and more people enjoy the convenience of being able to shop and buy by mail. More and more people want to be spared the lack of parking places, high fuel costs, irritable sales clerks, and crowded stores. They turn, therefore, to those companies that make their products or services available via direct mail. In 1982, 85 percent of Americans purchased *something* by mail.

Why direct marketing?

The complete honesty that results from direct-mail marketing is invaluable. Because it is so accountable, it lets you know if you have done a good job making your offer, pricing your merchandise, constructing your mailing package, writing your copy, timing your mailing, selecting your mailing list. Soon after you have accomplished your mailing you learn whether it worked or failed. That's what I mean by accountability. During the past few years, more of my work than ever before has been in the area of direct response. That is because companies are moving rapidly into direct-response marketing. They are learning that the feedback is instant and accurate when they employ this marketing vehicle.

Before studying the secrets imparted in these pages, you must honestly ask yourself whether or not your product or service lends itself to direct marketing. If you have a product or service, or are trying to select a product or service, to market via direct-mail or mail-order marketing, you should first consider several factors. You automatically consider them when asking and answering these questions:

The direct check

- Is there a perceived need for the product or service? ✓
- Is it practical? ✓
- Is it unique? ?
- Is the price right for your customers or prospects? ?
- Is it a good value? ✓
- Is the markup sufficient to assure a profit? ✓
- Is the market large enough? Does the product or service have broad appeal? ✓
- Are there specific smaller segments of your list that have a strong desire for your product or service? ?
- Is it new? Will your customers perceive it as being new? ?
- Can it be photographed or illustrated interestingly? ✓

- Are there sufficient unusual selling features to make your copy sizzle? ✓
- Is it economical to ship? ✓ Is it fragile? Odd-shaped? Heavy? Bulky?
- Can it be personalized? No
- Are there any legal problems to overcome? No
- Is it safe to use? ✓
- Is the supplier reputable? ?
- Will back-up merchandise be available for fast shipment on reorders? ✓
- Might returns be too huge? ?
- Will refurbishing of returned merchandise be practical? ✓
- Is it, or can it be, packaged attractively? ✓
- Are usage instructions clear? ✓
- How does it compare to competitive products or services? ?
- Will it have exclusivity? ?
- Will it lend itself to repeat business? ?
- Is it consumable, so that there will be repeat orders?
- Is it faddish? Too short-lived?
- Is it too seasonal for direct-mail selling? ✓
- Can an add-on to the product make it more distinctive and salable? ?
- Will the number of stock-keeping units — various sizes and colors — create problems? ✓
- Does it lend itself to multiple pricing? ✓
- Is it too readily available in stores? ✓
- Is it like an old, hot item, so that its success is guaranteed? ✓
- Is it doomed because similar items have failed? ✓
- Does your mother, wife, brother, husband, girlfriend, boyfriend, sister, or kid like it? ?
- Is direct mail the way to go with it? ✓
- Does it fill an unfilled niche in the marketplace? ✓

These questions were posed by Len Carlson, who for thirty years has sold about 10,000 different items from a direct-marketing company called Sunset House. They were listed in *Advertising Age*, in an article written by Bob Stone, president of Stone and Adler, a direct-response firm in Chicago.

You've got to ask yourself these hard questions and come up with answers that please you — and if you can't, you've got to discard the idea of direct mail for your particular product or service, or you've got to make some major changes in your offering. If as few as five of your answers to these thirty-six questions are not the right answers, you may be going in the wrong direction. This checklist can serve as a handy guide to direct-marketing success. Luckily, you have these questions to save you from spending money unwisely.

Only after you are satisfied that you ought to proceed into the world of direct marketing should you take the next step — which is to understand the relationship of direct-response advertising to non-direct-response advertising. Rather than giving you my words about that relationship, I would like to quote from a speech made in late 1982 to the Direct Mail/Marketing Association's 65th Annual Convention by David Ogilvy — the head of a major advertising agency that has offices worldwide. Keep in mind that David Ogilvy's agency is a standard agency, not a direct-response agency, although it now has a branch called Ogilvy and Mather Direct. Here is a portion of Mr. Ogilvy's talk:

> In the advertising community there are two worlds. Your world of direct-response advertising and that other world — the world of general advertising. These two worlds are on a collision course.
>
> You direct-response people know what kind of advertising works and what doesn't work. You know to a dollar.
>
> You know that two-minute commercials are more cost-effective than thirty-second commercials.
>
> You know that fringe time on television sells more than prime time.
>
> In print advertising, you know that long copy sells more than short copy.
>
> You know that headlines and copy about the product and its benefits sell more than cute headlines and poetic copy. You know to a dollar.
>
> The general advertisers and their agencies know almost nothing for sure, because they cannot measure the results of their advertising. They worship at the altar of creativity. Which means originality — the most dangerous word in the lexicon of advertising.
>
> They opine that thirty-second commercials are more cost-effective than two-minute commercials. You know they're wrong.
>
> In print advertising, they opine that short copy sells more than long copy. You know they are wrong.
>
> They indulge in entertainment. You know they are wrong. You know to a dollar. They don't. . . .
>
> Nobody should be allowed to create advertising until he has served his apprenticeship in direct response. That experience will keep his feet on the ground for the rest of his life. The trouble with many copywriters in ordinary agencies is that they don't think in terms of

selling. They have never written direct response. They have never tasted blood.

Until recently, direct response was the Cinderella of the advertising world. Then came the computer and the credit card. Direct marketing exploded. You guys are coming into your own. Your opportunities are colossal. . . .

Ladies and gentlemen, how I envy you. Your timing is perfect. You have come into the direct-response business at the right time. You are onto a good thing. For forty years I have been a voice crying in the wilderness, trying to get my fellow advertising practitioners to take direct response seriously. Today, my first love is coming into its own. You face a golden future.

David Ogilvy's speech was considered so important that he was the keynote speaker, and yet his entire speech was delivered on videotape. Goes to show that it's the content that counts. And the words just revealed to you are loaded with meaning. I hope you heed them. I hope you realize the enormity of Mr. Ogilvy's truth: If you don't know about direct-response marketing, you don't know about marketing.

According to technical experts in the field, direct marketing is not a fancy term for mail order. It is an interactive system of marketing that uses one or more advertising media to effect a measurable response and/or transaction at any location. We have the magazine *Direct Marketing* to thank for this definition.

That same publication reminds us that marketing is all the activities involved in moving goods and services from seller to buyer. Then *Direct Marketing* makes a crucial distinction. It says that direct marketing has the same broad function as standard marketing but also requires the existence and maintenance of a database. This database records names of customers, prospects, and former customers. It serves as a vehicle for storing, then measuring, the results of direct-response advertising. It also provides a way to store, then measure, purchasing performance. And finally, it is a way to continue direct communication by mail and/or telephone.

Looking into the future, *Direct Marketing* reminds us to consider interactive TV as an up-and-coming direct-selling device. This device, already in use in test markets, enables shoppers to see items on TV, then even order the items immediately. In about ten years, interactive TV will probably be the major vehicle employed by large users of direct marketing.

The value of direct response   You should, if at all possible, engage in direct marketing. The value to you is enormous. You get to pinpoint your prospects with amazing accuracy. You can be selective in regard to age, race, sex, occupation, buying habits, money spent on past direct-mail purchases, education, special interests, family composition, religion, marital status, and geographic location ranging from state to county to town to Zip Code to block.

If you have the soul of a guerrilla, you will have been compiling a mailing list from the day your business began. The list should naturally start with your own customers. From there, you can expand it to include people who have recently moved into your area, and people who have recently been married or divorced, or become parents. You can eliminate people who have moved away — and one in five Americans move each year.

You might engage in a simple direct mailing of postcards to customers, informing them of a sale you will have the next week. They will very much appreciate the early notification and will show their gratitude by purchasing from you. You might also engage in a full-scale direct mailing, consisting of an outer envelope, a direct-mail letter, a brochure, an order form, a postpaid return envelope, and even more.

Whatever you do, the process begins when you decide exactly what it is you wish to offer. How will you structure that offer? Then you must select your mailing list. If you haven't got the names already, you can purchase them from a list broker (look under "Mailing Lists" in your yellow pages). Take care. Be sure you buy a clean, fresh list. The broker (and the price) can give you clues on this. You must be certain that you know all the costs involved: postage, printing, writing the mailing, artwork, paper, personalization (individualizing each letter by name and address, rather than saying "Dear friend" or the like), and repeat mailing costs. Your gross sales, minus these costs and your production, handling, and shipping costs, will constitute your profits. Be sure you make financial projections and know your break-even point.

According to Lynn Atherton, who is a direct-mail executive in the direct-response arm of a major advertising agency and who helps mastermind mailings for some of the nation's largest direct marketers, the three biggest secrets that can be disclosed to a direct marketer are:

1. Pick your list with the utmost care.
2. Structure your offer in such a way that it is extremely difficult to refuse.
3. Plan your projections so that you earn a profit.

Ms. Atherton was also asked to describe the three biggest errors made by direct marketers. Never one to be inconsistent, she said they were:

1. Failure to pick the right list or lists.
2. Failure to structure an offer properly.
3. Failure to plan projections with enough foresight.

In the old days, a direct-mail campaign meant a letter. Today, it means a letter, two or three or five follow-up letters, perhaps a follow-up phone call or two, and finally, one more direct-mail letter. Many entrepreneurs engage in weekly or monthly direct mailings.

There are a multitude of decisions for you to make when you embark upon a mailing, so it is crucial that you know the right questions to ask. In addition to deciding about your mailing list, your offer, and your financial projections, you'll have to decide whether to mail first class or third class. Will you personalize your mailing? Will you have a toll-free number available for ordering? Which credit cards will you accept? Will you need to alter your pricing because you'll be selling direct? This seemingly simple subject becomes more complex as you learn more about it.

Mailing envelopes   The envelope for a direct mailing merits a chapter of its own. Executives should not be sent envelopes with address labels. Their names must be typed on the envelope. And for selling stationery, feminine products, or political candidates or causes, a handwritten envelope provides a wonderfully personal tone. Envelopes can be standard size (#10) or oversize (6 inches by 9 inches), manila, covered with gorgeous art, foil-lined, or window-type. They can have a return address, or, to pique curiosity, omit the return address.

One of the best devices you can use on an envelope is a "teaser" — a copyline that compels the recipient to open the envelope. Examples of successful teasers are: "FREE! A microcalculator for you!"; "Want to get your hands on $10,000 extra cash?"; and "The most astonishing offer of the year. Details inside."

As you can see, there are myriad ways to get a person to open an envelope. And that is the purpose of the envelope — to interest the recipient so that he or she will open it and read the contents.

You should almost always include a P.S. in your letter. P.S.'s get read with regularity, far more than body copy. Many direct mailings now include what are known as lift letters — little notes that say things such as "Read this only if you have decided not to respond to this offer." Inside is one more attempt to make the sale, probably a handwritten message signed by the company president.

Be sure you guarantee what you are selling, because you are not as "in touch" with customers as you would be with a store-sold product or service, and they will want the reassurance of a guarantee.

The most effective direct-mail efforts allow people to buy with credit cards. "Bill me" also works well as a rule. An element of urgency, such as "offer expires in one week," increases the response even more. Guerrillas always put a time limit on their direct-mail offers.

Whatever you do, make your offer clear, repeat it several times, keep your message as short as possible, and ask for the order. Don't pussyfoot around. Ask people to do exactly what you wish them to do. Then ask them again.

I also recommend toll-free phone numbers, which usually *triple* the response rate. Every day, half a million Americans order $180 million worth of merchandise by phone.

Toll-free phone numbers help

When you create a direct-mail ad with a coupon, make the coupon a miniature version of your ad, complete with headline, benefit, and offer. In short, make it a brief summary of the advertisement. Some direct-mail pros write their coupons or response devices before they write their ads.

Where should the ad appear in the publication? The best place, although relatively expensive, is the back page of a newspaper or magazine — where response can be as much as 150 percent greater than from the same ad inside the publication.

And while considering direct marketing, always consider including an insert with your bill. People certainly open bills, so that means they'll probably see your insert. And you'll get a free ride because the bill is paying the postage for the insert. Another type of insert is the free-standing type that often appears in newspapers or magazines. These are known to be very effective. So check with your newspaper or magazine rep to find out about their services with regard to inserts.

Freeman Gosden, Jr., president of Smith-Hennings-Gosden in Los Angeles, has come up with a direct-mail marketer's checklist. He offers these points for consideration:

- Look at the mail as your reader will.
- Keep your primary objective foremost in your mind.
- Does the number-one benefit hit you between the eyes?

- Does the number-two benefit follow close behind?
- Does the message of the mailing package flow?
- Does the outside envelope encourage you to open it — now?
- Is the letter the first thing you see upon opening?
- Does the letter discuss the reader's needs, product benefits, features, endorsements, and how to respond?
- Do graphics support the copy?
- Does the reply card tell the whole offer?
- Is there a reason to act now?
- Is it easy to reply?
- Would you respond?

The almighty catalogue   Catalogues are a whole different ballgame, part of direct mail, to be sure, but a very different part. As your business grows, you will probably require a catalogue to spur your direct marketing. When you do decide to market with a catalogue, be absolutely certain that your catalogue has the right positioning, the right merchandise selection, the right kind of merchandise, the right graphics, the right use of color, the right size (thirty-two pages is considered optimum), the right headlines, the right subheads, the right copy, the right sales stimulators, and the right order forms. Also be sure that you have formulated your projections correctly. Other than that, direct marketing with catalogues is a piece of cake.

If you run a mail-order business, your catalogue will be the heart of your business. It will be a mighty contributor to your bottom line. The success of your mail-order catalogue will be contingent upon your having customers who have already had one or more satisfactory transactions with you. That means that when they receive your catalogue they will trust you and will have confidence in your offerings. It also means catalogues are not for people just starting a business.

Be prepared to invest in your catalogue. A friend of mine who ran a successful mail-order company ($2 million in sales, with $500,000 in marketing expenses) spent 50 percent of his marketing money on direct mail, 30 percent on catalogues, and 20 percent on mail-order ads. Does it sound as if he believed in catalogues? Well, he didn't believe enough. Later, he changed his marketing budget so as to spend 15 percent of his marketing money on mail-order ads, 20 percent on direct mail, and 65 percent on catalogues. He had learned that his catalogues were the most important selling tools he had. In fact, he used to say he was in the catalogue business rather than the mail-order business. My friend became a millionaire in the business, so take heed of his words.

Think of your catalogue as a specialized form of direct mail. It is like a store on paper — a complete presentation of your merchandise. The items within your catalogue should reflect the interests of your audience and should be similar in nature. If you sell outdoor equipment, your customers won't want to buy gourmet foods from you. They look upon you as a specialist, and your catalogue must nourish that belief.

To print a catalogue you should have about 25,000 customers. That's a lot. But if you want to earn a whale of a lot of money, you'll have to start developing a customer list that long. The big money — the truly large sums — will come to you when you send those customers your catalogue. What if you don't have 25,000 customers? Create an inexpensive catalogue, perhaps a minicatalogue of eight pages, with just black and white photos.

Preparing a catalogue is quite a serious project. Once designed, it can be printed for 5000 customers or 5,000,000 customers. But the amount of work required to get the catalogue ready for the printer makes it cost-ineffective unless you print up 25,000 copies. That's just a rule of thumb, but it's a good one.

If your catalogue contains only 100 items, the cost of your art direction, copywriting, and photography, plus the charges for your type, photostats, and paste-up, will run about $5000. Your printer will charge about $1000 as a make-ready (getting ready to print) fee. The cost of the printing (in black and white plus one color) for an 8½ x 11 format on regular paper, sixteen pages, will run about ten cents per catalogue. Postage will run another ten cents. So the 25,000 catalogues will cost about $11,000 by the time they're in the mail — about $.44 each. Assuming you have a gross profit margin of 55 percent, you will have to sell at least $.80 of merchandise per catalogue mailed. You must sell $20,000 worth of goods just to break even. That's not easy. But if it's your first catalogue, breaking even isn't too bad. It builds business. And the next year, when you have 50,000 customers, most of your catalogue work will already have been accomplished. You can pick up most artwork and copy from the first catalogue, and your in-the-mail costs will be substantially reduced. Therefore you ought to make a very impressive profit on your catalogue the second year, even more the third year, and still more each succeeding year. But as with all other forms of guerrilla marketing, you must be patient, must not expect miracles, must consider your expenditures as an investment, and must remain committed to your catalogue marketing program.

Up till now, we've been talking about mailing your catalogue to your own list of customers. If you purchase outside lists, even exceptional ones, you should not figure on a return that is more than 85 percent of that realized by mailing to your own list. So test other lists very carefully before plunging in and mailing a million catalogues. Whatever you do, you *must* mail your catalogue at Christmas. People *want* to buy at that time, and you've blown an important opportunity if you do not mail to them then.

A few more pointers about catalogues: Work with your printer to determine the optimum number of pages, the paper stock, the format, and the print run. Naturally, your printer must be experienced in catalogue production to do this. Find one that is. Also, don't produce full-color catalogues until you can mail 200,000 or more of them. Use the front and back covers of your catalogues to sell merchandise. They are very effective. Stay away from group-item shots. Display your merchandise item by item and don't try to be artistic. Instead, be clear. Steer clear of models, because they can increase your costs more than is necessary. If you sell clothing, it's almost impossible to avoid using models, but do so if you can. Also, it is not a good idea to mix photos with illustrations. Choose between the two and stay with your choice.

Your copy should be simple, straightforward, and concise. Forget cleverness and give the facts, along with the benefits. Better to give the features and the answers to any questions that may come up than to be too brief. If you can possibly write the copy yourself, do it. You have a feel for the merchandise, or at least you should.

By all means, bind an order form into your catalogue. And offer some merchandise on that order form. Bribe people to order more than they ordinarily would. For instance, tell them that if they order $25 or more in merchandise, they will receive a free gift, and if they order $50 or more, they will receive a better free gift. And promise them a doozie of a gift if they order $100 or more. Try it. People just love free gifts. Don't you? Also include on your order blank a brief letter from you to your customers. Make it warm, personal, and not too long.

As you can tell, the business of producing and mailing catalogues is complex. But after the first year, it is exceptionally profitable — if you do it right. If you think you might ever offer a catalogue, start putting your name on as many catalogue mailing lists as possible.

Then you can expect your mailbox to be filled with informative examples every day but Sunday. Mine is.

Even if it isn't practical for you to use catalogues, I hope you will try direct mail if it is at all feasible for your business. If you do, you will get a head start by using the major marketing method of the future.

Try a small number of mailings first. Test always. Learn from each test. In truth, if you break even while testing, you are doing fine. The goal is to come up with a formula that can be repeated and expanded. If you ever obtain a publicity story about your business, consider enclosing reprints of it as a mailing.

In my own experience as an entrepreneur and as a direct-response writing specialist, I have found that envelopes with teaser lines get a better response than those without. I have found that short letters work better than long letters, that long brochures work better than short brochures, that postcards often make superb mailers all by themselves. I have learned that it is worth the time to check out many lists before selecting one, and that one's own customer list is a gold mine when it comes to direct mail. I know that a single mailing isn't nearly as effective as a mailing with one, two, or more follow-ups, and that a mailing with a phone follow-up is frequently best of all.

My own direct-mail experience

A guerrilla will either realize that direct-mail advertising is not the way for his or her business to proceed, or will utilize direct mail with intelligence, reading books about it, talking with direct-mail pros, and making it his or her most cost-effective marketing method. Strange as it may seem, the majority of people like to receive mailings from businesses; so don't feel self-conscious, and put the U.S. Postal Service to work for you.

What about a catalog for resort property renters? Sturdy yet romantic gear to make their places more saleable?

maybe start out selling at seminars?

IV
Non-Media Marketing

Now that you know you can market your products and services through mini-media and maxi-media, you should also know that you can succeed without using media at all. You can invite groups to your place of business to hear speakers. You can put on programs for these groups if they won't come to you. You can stage exhibits at fairs. You can display your offerings in model homes or auto showrooms or restaurants or other nonmedia places where groups of people will see them. You can participate in your local Welcome Wagon, which helps newcomers to the community and enlightens them as to products and services available. You can talk with fellow merchants and entrepreneurs and arrange to exchange information, assistance, and ideas with them when possible. You can hold sales training sessions for your own people. You can ask the manufacturers that supply you for their aid in marketing. You can develop incentive plans to spur your people to greater heights. You can hold open houses and parties. You can create dazzling window displays.

Coming up are even more ways that successful entrepreneurs can promote their businesses without using the media — at least not using it directly. Some of these methods ought to become part of your marketing plan if you are serious about success. They are hard to develop. They require painstaking detail work. They are far more complex than they appear. But they are worth your time and effort, and for many a guerrilla they pay off handsomely.

Is it possible to succeed using only non-media marketing? Yes. But it is easier to succeed with a combination of mini-media, maxi-media, *and* non-media marketing.

22
Advertising Specialties and Samples: If You've Got It, Flaunt It

ADVERTISING SPECIALTIES ARE THOSE items on which the imprinted name (and sometimes the address, phone number, and
theme line) of the advertiser appears. Examples of advertising
specialties are ball-point pens, matches, ashtrays, calendars, key
chains, paper-clip holders, caps, T-shirts, pins, playing cards, shopping bags, belt buckles, decals, banners, lighters, license-plate
frames, and more, lots more.

Consider these specialties to be the equivalent of billboards. That
means they are great for reminder advertising. They are usually
terrible as your only marketing medium. They do, however, put
your name in front of your prospective customers. And your prospects don't even have to leave home or office to see them. As part of
a marketing mix, that's a very good thing. As I've said before, familiarity is one of the keys to success. And there is no question that ad
specialties breed increased awareness.

On the other hand, advertising specialties don't do too much
more. They do make your prospects and customers feel good about
you, especially if the specialty items are valuable. I remember that a
businessman buddy of mine was ecstatic upon receiving a digital
clock-pen. He spoke with reverence of the supplier who gave it to
him, and he continues to show his loyalty to the man. A specialty
item with so much perceived value does breed a sense of obligation,
to be sure. And if you can purchase a breakthrough type of product
for your deserving prospects *and customers*, by all means give it
serious consideration. There are no particular industries or businesses that benefit more than others with this marketing medium.
But if, for example, you come across a unique and advanced
measuring device, and your prime prospects are contractors and
carpenters, you'd be well advised to give it a shot. Be proud to put
your name on such a gift.

Be proud to use sampling, too, if you sincerely believe that by providing exposure to your product or service you will win loyal customers. Choose sampling over advertising specialties every time, if it comes to making a choice. Both involve giving something away. Both win friends and create favorable associations. But sampling accomplishes these things by means of freebies that are more pertinent than advertising-specialty items.

I strongly suggest that you examine the use of ad specialties if they seem to lend themselves to your type of business. If, for example, you are a mobile auto mechanic, it's a dandy idea to give your customers and prospects key chains (for their car keys) with your name and number on them. On the other hand, if you are a computer consultant, handing out key chains makes no sense whatsoever. But handing out small guides to software makes a lot of sense.

What I would do, and what I have done myself, is to consider my line of merchandise or services very carefully. Then, I'd look in the yellow pages under "Advertising Specialties" and I'd find the name of a rep, call the rep, and ask him or her to pay me a visit, since I'm a prospect. Next, I'd ask the rep to recommend specialties that have worked for others in my line and to tell me about new ad specialty items that have not yet been used. I'd take the time to look through the rep's cumbersome catalogue of available specialties. Perhaps I'd get ten ideas that hadn't occurred to the rep.

I'd also learn about upcoming specialties, gift ideas, and specialties that I might recommend to my own clients. I might decide that none of the specialties are for me. But at least I'd know a lot more about what is available, what certain specialties cost, and what use other companies have made of these methods of non-media marketing. Perhaps I wouldn't want to use a specialty item now but would want to use one later.

I must admit to a prejudice toward calendars as an advertising specialty. I'm not talking about ordinary calendars. I'm referring to gorgeous calendars that most people will happily hang in their homes or offices, then look at almost every day. I have such calendars in my own home, and I have patronized the companies that gave them away. (I'm not really sure whether my business was instigated by the calendars; probably not, but one can't be too sure of one's unconscious thought processes.) And I have recommended the use of handsome calendars to my clients. They have used them and continued to use them. One of the reasons I like calendars as ad specialties is that people tend to look at them a lot. One of the reasons I do not like, say, playing cards, is that people tend not to look at them a lot.

If you do decide you want to distribute calendars, you've got to make that decision in the summer, at the very latest, so that the right calendars with the right inscriptions can be in your hands at the right time — probably in early November.

You might also look into the use of scratch pads. Personalized scratch pads have become very effective lead-generating gimmicks for salespeople, I'm told. What you do is pay a printer to stick a photo, your name, address, phone number, and theme line on a sheet of paper, then print up a bunch of sheets that are made into scratch pads — each sheet of the pad being an ad for you. Next, distribute those pads — free, naturally — to your prospects. Either hand them out or mail them. People tend to keep such pads by their phones or on their desks. They use the pads for writing notes to themselves. Every time they look at one of the scraps of paper, they see the name of your offering. Even the hottest of offers will not motivate them to pick up the phone and order whatever you are selling, unless they need it. But when they do need what you have to offer, chances are your name will come to mind first. And that's a big help to any guerrilla.

A good ad specialty

As with other types of marketing, the key here is repetition. Because it takes time to become known in a community, it's important to keep circulating new scratch pads.

I know of a real estate salesman in Southern California who estimates that he earns between $15,000 and $20,000 in commissions per year from listings generated by his scratch pads. He sounds like a real guerrilla in that he obviously tracks his sales leads like crazy, and then even translates them into dollar figures.

There are no hard and fast rules as to who should use ad specialties, when they should be used, or how they can be used best. But your ad specialty rep probably has many tips for you. If George, of Let George Do It, were to consider advertising specialties, he might like the idea of calendars and rulers, maybe ball-points pens, and possibly even scratch pads. Or George might let his altruism come shining through by giving away auto litter bags with his name on them. But George would probably not get involved in giving away freebies until his business was well established.

The cost of an individual advertising specialty is tiny. But the volume in which you must order each specialty is not tiny. I once gave away felt-tip pens for a business I was running. The cost of each pen was less than a dollar. But I had to order 300 pens before the manufacturers would put my name on them.

A client of mine who is very successful at fund raising for public schools gives away pens with his name, company name, and phone number on them. His costs are even lower than mine were, because he orders so many pens. His pens, by the way, are neither felt-tip nor ball-point. Because he's a real guerrilla, he gives away a new type of pen. People perceive it to be a breakthrough product, and they associate him with innovation as well.

In regard to the copy on your ad specialty, don't make the mistake of leaving it off entirely. I suggest that you include your name, address, phone number, theme line, and as much copy as will fit on the item. Not much will fit on a key chain or a pen. Quite a bit will fit on a calendar. But use restraint and remember that people won't hang a calendar if it looks like an ad. Nonetheless, it is possible to convey more information than the usual name and address. A guerrilla markets at every opportunity.

Final hint: Talk to people who give away ad specialties themselves. Ask them if they consider the specialties effective. Ask for the recommendation of a good rep. Ask about cost-effectiveness. Ask how long the person has been using ad specialties.

Every year, new advertising specialties are invented. Don't let any winners pass you by. If there is any potential reason for you to invest in this low-cost marketing method, see to it that you find out about the new specialties each year. They can't help you all by themselves — but they won't hurt you either.

Sampling, though, is a different matter. Sampling can help you all by itself. And it can kill you if your offering is at all shoddy.

I consider sampling to be the most effective marketing method available. Of course, I am assuming that you have an excellent product or service. If your product is wonderful, sampling will help it take off in a hurry. You've got to have the ability to service the people you sell, and you've got to offer true quality. But if you do, sampling works wonders.

My marketing idol, Procter & Gamble, spends a fortune on sampling. So do other large, successful, sophisticated marketing concerns. But that does not rule out guerrillas. In fact, before this chapter ends, you'll know of six instances where sampling helped small businesspeople realize healthy profits.

You'll have to examine your offering to see if it lends itself to sampling. Most offerings can be sampled. The first one that comes to mind is a car. You certainly won't want to give away a sample car. But almost all auto dealers offer free test rides. That's a sample. And it succeeds. Usually, and especially when you are offering a service, your sampling must be offered to one person at a time. But if you are offering a product, perhaps you can give away several of your items as free samples.

Since I've been living where I do, I've received in my mailbox free samples of toothpaste, detergent, shampoo, cigarettes, and chewing gum. I continue to use the toothpaste that was sampled. And we buy the new detergent. I doubt if any other marketing method would have persuaded me to switch brands so quickly.

Naturally, it costs a bundle to give away free samples. But if you can look upon the cost as a conservative investment, you might be tempted to engage in sampling rather than radio advertising. It's worth thinking about. I cannot think of a more guerrilla-like marketing method than sampling. Few companies do it. It is the essence of honesty, since it forces you to offer quality. It is relatively unique. People will appreciate you for it. Your competition probably doesn't do it. It is not for the lazy or unimaginative, but it is an optimum marketing vehicle for guerrillas.

The utterly honest method

Time for the first of my six examples of how sampling works. In the early days of waterbeds, people considered the beds to be a fad, a mere offshoot of the counterculture. This was understandable. But the beds were too good to be a fad. They would stick around. (Right now, they are a growing force in the bedding industry, and in some states one out of every five people sleeps on a waterbed.) An early waterbed retailer offered people a free thirty-night sleeping trial. He offered to deliver waterbeds to prospects, install the beds, and make a phone call thirty days later to see if his prospects wanted him to pick up the beds or were willing to pay for them. Ninety-three percent of the people were willing to pay for the beds. Sampling paid off.

Successful sampling

Another entrepreneur was launching a newsletter. He advertised in magazines. He engaged in direct mail. Both got mediocre results. Then he mailed free sample copies to prospects. Instant success. Sampling came through. Incidentally, it cost him a total of $500 to try the sampling; he realized $7000 in *profits* from the attempt.

A third guerrilla was marketing a large-screen television set of his own design. Very few people took the time to visit the showroom in which it was displayed. So he took out ads offering free home trials. Soon he had to discontinue the ads because the response was so great. And even better than the response to his offer was the fact that

90 percent of the respondents purchased from him after sampling.

A fourth guerrilla, an office manager who baked chocolate chip cookies and sold them at flea markets on weekends (earning more doing that than through her office-manager salary), engaged in sampling. She baked two sizes of cookies. The tiny ones were free samples. The large ones were $1 each. She gave away the tiny ones — one per customer. More than half the customers were then tempted by the enchanting flavor and crispy goodness of the sample to purchase one or more of the $1 variety. One more case of sampling that worked.

Thus far, I've told you about two samples of merchandise that were loaned rather than given away (waterbeds and large-screen TVs) and two samples that were given away permanently (newsletters and cookies). What you can learn from this is that it does not take a giant company to engage in sampling and sampling can be employed even if your product is too large or too expensive to give away. Free sampling can provide instant results that are not achievable via any other method of marketing. *If it is at all possible to allow your prospects to sample your offering, let them.* Are you a consultant? Offer a free one-hour consultation. If George wanted to show people how good he is at home repair, he would have no trouble giving away free samples. And he would, in all likelihood, benefit greatly from his sampling.

The large-screen-TV entrepreneur had to make his sampling come alive through advertising. His ads called attention to his sampling. So you can see that some sampling depends upon other methods of marketing. But some sampling can work on its own. My fifth guerrilla sampler, a person who washed windows for commercial establishments, frequently washed the windows of his prospects for free. This demonstrated his proficiency, his speed, his method of working. It also netted him several large customers. And it didn't require any advertising to get started.

It's hard to say no to "free"   Sometimes I see ads in marketing publications for writers who offer to write for free — just to prove how good they are. If they are indeed good, this advertising-then-sampling combination nets them quite a bit of business. Hardly anyone turns down something that is offered free. It seems that I'm seeing more and more ads of that type these days. It may be that the economy is tough as nails, but it also may be that people are catching on to the effectiveness of this method of marketing.

Example six involves a person who offered a service. He offered to come to my residence weekly and wash my car, and promised to wash my car that night, to show how good he was. I could see it the next day, realize how convenient his service was, and then, when he came back, sign up for his service. Was I ever tempted to say no to his offer? Of course not. In fact, he made it nearly impossible to say no. The next morning, my car was gleaming. The next evening, he knocked on my door and asked if I wanted the same service every week. That man had earned himself a steady customer with one free sample. It probably took him fifteen minutes to wash my car. But it demonstrated to me how good he was, how convenient he was, and what a nice fellow he was. That his price was definitely not competitive didn't even enter my mind.

By giving a sample of a great service, the car washer caused me to think positive thoughts about his offering. So I was won over quite easily. I wonder if he could ever have obtained my business via other methods. Let's see. He could have talked me into buying from him by canvassing. And in a way, his initial contact with me was a canvass. He might have also signed me up through telephone marketing, but I'm not so sure I would have signed. It certainly wouldn't have been as easy a sale as the sampling was, since he couldn't have proven his worth over the phone. A personal letter might have impressed me, but it wouldn't have afforded the give and take that the personal contact allowed. It also wouldn't have enabled him to prove his point. I would have read his circular or brochure with interest. But since I had never had a car washer who paid house calls, I might not have given the matter serious thought. A sign, a classified ad, or a listing in the yellow pages would not have won my business.

Why sampling works

None of the maxi-media marketing methods would have made me an instant customer. Newspapers, magazines, radio, TV, billboards, direct mail — I doubt if any of them would have made me an instant customer. Certainly if he had put his name on an advertising specialty, I would not have signed up so quickly. But sampling did the trick for him. And it might do the trick for you — in a hurry.

Such sampling is very expensive if you place a price tag on your time, but very inexpensive if you think of out-of-pocket expenses only. Sampling is quite different from other methods of marketing because it does not depend upon repetition. One great sample will do it all. Before you purchased this book, perhaps you looked through a few pages. Maybe you looked at the table of contents. If so, that was sampling on the part of the bookstore. And it worked. I bet sampling will work for you, too. Use it if you possibly can.

23
Free Seminars and Demonstrations: Show and Sell

I HAVE A CLIENT WHOSE business is computer education. His classes are unique, effective, and impressive. But standard marketing methods didn't attract many customers. So he decided to hold a free seminar on computers for people who knew nothing about them. He placed an ad and over 500 people showed up for the seminar.

Had he teamed up with a great salesperson, he might have sold his program to as many as 50 percent of the people attending. But he'd never dreamed so many people would show up, so the number of people he sold on his series of lessons was closer to 5 percent. Next time he holds a free seminar, he'll be a lot better prepared to close his sales. In fact, he might even hire a professional salesperson to maximize the number of people who sign up for paid lessons following the demonstration lesson.

Many people who give paid seminars or courses for a living advertise free miniseminars with ads in the business sections of newspapers. One speed-reading school advertises its free miniseminars with television commercials. An income tax expert markets his free seminars by means of publicity stories coupled with radio commercials on talk-oriented stations. Many entrepreneurs earn a great deal of money with paid seminars and courses. But they cannot attract large numbers of people to paid seminars and courses merely through newspaper ads, so they attract them to free seminars, then convert them to paying customers.

As one guerrilla to another, I sincerely recommend the same tactic to you. I recommend, if it is at all feasible for your type of product or service, that you advertise in the newspaper that you are holding a free seminar on the topic most closely connected with your product or service. Then obtain as many customers for your free seminar as you can. They may purchase your products or they may sign up for your service. If you hold a decent seminar, they will.

When I say seminar, I really mean lecture. Give your audience valuable information and demonstrate your expertise or your product's efficacy for, say, the first forty-five minutes. Then, spend the next fifteen minutes selling whatever it is you wish to sell. What I am talking about is a fifteen-minute, straight-from-the-heart commercial — delivered by you or by someone you hire. The entire process takes one hour. After that, you sign up the prospects. Unlike professional seminar leaders, you probably won't be signing them up for a paid seminar. But you will be allowing them to buy your offering. And they'll want it because your message, your demonstration, your enthusiasm, and your proven expertise will have created within them a desire to purchase from you.

The shape of the seminar

There is no question that an in-person commercial is better than a radio or TV commercial. Certainly a fifteen-minute selling opportunity will pan out better than a thirty-second selling opportunity. For this reason, seminars and demonstrations are being utilized more and more to market products and services.

In a sense, a lecture or demonstration is very much like a sample. Your prospects get to see for themselves what you have to offer. They probably get to touch it, if it's a product, and they get to ask questions, whether it's a product or a service. They get to learn more about your offering this way than they do by standard marketing methods. And just as sampling convinces many people that they should buy a good product, so can your seminar.

Before I write one more word, I should emphasize that a free seminar/demonstration amounts to marketing in a vacuum unless two other factors are present. First, your free imparting of information must be advertised, so that you'll have a large group of prospects. Advertise in the newspaper, on the radio, or on TV. Go for the free publicity that is readily available when you're offering a free seminar. Tell the truth in your ads as to the contents of the seminar, and try to attract honest prospects, not just warm bodies. Second, be sure that either you or an associate can sell your offering to those prospects after the seminar is over. My client was a brilliant lecturer. People listened intently to his every word. They enjoyed looking at him and listening to him. As a lecturer, he was first rate. But as a salesman, he was eighth rate. He had no inkling of how to close. He had no instinct for blood. He didn't have the kind of personality that could take advantage of the momentum his lecture had built. So he signed up only 5 percent of the audience, rather than the 50 percent that was possible.

The three factors

If you can, demonstrate your product or service at your seminar.

Keep in mind that although what you are offering is free, people are giving up their time. They are traveling to the place where you are holding your seminar. And they have expectations, based upon your ad. You must give them value in exchange. You must live up to their expectations and move beyond them. You must treat them as though they have paid to hear you. You should make sure that even if they do not buy from you, they still feel that their time was well spent. Perhaps they'll buy from you later.

Where should you conduct your seminar? At your place of business, if possible. Just rent the chairs you'll need. Perhaps you'll conduct it outdoors, if you are demonstrating gardening skills or the like. Perhaps you'll conduct it in a gym, if you want to show and sell exercise equipment. Most seminars, however, are held in motels or hotels, where seminar facilities are readily available. Such facilities include a lectern, a microphone, a blackboard, chairs, and easily available coffee. It is also advisable to offer free parking. If you have a store, a free seminar held there will work well. It will show your prospects where you are and what you sell. For instance, a seminar on decorating held in your furniture showroom is a natural.

People appreciate useful information. They appreciate it all the more when it is free. When you conduct a seminar or workshop, when you give a lecture, when you demonstrate a product or service, you prove your expertise. You establish yourself as an authority. You gain credibility. Even if people do not buy from you right then and there, they very well may buy from you later. There is a tactic, however, that some very successful (and very high pressure) businesses employ to get the maximum number of people to buy right then and there. They establish three "sales points" on the way to the exit. Upon conclusion of the free seminar, the speaker tells the customers that they can either sign up for the paid seminar at a particular table or with specific representatives located throughout the room. Probably four reps are present to sign people up. Prospects who do not buy must then pass the three sales points prior to leaving the room. At each, they are given a different sales pitch, stronger each time. Some people sign up in the main room, others at the first sales point, and still others at the second sales point. Another group signs up at the third sales point. Only a tiny group — who have world-class sales resistance — leave the building without putting their hands to their wallets.

This practice is common among some consciousness-raising groups. It is the hardest of all possible sells, and it is not easy to resist.

As you can see, it takes several people to accomplish this tactic. But it does work. And if you care about profits more than you care about social propriety, you might put this practice to work.

Free seminars, even without triple-teamed closes, can be a bonanza for you, and you should try to market with them if you possibly can. It may be that your business just doesn't lend itself to seminars. If you operate a window-washing business, a car-washing business, or a mail-order publishing business, perhaps seminars are not for you. But if you run an income-tax-preparation, instructional, or retail-furniture business, perhaps they are.

Think about the field in which you operate. Can you give a lecture for forty-five minutes on any aspect of it? Which aspect? How will this tie in with your offering? Do you have the showmanship to lecture for forty-five minutes and hold the attention of your audience, or should you delegate that task to someone else? Do you have the salesmanship to close sales right then and there, or should that, too, be the job of an associate? What will you be selling at the seminar? Will it be products? Services? Books? Lessons? A paid seminar?

As with sampling, if it is at all possible simply to try one free seminar to market your business, do it. It can be a lot of fun. And it can be extremely profitable, with a lower cost per sale than advertising in any newspaper or on any radio station. It will give you both immediate and long-term benefits. You'll get to mention, in future marketing, that you have lectured in your field, led seminars in your area of expertise. Giving free seminars is a very innovative way to market.

The cost of giving a seminar that's not at your own place of business is about $25 to $100 for the room, plus whatever it costs to provide coffee for the people attending. If you'll only keep them for a one-hour period, you need not provide coffee or water, merely seating. If you plan to keep them longer, it's only fair to make coffee or water available. Some morning seminars also provide free donuts. Even donuts are weapons in the arsenal of a practitioner of guerrilla marketing.

Seminar costs

To the cost of the room and refreshments, add the price of the ads you'll be running and any seminar materials you'll be handing out. After your seminar and sales pitch are completed, you can total up your receipts, then divide them by the total cost of the room, the ads, the refreshments, and the materials. That will give you your cost per sale. If it is low enough, continue to market this way. In fact, it doesn't have to be low. Even if you sell ten people a $1000 product and it costs you $1000 for your room and ads and handouts, you will have earned $10,000 while spending $1000 — a cost per sale of $100. This is a high cost, but it's teeny-weeny when compared to your probable profit on a $1000 product. That is why so many free seminars are being offered these days. That, plus the opportunity to talk to honest-to-goodness prospects, people who have already shown that they will expend time and effort to learn more about the field in which you operate.

Demonstrate   Demonstrations can be given not only at seminars but also in homes, at parties (be sure you consider party-plan marketing for your business), in stores, at fairs and shows, in parks, at beaches, almost anywhere. People are attracted to small crowds, and a free demonstration will almost certainly attract a small crowd. At a free demonstration, which is much less lengthy than a seminar — no more than five minutes — be prepared to sell and take orders immediately afterward. Folks who give seminars and demonstrations often have cohorts all set to accept customers' credit cards, checks, and cash. The person giving the demo or seminar is usually too busy answering questions to take orders. So be sure you have that base covered.

A free demonstration need not be marketed in the same way as a seminar. Just showing up at a high-traffic location, or placing some well-conceived signs, may do the trick. Of course, it is okay to advertise. But it may not be necessary. It will be necessary to provide the showmanship and salesmanship, though.

Can you demonstrate your product or service effectively? Be sure you ask yourself and answer honestly. If you can say yes, by all means give it your best shot. Rarely will you be afforded so golden an opportunity.

Throw a party   A few moments ago, I mentioned the idea of giving your free seminar or demo in a party situation. More and more items every year are being marketed through party-plan marketing. Here's how it works: A person becomes a party-plan representative for a company. Let's say it's an art gallery. This person then throws a party for all of her friends. (I use the feminine gender because I associate party plans with women and with Tupperware. Good going, Tupperware!) At the party, the woman serves coffee and pastries, maybe even little sandwiches. She also gives a well-planned sales spiel about the art she is selling. She shows twenty original oil paintings to the assembled throng. The lighting is optimum. Music especially selected for the occasion is playing in the background.

The woman's enthusiasm is bubbly and contagious. She *loves* those paintings. It shows. Her friends start to love them, too. And the prices! They sound so low. A buying frenzy starts. Fifteen of the paintings are sold. They sell for an average of $100 apiece. The art gallery purchased them for $25 each, including the frames, from artists skilled at rapidly creating oil paintings that look expensive and do have a degree of quality.

Each $100 sale results in $25 for the woman. She is glowing with delight. She made $375 for the night and spent only $50 for refreshments — a $325 profit. And that's just the start. She tells her friends that they can do the same. And they do. The word spreads. The parties spread. The woman who threw the first party gets a cut of sales from the parties thrown by the women she signed up. She's raking in the bucks. Her friends are raking in the bucks. The quickie oil-painting artists are raking in the bucks. And the art gallery — well, its owners are very, very, very happy that they engaged in party-plan marketing.

Can you? Here's the type of companies that do already: exercise-machine companies, art galleries, kitchen-equipment companies (such as Tupperware), womens' clothing manufacturers, vitamin manufacturers, X-rated product companies (the burgeoning "pleasure" industry), cosmetics manufacturers, computer companies, and lingerie manufacturers.

Such parties are ideal places for demonstrations. And the people attending *are already conditioned to buy.* You can't beat that kind of situation if you're a practicing guerrilla. Of all the places at which free seminars or demonstrations can be held, parties certainly rank up there near the top.

About the only disadvantage — if it can be construed as such — of free seminars and demonstrations (except for parties) is that you must do quite a bit of traveling. Either you or a person you delegate. You can't keep holding free demos and seminars in the same area over and over again. You've got to go on the road and talk to fresh prospects. But you can make these free sessions part of your marketing plan and give one or two per year, in your area only. A guerrilla would find some way to utilize them. Et tu?

24

Trade Shows, Exhibits, Fairs: Making a Public Spectacle

SOME WILDLY SUCCESSFUL ENTREPRENEURS employ only one major method of marketing: They display and sell their wares at trade shows, exhibits, and fairs. They realize that many serious prospects will attend these gatherings, so they put all their efforts into exhibiting and selling their merchandise (they usually sell products rather than services). This is not to say that their show booths are their only marketing vehicles. But they are their primary ones. And in a few instances, this is the only way a person needs to market.

The marketing plan of many a guerrilla consists of appearances at four major shows or fairs, plus circulars or brochures to be distributed at the shows. Nothing else. And to be sure, nothing else is needed.

I once attended a large national furniture show with a client who owned a chain of furniture stores. He very much wanted to be one of the first people through the doors at the three-day event. When I asked him why, he told me that he would first breeze through the show, making notes and looking at all the exhibits. Then he would quickly return to those displays that had caught his attention and order a full year's worth of items, making certain to get agreements that he would be the exclusive outlet for each item.

The $50,000 minute Sure enough, it took him, with me hot on his heels, a mere thirty minutes to walk the miles of aisles. Then he spent the next two hours dickering with those manufacturers or distributors that tickled his fancy. At the end of two and one-half hours, he was delighted, having signed up for a year's worth of purchases, all with exclusive arrangements. And just as happy as he, maybe even happier, were the handful of entrepreneurs who had attracted his attention with their merchandise, their displays, their salesmanship, and their readiness to grant concessions. I well recall the look on one man's face when he realized that in only ten minutes he had sold half a million dollars' worth of goods. Fifty thou per minute is a pretty luscious sales rate.

I suggest that you browse through a copy of *Tradeshow/ Convention Guide* at your library, or order a copy from Budd Publications, P.O. Box 7, New York, New York 10004, to learn of a plethora of shows at which you can display your offerings. You'll find more than you think, and believe me, the shows will be worth checking into.

There are a couple of ways to display what you sell at such shows. One way, the standard way, is to rent a booth for several hundred dollars, set up a display, and give it your best. Another way, guerrilla-like in character, is to visit a show, find a display booth that offers merchandise compatible with yours, and strike up a deal with the exhibitor whereby you share a portion of the next booth the exhibitor rents. That means you pay part of the rental fee, assume part of the sales responsibility, and allow your items to be displayed and sold along with those of your new compatriot.

Cutting costs

Visiting such shows is a revelation to the astute guerrilla. When you visit one or two, you will learn of products that compete with or complement yours. You will also discover products that knock your socks off — products with which you would love to become associated, and possibly can. You'll learn the right way to display goods, and the wrong way. You'll pick up some dandy ideas for brochures, signs, and demonstrations. You'll learn a heck of a lot from the mistakes of others — people who have great merchandise but don't know how to market it. And you'll meet people who may be able to help you distribute whatever it is you sell.

An educational experience

Let's look at a case in point. A man-and-wife team who marketed greeting cards all by themselves by calling on stationery stores were soon alerted to the existence of stationery shows at which greeting cards were displayed. There, they were told, they could display their own cards and make sales, they could team up with other card manufacturers, and better yet they could meet distributors who could distribute their cards throughout the country. The two budding entrepreneurs went to the show, checked out the cards and displays of others, and met several representatives who offered to distribute their cards. Because they were greenhorns at the business, they were delighted, and they signed on with several of the reps.

Business picked up for them that next year. But in talking with a few fellow card sellers, they learned that there are basically two kinds of reps one meets at shows. Some are ordinary reps who conduct an ordinary amount of sales activity, and achieve ordinary distribution in ordinary stores. Those, alas, were the kind of reps the man-and-wife team had signed up. The other kind of reps are known as Rolls-

Royce reps. They have the ability to move prodigious numbers of greeting cards by distributing only in high-volume stores and expending a great deal of selling energy.

The next year, the man and wife went to the stationery shows and signed up with only Rolls-Royce reps. By signing with them, the man-and-wife company increased its sales fivefold over the year before, propelling them into a deliriously wonderful tax bracket. So if you are looking for national distribution of your goods, look for Rolls-Royce reps at major trade shows.

Maximizing the marketing opportunity

While displaying your products in your own booth — something you will most likely want to do after you are ready to take on large orders — you will have a great opportunity to engage in four other types of marketing at the same time:

1. You'll be able to hand out circulars. I suggest that you hire someone, preferably a gorgeous woman (or a gorgeous man, if women are your prime prospects), to distribute your circulars while walking through the show. The cost to hire the person will be about $50, and for that, she or he will pass out as many as 5000 circulars — all inviting people in attendance to visit your booth. If you do that, you will instantly rise above most of the other exhibitors, since they will not be practicing such a guerrilla-like tactic. You'll also attract more prospects.

2. You'll be able to give away brochures. Because brochures are more costly than circulars, you won't want to give as many away. But by disseminating them at your booth only, you'll be able to narrow the distribution down to serious prospects only. And your brochures will do heavy-duty work for you. Many people attend shows and exhibits merely to collect brochures. Then they study the brochures and place their orders on the basis of the information they've gleaned. So this is a chance to make your brochure a powerful sales tool. Be sure to get the names and addresses of the people to whom you give brochures.

3. You'll have a great chance to demonstrate your goods to real prospects who are in a buying mood. You can demonstrate your offerings to large groups of people. And since your competitors will probably be at the show too, you'll have a good opportunity to prove the advantages of your product.

4. You'll have ample opportunity to give away free samples. Rarely will you be afforded the chance to give samples to so many potential customers. So if it's possible to let people sample your merchandise, a show or exhibit is the place to do it.

Perhaps now you can see how entrepreneurs avail themselves of the opportunities at shows with 100 percent effort, and why they concentrate their marketing energies and dollars on shows.

Pay close attention to this next guerrilla secret. It frequently spells the difference between astonishing success and depressing failure. It is quite obvious, or so I thought until I saw exhibitors who didn't understand the concept at all. So let me make it even more obvious right here and now. Your main purpose in having a booth at a trade show, fair, or exhibit is to *sell your product*. Sure, you want to display, to demonstrate, to educate. But you really want to *sell*. So you've got to have the means to take orders right there at your booth. You've got to have a person there who is dedicated to selling. You should aim for a large volume of sales at the show itself, in spite of the fancy brochures you will be passing out. Don't forget the furniture-store entrepreneur I wrote about at the start of this chapter. He visited the shows to look and then to *buy*. He didn't care about brochures. He wanted to place his orders at the show.

The main thrust

If you do not sell a lot of what you want to sell at a show, you have failed in this marketing effort. Don't feel great because you have given away cartons of brochures, made gobs of friends, obtained loads of contacts. That's fine, but if you have not sold a large volume of what you are selling, you have not taken advantage of the glorious opportunity afforded you by such shows. I recall two competitors at a national show. Both had attractive displays. Both gave imaginative demonstrations. Both handed out compelling brochures. But the first company figured that the show was a place to display — so it made zero sales. The second company, a new, small, young partnership, figured that the show was a place to sell — so it made $4.5 million in sales during a three-day period. I believe I've made my point.

Many craftspeople sell all the crafts they make at one or two yearly shows. They spend most of the year making their items, then spend a few weeks — at two three-week shows — selling them. Often, no other marketing is necessary for them. But generally, to succeed at marketing in a show, exhibit, or fair, you need a combination of marketing tools: a professional-looking and beckoning display; a supply of informative brochures; a larger supply of enticing circulars to be passed out to the people at the show; a method of demonstrating, sampling, or showing off your goods; and at least two high-energy salespeople. If you have all of those, you are a guerrilla and you have primed yourself to succeed.

The winning combination

Your exhibit at the trade show should be as professional as you can afford. New technology in audio-visual presentations makes it possible for you to stage a continuous multimedia extravaganza — including slides, film, videotape, and music. Lighting can be combined with this multimedia display to literally spotlight your products as they are being featured in your multimedia show. As the visual images dance before the eyes of your prospects, and as music soothes their conscious minds and gains access to their unconscious, the tape-recorded voice of a master motivator tells your audience that they should buy from *you*, that they should trust *you*, that they should give their money to *you*. And there you can be, order pad at the ready, all set to sign, seal, and deliver.

That's the best possible scenario for a trade-show exhibit. If you can't afford it, work down, step by step, including as much as you can.

In most big-city yellow page directories are several columns of "Display Designers and Producers." These businesses offer such lovelies as modular exhibit systems. They will construct or they will rent, and they will even store your exhibit while you're not using it. They'll make a miniature model of your exhibit before you give them an okay to built the real thing — or ten real things. They craft handsome exhibit displays of wood, plastic, cardboard, or metal. They make displays of any size, wired and ready to go.

I'm always impressed and educated when I walk through a display warehouse. I discover great ideas for future displays. I get a good fix on current prices, both for renting and for purchasing. Because the technology is moving so rapidly, it's a good idea to make a yearly visit to one of your area's largest display companies. Ask to see the best they have. And remember — you may be able to afford it if you go in with a few other compatible companies. Case in point: At a recent waterbed trade show, the best exhibit was a multimedia display using holograms and laser technology. It was paid for by a mattress maker, a heater manufacturer, and a bed-frame company. Each of these three compatible companies got a first-class reputation for 33 percent of the first-class price.

Of course, you can always build your own display. If you have the time, talent, and equipment, give it consideration. But do me a favor. Before you do it yourself, look at what is available to you now. That's what your competitors will probably use. Can you do better? Can you keep abreast of new developments?

Staffing your booth Just as important as an award-winning display are the people who man — or woman — your booth at the trade show. They should be talented in several areas. Here are a few tips:

1. Staff your booth with *enough* people. Not doing so can be fatal. I recall a show booth that was manned by two wonderful company reps. They were backed by a beautiful display. At one point, one of the reps was having lunch and the other was visiting another booth. The only person left was a lackadaisical fellow who didn't really understand the company's business and was really around as a gofer. Naturally, that was when two of the biggest customers in the industry visited the booth. They couldn't get answers to their questions, couldn't get an explanation of a new product being introduced, so they moved on and gave their business to someone else. Don't blow your opportunities. Be sure that a top-rate person is *always* at the booth. To do that may require at least two, and, if you can arrange it, even three top-rate people to attend the show and attend to the exhibit. One of those people must *always* be on hand to answer questions and take orders.

2. Be sure the people staffing your booth are *personable, extroverted*, and *friendly*. You don't want an introverted genius up there on your stage. Some people serve best from within the inner sanctum of the company. Others are made for the road.

3. Do what is necessary to staff your booth with *knowledgeable salespeople*. Knowledgeable alone isn't enough. Sales-minded alone isn't enough. At a trade-show exhibit, your stars must be both.

4. Ascertain that the people staffing your booth have a *high energy level* and won't burn out too soon. Trade shows are exhausting. It's hard to stand up and be bright and charming all day, three days in a row.

5. Carefully select people with the *proper social graces* to represent you at trade shows. Trade shows invariably mean parties. I've seen enough people get embarrassingly drunk at such parties to realize that their energies on the exhibit floor were wiped out by their antics on the sixteenth floor.

At trade shows, marvelous things can happen for your company. It is possible — and I know of at least one instance in which this happened — to make one contact who will place an order so large that it will put you on easy street for at least a year. A woman who invented a paper-towel dispenser printed her circulars on paper towels, then gave them away at her booth — dispensed from the dispenser she had invented. One buyer placed an order with her for 250,000 units. Was this due to her unique way of supplying information? Maybe yes, maybe no. But she sure wouldn't have made a sale that size had she not been at the show. And she may not have attracted attention had she not developed such a unique way of sampling, demonstrating, and providing information.

Perhaps your business simply cannot make sales at such public gatherings. But if there is any way you can utilize this marketing tool, do it. Making a public spectacle of yourself is more of a virtue than a vice at such events.

25
Miscellaneous Marketing Tools: Searchlights, Contests, T-Shirts, and More

EVERY FEW MONTHS, NEW MARKETING tools are developed. Some are ingenious. Some are ridiculous. All are worth examining. Just because a marketing device is new doesn't mean it is bad. Probably the most amazing moment I spent during my career in big-time advertising agencies occurred while I was working in England. We had persuaded a large manufacturer of anti-acne products, the largest in the country, to experiment with television advertising. This was in 1968, hardly the Dark Ages.

After a three-month test, during which sales went right through the roof, we prepared a plan calling for the year-round use of television. When we presented it to the client, he told us he did not plan to include television in his marketing program. We wanted to know why, since our test had been enormously successful. "Because frankly, gentlemen," the client countered, "I am not convinced that television is here to stay."

I suppose you can take the same attitude when examining new methods of marketing. But even if a method is hot for only one year, a guerrilla should avail himself or herself of it during that year. It doesn't have to be "here to stay" in order to help your business. Any help you can get should be gratefully accepted.

Recently, I heard of moped advertising. That's a type of marketing in which you pay a company and provide them with a sign advertising your product or service. Then they have one of their employees drive a moped into high-traffic areas where your sign can be seen by large numbers of people. If you are marketing sunglasses, tanning oil, or soft drinks, it makes a lot of sense to employ this medium at beaches. Mopeds can go where buses and cars cannot. They can go to parks and ballgames and parades — wherever lots of people congregate. This is a new marketing medium. It may or may not be here to stay, but it can be of help to you.

There are other less obvious marketing tools that you probably

Moped marketing and more

have heard of. Matchbooks, for one. Package inserts, too, though they are really part of direct marketing. Searchlights are successfully used by many a retailer. But if you live in a community that frowns upon their use, better steer clear of them. Bench advertising is another medium that is available in certain towns, but not many. Might it be right for you? What about T-shirt advertising? If your business might benefit from this method of marketing, give it consideration: Some businesses (but not small businesses) get impressive results from commercials run in movie theaters and drive-ins. Can this medium influence your prospects? If they are moviegoers, maybe so.

In addition to these marketing tools, you can use bumper stickers to broadcast your message. And buttons. And decals. And imprinted sun visors. There's skywriting. And you can use banners that are towed by airplanes. Another popular device is A-frames, known as sandwich boards. These are worn by people parading in front of large groups of other people, and they tell of the benefits of buying from you or announce special offers. As a guerrilla, you have an obligation to give serious consideration to many of these off-the-wall marketing devices.

I recall being approached by a company called Johnny-Ads. They told me that they placed signs on the inside of doors in rest-room toilet cubicles. That explained their name. It also seemed to me to be an invasion of privacy. I mean, if you can't be free from advertising while on the john, where can you be? Although I did not sign up for a three-month trial of ads in latrines, I did hear some glowing stories of success achieved by others using the medium. Since that time, however, I have heard nothing about the company.

There are now several companies that offer to market your services with picket advertising. One of these is called Rent-a-Picket. You pay them a set amount and they have their employees parade in front of your place of business carrying picket-type signs that say wonderful things about you. It's unique, all right, and it may even be here to stay. It is certainly marketing. And for you, it might be worthwhile.

Such advertising methods — searchlights, skywriting, pickets, john ads, and the rest — should be perceived the same way you perceive billboards. They are reminder advertising. They help keep your name in the public eye, and they call attention to your prime attributes. But they probably can't do the job all by themselves. Still, one or more of them might be made part of a smart marketing plan.

If you have a place of business where you occasionally run promotions, a searchlight to call attention to a late-night sale may work as an attention-getter for you. I know of a waterbed retailer who once filled a waterbed mattress with helium and tied it to a rope. Then he let it float over his store, where it could be seen for miles. The cars that drove by didn't all stop, but many slowed down and noticed the store. The owner of the store says that the stunt enabled him to equal his average monthly volume in one day and to double it within one week. Crazy, but it worked.

And so it is with many unusual marketing methods. As a small entrepreneur, you can take chances that many well-established large companies wouldn't try. Take advantage of your smallness. Experiment. Try making up your own advertising implements. If you make up ten signs, you can hire ten high school students to affix the signs to their bikes, then ride the bikes wherever your prospects might be. Would this work for you? Or perhaps you could arrange to have a truck with bells drive through neighborhoods alerting the community as to your offerings. Ice cream companies do. Political candidates do. It's worth looking into if you think it might work.

Just because certain marketing methods are rarely used, or because you've never heard of them, doesn't mean they won't be effective for you. During the next year, two or three fascinating ad vehicles will be invented. Keep your eyes peeled for them. If you honestly feel that they can help you — not just as gimmicks, but as sales tools — give them a try. For example, if you are marketing a rock concert and you know of a beach where lots of potential concert-goers hang out, it might make a whole lot of sense to market your concert on a banner pulled by an airplane. And it shouldn't be too tough to find a plane owner who offers such a service.

Also consider contests and sweepstakes. These definitely do attract **Contests can help** people, even though they may not be attracted to your primary offering. Those who enter do become *involved* with you, and involvement can lead to sales. Certainly you've seen ads or received mail that screams, "You have been selected," or "Fabulous Sweepstakes," or "You may have already won $1,000,000," or "Be a winner." Some sweepstakes experts believe that although people may not have money for food, they do have money for sweepstakes. In fact, the experts say, "When times get bad, sweepstakes get good."

In 1982, sponsors spent an estimated $170 million on prizes, plus far more than that advertising the sweepstakes. Between 1979 and 1982, according to the Promotion Marketing Association of America, the number of contests and sweepstakes grew by more than 27 percent. Contests and sweepstakes used to be shunned as legally and morally dubious. But they have now become a mainstay of

American marketing. For that reason, they are worth considering. If you do get involved, be sure you do everything on the up and up. Check with your lawyer to be sure you are not conducting an illegal lottery when you are asking folks to guess the number of coins in a bottle.

If you want to attract a lot of foot traffic to a particular location, give thought to running a contest that requires people to come to your place of business to enter, and to return to see if they have won. These days, smart marketers are learning that everyone should win *something*. Whatever that is, it should be enough so that they do not resent you and associate your offering with their loss. The best prizes of all, better than cruises and convertibles and round-the-world trips, is *cash*. No surprise there.

People seem to want to gamble; even charities are jumping onto the contest bandwagon. So let your imagination run rampant. I know a retailer who filled a gigantic container with goldfish. Then he advertised his contest: "Guess the number of goldfish in the container and win $1000!" His traffic count (and his sales) rose so dramatically that the $1000 prize didn't even put a minor dent in his budget. Because he was a guerrilla, he gave twenty-five-cent plants to everyone who entered — after the prize winner was announced. Again, people came in to collect their prizes, and while they were there, well, they purchased something else.

Different communities have different laws regarding contests. I'm sure you've seen the disclaimer "Void where prohibited by law" appended to many a sweepstakes entry form. So don't leap into this type of marketing without first consulting the local authorities.

Contests always attract attention. What you want to do is attract the attention of *prospects*, and not just people. Because people want not only to make money but also to save money, try marketing with price-off coupons. If you're a retailer, use creative tags on your merchandise. Perhaps each tag can offer a different-percentage discount. Then, you can advertise a "Mystery Tag Sale." It's not a completely new idea, merely a variation on an old one. But it can, and does, work.

Giving "spiffs," or special commissions, to salespeople who surpass a certain goal or sell a specific item is also an effective method of marketing. Can you put it to work to increase your own sales?

Exciting, ever-changing window displays can also be effective. You're in luck if you can use them. And even if you don't have your own display window, you may be able to strike up a deal with someone who does. Just imagine the difference between a store that has a window display and one that doesn't. Enormous!

I know of a fancy hairstyling salon that kept a poster in its window advertising a nearby clothing boutique. The boutique displayed a poster for the salon. Both gained extra sales as a result. The cost? Nil. The only price was the few seconds it took for someone to come up with the idea.

All of these miscellaneous marketing methods are valuable to one entrepreneur or another. They very often make the difference between a profit and a loss. But they rarely can serve as the foundation for a marketing program. They should be used as adjuncts to a solid mass-media program. You've got to prevent your public from becoming callous to your marketing, and these miscellaneous marketing tools do the trick.

Although many miscellaneous marketing tools remain forever miscellaneous — that is, never enter the marketing mainstream — they are not to be ignored. Guerrillas look under every rock, peer around every corner, examine every opportunity. You never can tell when you might make a flurry of sales from a moped sign displayed before thousands of prospects in a park on a sunny day.

26
Public Relations: Instant Credibility

PUBLIC RELATIONS MEANS EXACTLY what it says. But it is also accurate to say that it means publicity — free stories and news about you and/or your company in newspapers, magazines, newsletters, and house organs, on radio and TV, and in any other type of media.

Here's what is good about publicity: It is free. It is very believable. It gives you and your company a lot of credibility and stature. It helps establish the identity of your business. It gives you authority. It is read by a large number of people. It is remembered.

Many smart entrepreneurs feel that there is no such thing as bad publicity; that as long as you get your name out there before the public, that's a fine thing. But there are some bad things about publicity, though I only mean bad in a relative sense. You have no control over publicity. You have no say-so as to when it runs. You have no control over how it is presented. It is rarely repeated. You cannot buy it. You cannot ensure its accuracy.

On balance, however, publicity is a wonderful thing. And any marketing plan that fails to include some effort at public relations is a marketing plan that isn't going all out.

$10,000 per story When I was advertising my self-published book *Earning Money Without a Job* (since published by Holt, Rinehart & Winston and available in bookstores) in various magazines and national newspapers, I was spending about $1000 per ad. Each ad was bringing in about $3000 in sales. The book was not available in bookstores and could be purchased only through my mail-order ad. Then, a reporter from the *San Francisco Chronicle* purchased a copy of my book. Because I lived in the vicinity, and because he took a liking to the book, he called to see if he could come to my home and interview me, and asked if he could bring along a photographer. It didn't take me long to extend a warm welcome to him and his camera-bearing associate.

The interview lasted about an hour and included a brief photo session. A few days later, an article about me and my book appeared in the main news section of the newspaper. Accompanying it was a photo of me. Well into the article was the address to which the $10 purchase price (now it's only $4.95) could be sent. Within a week, I received over $10,000 worth of orders. The article had not solicited orders, did not really try to sell the book, and mentioned the address and selling price in a place where only serious readers of the article would find them. More than $10,000 in sales, and the marketing didn't cost me one penny.

As wonderful as I felt about the results, I felt just as frustrated at not being able to repeat the process. I sent the article to other newspapers, letting them know I was available for interviews. I continued to advertise the book, still achieving a fair degree of success. But never again have I been able to earn so much money with so little effort. Because my mama didn't raise a moron, I have made reprints of the article and used them as parts of mailings and press kits. So I have received a bit more mileage from the publicity. Although I know of similar stories, and indeed have arranged and taken part in them, never has the value of PR hit home as sweetly as in that instance.

The reporter felt that my book was newsy, since it promised honest information on how people can earn a good living without having to hold down a job. And that is probably the single most important factor in obtaining free publicity: providing *news* worth publicizing.

The most important factor

Let me clarify here that if you want, you can pay for public relations. You can hire a PR person, pay him or her a monthly or project fee — anywhere from $500 to $5000 per month — and let that person do what is necessary to secure free publicity. PR people are experts at it. They have the contacts, the experience, the insights. They have made all the errors, they have learned from them, and they are usually well worth their fees. But because you are a guerrilla, I want to let you know in this chapter of ways you can do what PR people do. That way, you'll be able to get the publicity and you won't have to pay anyone a dime.

Make no mistake: A public relations pro works very hard and very intelligently. So you'll have to put in the same kind of effort and intelligence. To succeed at gaining free publicity, you must have three attributes: the imagination to generate real news that is worth publicizing; the contacts to whom you can offer your news for publication or broadcast; and the persistence to follow through and see that you get the coverage you want.

The PR pro

Believe me, I was very lucky when I received the free publicity for my book. I had done nary a thing to get it. Didn't use much imagination. Had no contacts. Wasn't persistent. But I reaped rich rewards. Unfortunately, life does not usually work that way. You've got to knock yourself out to get the "free" publicity that helps so many companies. Instead of paying for the publicity with money, you pay with work: phone calls, writing, time, and determination. But all that effort will be worth your time. People who expend it say that PR really stands for profit.

If you do something good, you should get credit for it publicly. If you contribute money to charity, that's good — and it is a basis for PR. If you donate merchandise, that too can result in a publicity story. Just be sure you let your local media know of your altruism.

One of the most important public relations tools is the annual report. As a rule, entrepreneurs don't publish one. But why not? It need not conform to the usual annual report sent to shareholders. It need not talk money. It can be a report that contains information valuable to your customers. When you do publish such an annual report, send some copies to the media. Let them enjoy your creativity. Nudge them to give that creativity some "ink."

When you give a speech — and I recommend that you give them when you can — on a topic related to your business, see to it that there is press coverage. After all, you are speaking because you are an authority on your topic. If the public learns that, they'll probably reward your expertise with their patronage.

Recently, I went to a restaurant that was jammed. I hadn't seen any advertising for the restaurant, so I asked some friends there how they had heard of it. They told me they had been invited to an opening-week party — all the food they could eat. The restaurateur must have lost his shirt that week. But he gained it back — and then some — in the following weeks. Most likely, he wrote all that free food off as a marketing expense. That's what it was.

Members of the press are frequently invited to "press parties." At these parties, cocktails and hors d'oeuvres are served, and frequently a presentation is made. It's a short one, but attractive and hard-selling. The purpose is to woo the press with wining and dining, then win their hearts with a dramatic presentation of the facts. Naturally, the facts are about a new business or a new direction for an old business. It's no surprise that the press coverage following these parties is tremendous. Guerrillas hold their press parties at unique places such as ferryboats, railroad cars traveling to interesting destinations, penthouses, haunted houses, parks, baseball diamonds, and art galleries.

If you have a relatively momentous announcement to make, consider holding a press conference. Attract the press by letting them know you will tell them something newsworthy. Be sure, however, that you live up to that promise. And be sure you can answer hard questions.

When a crisis develops in your community, do what you can to alleviate the problem and gain free publicity at the same time. When a flood hit the area in which I live, an enterprising businessman furnished free hamburgers to the people helping out. He must have given away 600 burgers. But his business was written up in five newspapers, mentioned on three radio stations, and shown on television. Well worth the 600 burgers. This is not taking advantage of an unpleasant situation as much as it is being "publicity aware." A guerrilla smells opportunities like that every time.

A major-league PR pro once told me that about 80 percent of the news is "planted" — sent to the media by publicity firms. Sometimes planted news deals with political topics, sometimes it deals with industrial topics, and sometimes it deals with products or people. That same person told me that newspapers are hungry for real news. If you can furnish it to them, they'll gladly publish it. But telling a newspaper that you are having a sale is not news. Informing a radio station that you have started a business is not news. News needs a   **The hook**
slant to it, a hook that will interest people. If I wrote a publicity release saying that I had written a new book called *Earning Money Without a Job*, that would not really be news. But if my release stated that now there is a new way to combat unemployment, it would be news. And that might be a reason for a newspaper to write about my book.

The way you communicate the news you wish disseminated is by writing a piece called a publicity release. Address your release to as specific a department as you can — Sports, Entertainment, Business, whatever — and use the specific name of the editor of that department. Get it by phoning the newspaper and asking. If your news is really hot news, send it to the news or city editor. If your news item is homier than hard news, send it to the feature editor. Tailor your publicity release to the personality of the medium for which it's intended. A release for a newspaper might be longer and more detailed than a release for a radio or TV station. The latter media probably require more brevity and spice.

The release   When writing a publicity release for any medium, you should use the format that is generally followed and that is appreciated by most media. Put the date in the upper right-hand corner. Type in the name of the person to contact for more information, probably yourself. Be sure you include your phone number. Write the release date next. The item may be for immediate release, in which case you say that — using those words. Or it may be for release after February 10, 1984, in which case you say that. Next, you have the option of providing a headline. I always do, and I recommend that you do the same. But if you don't want to, the newspaper will do it for you. And even if you supply a headline, the newspaper will probably change it.

Then type your release. Double-space it. Use 8½ x 11 paper and leave wide margins. Begin one-third of the page from the top. When you move on to a second page, identify your story at the top of that page, in the left-hand corner. Write in short, clear sentences. Do not use long words or adjectives. Do not give opinions. State facts. To indicate the end of your release, type either a ##, a ***, or a -30-, centered, below the last line.

What do you say in your release? Say *who* it is about, *what* it is, *where* it is, *when* it is, *why* it is, and *how* it came about. Say all that in your first paragraph if you possibly can. Read your local newspaper and notice how deftly most reporters can work that who, what, where, when, why, how data into the very beginning of most articles.

It also helps immensely if your release is accompanied by a *very* short note. It's okay if that note is handwritten. On the note, explain in as few words as possible why you are sending the release. When you can, and when it is appropriate, enclose a photo. Make it an interesting photo, because newspapers want to be as interesting as they can.

Making contact   Even if you are armed with a perfect release and send it to the right person, there's a good chance it will be ignored. If you *hand* it to the right person, there is less chance of it being ignored. If you give it to the right person over lunch, that's even better. And if you give it to the right person over lunch and that person is an old friend of yours, that's best of all, though no guarantee of publication.

That's why I say that contacts are so very important. If you lack those contacts and the time to have lunch with all the editors and news selectors at the various media, you'll have to keep phoning the person to whom you mailed your release until it gets published. That's where persistence comes in. Don't forget, there are many people trying to get their stories in. Squeaky wheels receive the oil.

Send out your release about ten days in advance of the date you
. wish it to appear. This gives you time to phone the editor and suggest
that the newspaper or other medium cover your story, and allows
you to make suggestions for picture possibilities. It gives the paper —
or the station — time to fit the story in, thereby increasing its
chances of being used. And it lets you be absolutely certain that the
release gets delivered in time.

Suppose you are George of Let George Do It. You want free
publicity. You decide it would be newsworthy to build a unique
barbecue pit in the local park. You secure permission, then write
your release. Accompanying it is a photo of you working on a project
of which you are very proud. You include a cutline or caption pasted
(not clipped) to the bottom of the photo and folded back. It says,
"Award-winning patio being built by patio designer George
Richards, owner of Let George Do It, Hessel Avenue." The accompanying release says:

February 1, 1984

Contact: George Richards (707) 555-3463
LET GEORGE DO IT, sponsor
115 Hessel Avenue
Sebastapol, CA 91554

FOR IMMEDIATE RELEASE

DESIGNER TO BUILD BBQ PIT AS GIFT TO CITY

George Richards, of Let George Do It, a local contracting firm, will
construct a barbecue pit of his own design in Marvin Park on Friday,
February 10, as a gift to the city.

Richards, whose patios, sun decks, and barbecue pits have won
awards for design excellence, said, "I've drawn up a design that will fit
right in with the city's personality. I don't think there's a barbecue pit
in America quite like it."

The gift to the city, to be constructed on the third anniversary of
Let George Do It, has been approved by the town planning commission. "The people in this town have been very receptive to my designs," said Richards. "I feel it is high time I express my gratitude."

Richards will cook and serve hamburgers on the newly designed
barbecue pit when it is completed Friday evening. The public is
invited to view the new addition to Marvin Park and to enjoy the
hamburgers — while they last.

* * *

The best thing that could possibly happen would be for the newspaper to publish the release as sent, then do a follow-up story on the celebration following the completion of the barbecue pit, complete with a photo of George and his creation.

Make it newsworthy

Perhaps you can't build a barbecue pit for your city, but you can still gain free publicity if you do things such as teach classes in your area of expertise, publish a newsletter on it (a nifty marketing tool in itself), or write articles. All of these things help establish you as an authority. Because of the free media coverage you'll get for your work, word of your expertise will get around, and it will sink into the minds of your prospects.

The best marketing plans usually call for a *combination* of advertising and public relations. The two go hand in hand. One is highly credible but gives you no control. The other has less credibility but gives you complete control. Together, they supply most of the pieces of the marketing puzzle.

Even if you have the best of contacts and the most dogged of attitudes, the bottom line is still that you have to provide news to get a free publicity story or interview. If a Martian lands on the roof of your store, you'll have made that news without even trying. But usually you've got to generate the news, as George did when he built a barbecue pit for the city. There are eight ways guerrillas can create news all by themselves. Most likely, you can garner free publicity by employing at least one of them.

How to be newsy

1. You can tie in with the news of the day. If you're a computer tutor, a person who teaches people how to operate computers, you can issue statements that pertain to the news stories about them.

2. You can stage an event — a computer fair or a free computer seminar — during which you show the public how computers work.

3. You can release useful information. In your professional reading, maybe you'll come across an item in which your community will be interested. Include it in your press release.

4. You can form a committee to study how computers can help the community — by lowering taxes, for instance. It need not be that, but find some slant.

5. You can give an award or a scholarship each year. People love awards, and perhaps you can invent one that ties in with computer education.

6. You can make a prediction using your computer. If it is startling enough, and pretty likely to be true, it will be news and will enhance your reputation as an expert.

7. You can celebrate your own business anniversary by providing free computer lessons for a week. This is the same principle as George's donation of a barbecue pit.

8. You can do something incredible. Maybe you could keep a talking parrot at the place where you give computer lessons. The parrot, naturally, would talk computerese ("Polly wants a print-out"). Maybe you could get married in your computer classroom. Maybe you could paint a mural of a computer on the outside of your building. Keep it in good taste, but make it amazing.

Another part of public relations is the joining of civic clubs and community organizations. That may be your most important marketing tool. Although you will be doing your duty as a member of the community, you will also make lots of contacts with people who can give you business and with people who will refer business to you. I hope you don't join just to obtain business. In fact, if you do, your true motivation may be discovered, causing you to lose business. But if you join to aid your fellow man, you'll most likely end up with important contacts.

Joining in

Despite all the other marketing you do, possibly the most effective will be the joining of organizations. The only marketing many successful entrepreneurs do is to join as many clubs as possible. I'm sure you've heard that a lot of business is conducted on golf courses. Just as much is conducted in meetings, at lunches, in steam rooms, at dinners, and over cocktails with fellow members of a club.

A true guerrilla puts as much effort into public relations as possible. To a guerrilla, everything that one does publicly is really public relations. That includes the sponsoring of events, teams, floats, tournaments, and more. You'll obtain sales much more slowly from sponsoring a Little League team, bowling team, or homecoming float than you will from some other marketing methods. But some entrepreneurs report that although the sponsorship of events does not result in quick sales, it does help their other methods of marketing take effect more quickly. There's no question that you will make sales. You will gain credibility, too, and you will become known as part of the community. And you'll cause folks to feel good about you. Don't underestimate the power of favorable association. Some major advertisers who spend millions on TV commercials test those commercials to find out only if they have resulted in the company's product having a more favorable association in the minds of viewers. So it is true that sponsoring events will cause more favorable public association in a hurry. But sales in a hurry? No way.

A respected member of the community

Still, if you want to establish yourself as part of the community, consider sponsorship. Sponsor a turkey race at Thanksgiving, a toys-for-the-poor collection at Christmas, Little League teams during the summer, and bowling teams during the winter. This will do everything good for you — except win instant sales. Because you are a guerrilla, however, you will be gaining those sales from other marketing methods. And since that's the case, perhaps you should spring for a sponsorship. It doesn't cost all that much — just a few hundred bucks, in most cases. And what it does not buy in quick profits it does buy in good will.

Among those who should consider sponsorship are new businesses that need to establish their identity, companies that sell items intended for the audience of the events sponsored — for example, sporting goods stores sponsoring any type of athletic team — and companies that feel they must become more involved with the community. Sometimes community involvement is beneficial for political reasons.

Consider your own business. If there is not a good reason for you to sponsor teams or events, you probably should not do it. Don't do it just for your ego, and don't do it merely because your kid asked you to. But do it if you can, for a true guerrilla utilizes as many marketing tools as can be properly employed. And it doesn't take much cash to employ this particular tool properly.

Actually, doing it for your kid isn't always bad marketing. If your company has been earning money for many years within the community, there is absolutely nothing wrong with giving some of those profits back. By putting a Little League team on the field, outfitted in snazzy uniforms heralding your company name, you will be making a charitable contribution and marketing at the same time. Nothing wrong with that.

Frankly, many teams and events *are* sponsored for the benefit of the sponsor's ego. If you want to massage yourself the same way, just be sure you know why you are doing it.

It may be that you can take advantage of the timing of certain events. For instance, if a homecoming parade, featuring floats and queens and brass bands, ties in with a specific promotion you are having, join right in. Sometimes you can collaborate with a fellow entrepreneur and co-sponsor a float.

Many bright people believe that you should not become involved in community relations for the profit motive alone. They believe that if you sponsor teams or events for the sake of the community you will prosper, but that if the sole purpose of your sponsorship is to earn extra dollars you will fail to prosper. Give that some thought. I believe it to be true. Deep down, I feel that you do owe something to your community if you are succeeding.

What sponsorship really does is lubricate the marketing wheels that are already turning for you. People aren't going to buy from you because they saw your name on a uniform. But they may buy from you if they saw your ad in the newspaper *and* your name on a uniform.

The reasons for sponsorship

There is still another reason why some companies sponsor events: They may be resented if they do not. If you are operating in a small town where most of the businesses sponsor teams, you'll just have to pay those civic dues — or run the risk of offending the members of the community.

It is also true that the success of your business may depend upon the health and stability of your community. And your sponsoring of an event or a team will contribute to that health. That helps you in two ways. It helps your region and it helps your business. Without doubt, sponsoring events or teams or causes or floats gets you recognized as a solid citizen, as a kind, generous, helpful, friendly human being — a pillar of the community. And that helps your business, regardless of your intent. Guerrillas can be altruists, too. No law against it.

The cost of sponsorship is going to be time as well as money. Not too much of each, but some of both. You can't sponsor a team and fail to show up for their games. You can't back an event and then divorce yourself from it entirely. Word will get out that you are in it for the money alone, and that will cause you to lose more sales than you'll gain.

In some cities there are no events or teams to sponsor. You may want to add this weapon to your marketing arsenal but cannot. If that's the case, perhaps you can invent an event. Think about doing that if you have the opportunity. If yours is a growing community, your initiative, which costs very little now, will be worth a lot later. You will have positioned yourself in the right way, in the right place, at the right time. Perhaps you'll never again have that chance. Perhaps one of your competitors will start a cause, a league, or an event and assume a leadership position.

The reason to start a program

The payoff from sponsorships will differ from that connected with other marketing tools. Don't shortchange that payoff, however. It might be a feeling of warmth toward your business by the community at large. It might also be a new contact, a new customer, a new source of profits for your business. Perhaps at a league meeting you'll meet someone who can direct fifty new customers your way.

By sponsoring events, you create the opportunity to meet new people, make new friends. And because your business, rather than you, is doing the sponsoring, it will probably be the benefactor of the gratitude. Little political favors may fall your way, such as better positioning in the local newspaper for your ads, better timing on the local radio station for your commercials, new contracts coming your way. None of this will be measurable, in the classic sense, but little of it will be accidental. Your sponsorship will be the cause. Increased profits will be the effect. Will it always work that way? Not always, but sometimes. Now that you know the value of sponsorship, look into it.

27
Producing Professional Marketing

IT IS POSSIBLE TO HAVE a first-rate product or service, a well-conceived marketing plan, brilliant positioning, a dynamite creative strategy, a topflight business location, a gorgeous package, a wonderful name, and a memorable theme line, and still have your business fall flat on its face. It is not only possible but commonplace.

The reason? Your marketing materials look just awful. Your words sound horrible. Your advertising is a real turn-off. You have sunk all your money into media, and you have skimped on production. That is a mistake no guerrilla would ever make. A diehard practitioner of guerrilla marketing knows that marketing has an intangible quality that defies number, defies logic. It is the way marketing "feels." And that "feel" is determined by the *look and sound* of the marketing. If it is bad, you can't hide it. You can't hide it if it is good, either, but you won't want to.

Non-guerrillas measure advertising strictly by CPM. That stands for "cost per thousand," and it refers to the cost in media dollars to reach one thousand people. If a radio commercial costs $100 and it reaches ten thousand people, your cost per thousand — your CPM — is $10. That is considered a relatively high CPM. Some CPMs get down to $2.50, as is the case with widely viewed TV shows. And $2.50 is not a high price to pay to reach one thousand people.

But true guerrillas look far past the CPM. First, guerrillas realize **Beyond CPM** that the *cost per prospect* is more important than the cost per thousand. Second, guerrillas are highly sensitive to the metamessage of their marketing. The metamessage is the unspoken part of the marketing process. It is the true emotional impact of the advertising, which really cannot be measured at all.

The metamessage of your marketing reaches not merely the conscious mind of your prospects but also the unconscious. That is why it is so difficult to measure. I suppose it can only be gauged by sales results over a long period of time. One thing is certain: *You have complete control over it.* That's the good part. Here's the not-so-good part: It costs to send out a positive metamessage. Producing professional marketing materials costs quite a bit of money. On the other hand, it costs very little to produce unprofessional marketing materials. In fact, it costs so little that many would-be guerrillas are wooed away from success by the temptation to save a buck on production.

Reflecting on my own experience with clients over the years, I realize that 40 percent of them, usually the big ones, spent too much on production. This did wonders for their egos, but not their sales. They confused their prospective customers with too much form and not enough substance. Their electronic marketing — radio and TV — reeked with so much fluff and unnecessary window dressing that the message became cloudy. Another 40 percent of my clients, usually the smaller ones, spent too little on production. They invested in media advertising but not in artwork. They bought a lot of time and space but not a lot of talent. They decided that they could write the copy themselves, that their girlfriends could do the artwork. They allowed radio stations to write their radio spots. They allowed newspapers to lay out their newspaper ads. The result was usually schlocky-looking advertising that had an amateurish feel. They produced marketing like cheapskates, and it showed. That means that only 20 percent of my clients spent the right amount on production.

How to spend   Keep in mind that it is very easy to overspend, and even easier to underspend. You will be advised to spend far more than you ought to, possibly by a friend or associate, frequently by a production facility, maybe by an advertising agency. You will also be advised to spend far less than you ought to, probably by a media rep who wants those extra dollars for a commission and for more ads or commercials for you, or by your accountant. Bad advice, all of it. Don't let it ruin an otherwise good marketing effort.

Here's some good advice: *Reserve about 10 percent of your marketing budget for the production of marketing materials.* That means you should set aside quite a few dollars for creating professional ads and commercials, handsome signs and brochures, and motivating messages. Most likely, you'll spend a lot of that production budget up front. That's how it usually works out. You can amortize those funds over a long period of time. Let's say you plan to spend $36,000 over one year to market your product. That comes to $3000 per month. This means that you should spend $3600 producing ads and marketing materials.

If you are a new company, or if you are an old company just

coming to your senses, you may want to invest in a logotype, or logo. That is your symbol, and it should include your name. It will appear on your signs, in your ads, on your business cards, stationery, and brochures, in every single place you can think of to put it. It will become associated with you. To produce a logo, a good art director will charge anywhere from $500 to $50,000. You'd be overspending if you went the $50,000 route — though large corporations have spent double that — and you'd be underspending if you paid a mediocre art student $150.

Because you'll be using it for so long and in so many different applications, invest in a first-class logo. If this means you write a check for $750 to $1000 up front, you can amortize that $750 to $1000 over the length of time you are in business. In the long run, it may come to only a few dollars per month. Truth is, you should not even consider the money you spend for a logo as part of your production budget. It's above and beyond that budget.

Say you are quoted a price of $500 to produce an ad. Sounds like a lot. But if you run that ad over the course of four months, it comes to only $125 per month — a small sum for production. And $500 should buy you a darned good-looking ad. Naturally, you won't want to spend a lot of money on an ad you will run but once. But remember, guerrillas run their ads more than once, more than twice. They run them until the ads stop pulling in business. If you let your newspaper lay out your ad, and if you write the copy, it may only cost you $50 to produce an ad, but the ad may never pull in any business. So it's really not much of a savings for you. It amazes me when a person signs up for a $10,000 TV schedule, then wants to run a $150 commercial. Seems to me that's a savings in the $150 department and a waste of money in the $10,000 department. Don't let it happen to you.

There are three ways that you as a guerrilla marketer can produce advertisements or commercials. One way is to do it all yourself. You handle the graphics, the writing, and the ad production. If you are a creative genius and have experience producing ads, that will save you a lot of money. It may eat into the time you spend running your business, but if you're the best person to write your copy and create your layout, go to it.

Three paths to effective ads

A second way to have your advertising production done is to turn the work over to an advertising agency. For many entrepreneurs, that's a good idea. Advertising agencies earn 15 percent of your media dollars. In effect, you get their services free. If you buy

$10,000 worth of radio spots, it will cost you $10,000. If you use an ad agency, it will still cost you $10,000, but it will cost the ad agency only $8500, since as an accredited advertising agency it gets a 15 percent discount from the media. So you get the ad agency's expertise, its planning ability, the time it invests placing the advertising for you, and even its writing talents — and you don't pay anything for services rendered. You pay only for type, illustrations, and a camera-ready mechanical. On the other hand, as a guerrilla you will probably set up your own house ad agency so that you yourself can earn the 15 percent discount. So it may be that an ad agency will charge you for time only. Most of them charge on a fee basis, the fee depending upon the amount of work and time required to service your account. If you have a too-tiny budget, most ad agencies will turn up their noses at you. But if your budget is hefty, advertising agencies can save you a lot of time and trouble. And they provide a great deal of much-needed expertise.

Most entrepreneurs, however, produce their marketing materials a third way. They use independent contractors to fill in the gaps in their marketing ability. A success-oriented entrepreneur will hire a smart marketing consultant to help draft a marketing plan and a creative strategy. The consultant is paid a fee — one time — and that's it. If he or she is needed down the road, then another fee is charged. Maybe you'll want to keep a consultant by paying a monthly retainer fee for continuing counsel.

A smart entrepreneur might also have an ongoing relationship with an art director. That person designs the logo, the ads, the brochures, the circulars, the yellow pages ads, the mailing pieces, the signs — everything that needs designing. The art director is paid by the hour, by the ad, or by the project. Usually, it is by the hour.

You might also hire a copywriter who charges by the hour or by the ad. And you might employ a media-buying service to place all of your ads for you, at a charge of from 3 percent to 5 percent of the cost of the ads. Since a media-buying service can save you 15 percent, the 5 percent it charges actually amounts to a savings of 10 percent for you. At times, you might also wish to hire a professional research firm that charges by the project. And you might need the services of a photographer or an illustrator. Be sure they all follow your marketing plan and pull in the same direction.

As I have mentioned a number of times, and will continue to mention because it is so important, you should utilize as many methods of marketing as you can properly utilize. The same holds true for marketing production. Do as much of it yourself *as you can do properly.* Farm out the rest to talented professionals. In all likelihood, you are a pro at your business. And you should use people who are pros at the business of advertising production. That combination of pro and pro is a tough combination to beat.

An effective printed piece, be it ad, brochure, circular, or point-of-purchase sign, requires expertise in seven different areas.

Seven areas of expertise

The first area is that of the *idea*. Don't forget that all marketing starts with an idea. It is not important that you be the person who gets the idea. It is very important that you be able to *judge* the idea. If you can't distinguish a good idea from a bad idea, find someone who can. That's the most important part of marketing.

The second area is *copywriting*. First of all, somebody has to come up with a winning headline. To be successful, the headline should either state the idea succinctly or interest people so much that they'll want to read the copy. The copywriter must have the ability to write flowing, motivating copy. No particular style is right or wrong. But in general, copywriting should be clear, easy to follow, crisp, and believable. Many people believe that because they can write, they can write copy. If that were the case, there wouldn't be such a large number of copywriters earning in excess of $50,000 per year for their golden prose. There is a huge difference between writing in the English language and writing advertising copy designed to create a desire to buy.

The third area is *graphics*. The most important aspect of graphics is the design and layout. An art director must take the words and pictures and arrange them in such a way that the reader's eye will flow from one element to the next, free and easy. There must be no hint of confusion. The ad should look appealing, should invite readership by its look. It is not easy to create such ads. That's why some art directors are paid fancy salaries, also in excess of $50,000 yearly, to lay out advertisements. They possess a graphic sense that combines aesthetics with motivation, art with psychology. You need an ad maker to design ads, not merely a designer. An ad that merely looks good is a bad ad. The ad must look good and also communicate exactly what you wish to communicate.

The fourth area is *pictures*. The pictures may be illustrations or photos, black and white or color, small or large, one or many. The art director makes that decision. The illustrator or photographer then takes over and draws or shoots the picture that helps bring the marketing plan to life. I have had clients pay $5000 for a single photo session and feel that the shots were worth every cent. If you are handy with a camera or if you can illustrate with pizzazz, perhaps you can handle the picture portion of your advertising. But chances are, you'll be better off hiring a pro. Fortunately, most people recognize their lack of talent at art. Unfortunately, most people fail to recognize their lack of talent at writing.

The fifth area is *typography*. There are books and books of typefaces you can select. With such a wide selection, which is the right kind of type for your advertising? Should it be a serif typeface — one with letters that have little tails and curlicues? Or should it be a sans serif typeface — one with clean, streamlined letters? Should you use italics? Boldface type? All capitals? What is the right size of type for the headline? The subhead? The body copy? The theme line? A type expert or art director must be able to answer all of those questions and answer them correctly. Otherwise, a lot of money may go down the drain. I've seen many ads that had everything right except that the type was unreadable — either unclear or too small. And any ad with unreadable type is a sad waste of money, space, time, and energy.

The sixth area is *paste-up*. That means pasting on a board or sheet of paper the type that has been set, the headline, the illustration or photograph, the logo, the border, and any other element that goes into the ad. The paste-up person, when preparing the mechanical — a term used to describe the pasted-up ad — must place and paste with precision. He or she follows the design formulated by the art director and pastes all the pieces together to make a camera-ready ad.

The seventh area is *photostating*. Once an ad has been thought up, written, laid out, illustrated, set in type, and pasted up, it must be photographed and a photostat of the ad must be made. That's what you send to the newspaper. That ensures that the ad will appear as you want it to appear. The art director should already have contacted the newspaper to find out their printing idiosyncracies, so that the ad will print well. Once that is done, your ad quality is assured if you send a perfect stat to the paper.

It is the rare guerrilla who possesses expertise in all seven areas. Even the most proficient ad makers are expert in but a few. Generally, one person thinks up and writes the ad, a second person serves as art director, paste-up person, typographer, and stat maker, and a third person handles the photos or illustrations. That, as I said, is generally the case — meaning more than 50 percent of the time. In many cases, however, the art director thinks up the ad. In some cases, one person does the writing, a second person handles all graphics and production responsibilities, and either of the two people gets the idea for the ad. It doesn't matter where a good idea comes from.

Your job, as a guerrilla, is to exercise the right judgment in all of these areas. You need not be able to do any one of these tasks, but you must be able to distinguish good from bad in all seven areas.

Judgment is all

One of the most successful entrepreneurs I have ever known, a true guerrilla in absolutely every sense of the word, had zero talent in all seven areas but had exceptional judgment and resourcefulness. His judgment helped him recognize his own limitations, helped him distinguish a good ad from a bad ad, a good commercial from a bad one, good copy from bad copy. His resourcefulness led him to the people who could supply the talent he needed to run prime-quality ads. Although he didn't contribute one word to his copy, he never ran a bad ad. His success both financial and personal, was astonishing. He built a company that used all of the media — and I mean all. There was not a single major marketing tool that he failed to use. And yet he had no built-up marketing talent, merely good marketing judgment and instincts. That's all you need to be a guerrilla. That plus aggressiveness.

Needless to say, it will cost you money to secure talent in the seven areas required. And remember, I'm just talking about printed marketing materials. You'll require even more talents for television marketing. And radio advertising calls for professionalism in five areas: the idea, the writing, the announcing, the music, and the sound effects. As with print advertising, you yourself don't have to have talent in these areas, merely good judgment. And you must know how to locate expert production studios.

In my part of the world, seminars are often presented for entrepreneurs. Some seminars are geared to teaching you how to produce your own marketing materials. If such seminars come to your area (check with a local community college), sign up for one.

Now that you are taking the marketing process seriously, start developing a radar for good marketing and bad marketing. Both kinds are all around you. The more you observe, the more you learn, and the more you learn, the better you'll be able to market.

Marketing radar

I encourage you to hire a pro to design your work. Unless it is something at which you really excel, you are usually far better off giving it to a pro — or to several pros. To find them, merely set aside a few days to visit graphic-art firms and view the work they have done for others. Visit writers and art directors and look at ads they have created. Listen to radio spots they have written and produced. View TV commercials for which they have been responsible. Only if you do it that way will you get a feel for the marketplace. When looking at the work of these people, ask two questions: (1) How much did it cost to produce? (2) What were the sales results? Concern yourself more with the answer to question two than question one.

You can save sacks of money and get to use beautifully produced ads, commercials, brochures, and signs if you make use of co-op advertising. If you are a manufacturer, you can gain a lot in local sales by joining a good co-op program. If you are a retailer or distributor, you can gain welcome funds for your marketing budget by obtaining co-op money. Co-op funds and materials are made available to entrepreneurs by large companies. To learn all there is to learn about co-op advertising, write the Co-op Resource Center, Box 2243, North Mankato, Minnesota 56002. Should you wish to call for free details, the phone number is 507-625-2667. If you wish to obtain first-class marketing help in the way of money, ads, and more, co-op advertising is definitely an area worth exploring.

Only after you have assembled the proper marketing aids will you be able to combine the best stated message with the best metamessage. It is the combination of the two that will result in success. One without the other just won't do it.

Marketing mileage   When thinking about marketing — an activity in which you should engage more and more — try to think long-term while you are thinking short-term. Don't just look at the week ahead. Look also at the months and years. Your marketing efforts will add up. Your identity will not come easily or quickly but will be built over time. And everything you do in the way of marketing will contribute to that identity. If you see that you may have to spend $1000 to produce an advertising piece, think of other ways the piece can be used. Maybe you can turn it into a sign. Perhaps it can also serve as a customer handout. Possibly it can be the basis for a brochure. Maybe it can be used with interchangeable headlines and become two ads. Perhaps it can be the major part of a mailing. And you may be able to use it for five years or longer. By getting the most mileage out of your marketing materials, you will save a lot of money. Suddenly, that $1000 figure looks a lot more reasonable. Why, with enough deep thought on your part, it might even seem inexpensive.

Brand names   In addition to getting as much mileage as possible from your marketing, do everything you can to create brand names for your products. People trust brand names. They have confidence that a brand-name item will perform better than a non-brand-name item. Don't make the mistake of thinking that brand names belong only in the province of the big guys. Brand names can be used by anyone who wants to create them. Smart marketing people, big and small, want to create them. A friend of mine, who has one store, has created a brand name for his interior furnishings. He calls them the Europa 2000 Collection. He has marketed and advertised and promoted them so long and so hard that people in his community now ask all over town for items from the Europa 2000 Collection. The collection is available only at his store, of course. He has created a line of goods that people ask for by name.

According to the *Harvard Business Review*, entrepreneurs are going to have to start developing their own brand names. There is a new selling environment. People want uniqueness, want names they can trust. Creating a brand name gives the people what they want and gives you what you want: consumer confidence. A good approach to take is to give your customers more than their money's worth. If you sincerely try to do that, to go the extra mile, provide the extra service, give the extra quality, you'll be able to convey that attitude in your marketing. You'll be a better marketer if you think that way. And word will spread, too.

There is no mystique to marketing, as you have seen. It is nuts and bolts and is fairly easy to dissect. But marketing is difficult to do properly. Never forget that no matter what your business really is, *people will think of it as your marketing portrays it.* If you run cheap-looking ads, that's what people will think of your product or service. Don't believe those people who tell you that you'll never go broke underestimating the intelligence of the American public. Instead, figure that the American public is about as intelligent as your mother. And you know that she is no dodo. In reality, she is a good representative of the public.

If you have employees, make sure they are completely aware of your marketing program. They must reflect all that is conveyed in your marketing. After all, people will come to you because of that marketing, and they will expect certain things from you. Your salespeople or representatives must have attitudes that are consistent with the messages you have been putting forth. Guerrillas not only have all employees and associates read their marketing plans but also insist that all employees read every ad and hear every commercial. If they do, they'll be able to relate that much better to customers and will know what the customers are looking for. They will know what is

Tell your employees

being communicated in advertising and will be able to help the business live up to its marketing.

One of the most important attributes a guerrilla can have is patience. Wait for that marketing plan to take hold. Stick with it. If you have thought it through, it will pay rich dividends. If you expect instant results, your plan will never have a chance to shine, to motivate, to sell. Lean on your marketing materials as much as you can. Post your ads on your door, in your window, on your walls. Be proud of them. Create each ad with the care you would use if it were your only ad.

You are probably reading this book because you own your own business or because you are considering owning your own business. I doubt that many people would invest in a marketing book unless they were involved in the marketing process. It may be that you are in the marketing department of a company. But it is more likely that you have your own company. Merely by purchasing or taking the time to read this book, you have proven that you already know the crucial importance of marketing. In our competitive society it is more important now than ever. Because you purchased a book dealing with guerrilla marketing, you are a person who wants to market more effectively than your competitors. You are now equipped to put better marketing to work for you.

Entrepreneur magazine, a worthy publication for any person who considers himself or herself an entrepreneur, publishes an entrepreneur's credo at the beginning of every issue. Because I suspect that you are a small businessperson who wishes to become a big businessperson, and because I believe you are an entrepreneur, I will repeat the credo by which you may already live:

> I do not choose to be a common man. It is my right to be uncommon — if I can. I seek opportunity — not security. I do not wish to be a kept citizen, humbled and dulled by having the state look after me.
>
> I want to take the calculated risk, to dream and to build, to fail and to succeed.
>
> I refuse to barter incentive for a dole; I prefer the challenges of life to the guaranteed existence; the thrill of fulfillment to the stale calm of Utopia.
>
> I will not trade freedom for beneficence nor my dignity for a handout. I will never cower before any master nor bend to any threat.
>
> It is my heritage to stand erect, proud and unafraid, to think and act for myself, to enjoy the benefit of my creations and to face the world boldly and say: This . . . I have done. All this is what it means to be an entrepreneur.

Now, you have risen above the level of entrepreneur. Just as the entrepreneur has advanced beyond the wage slave, being freer, more responsible, and a greater taker of risks, the guerrilla has advanced beyond the entrepreneur, being a mite harder working, a bit sharper, slightly more of an explorer, often more successful. As the age of the entrepreneur and individual enterprise comes more and more into the forefront in America, the need to be a guerrilla is more and more acute.

Regardless of your lofty achievements, regardless of your successes, regardless of the size to which you grow, it will always be possible to bring to marketing the imagination, the ingenuity, and the comprehensiveness of thought of a guerrilla. If you are armed with these, I'll see you in the trenches. And at the bank.

A Guide to Further Information

Index

Books

Applegath,
New Y...

Baty, Gor...
lishing, 19...

Daniells,
Califor...

Day, Wil...
N.J.: P...

Dean, Sa...
Wilmi...

Dible, D...
Entrep...

Hisrich, ...
Cumm...

Joffe, Ge...
San Fr...

Kamaroff,...
1981.

Kuswa,...
Dartn...

Louis, H...
Nelso...

Malicksc...
Kind...

Ogilvy,...

Phillips,...

Ries, Al...
McG...